Captain Joshua Slocum

SAILING ALONE AROUND THE WORLD

THE COASTLINE COLLECTION

VOLUME I
Captain Joshua Slocum
SAILING ALONE AROUND THE WORLD
with an introduction by
Donald W. Davidson

VOLUME II
Henry Beetle Hough
COUNTRY EDITOR
with an introduction by
Walter Cronkite

VOLUME III
Henry David Thoreau
CAPE COD
with an introduction by
Joseph Jay Deiss

THE COASTLINE COLLECTION

Captain Joshua Slocum

SAILING ALONE AROUND THE WORLD

Illustrated by Thomas Fogarty & George Varian

WITH AN INTRODUCTION BY

Donald W. Davidson

The Peninsula Press

Cape Cod · Nantucket · Martha's Vineyard
New Bedford · Plymouth

This edition commemorating the centennial of the captain's voyage is
Volume 1 of *The Coastline Collection*
published by
The Peninsula Press · Cape Cod 02670 USA

Visit The Peninsula Press online:
www.capecod.net/peninsulapress

This edition first published in 1995 by The Peninsula Press.

Library of Congress Catalog Card Number: 95-067094
Slocum, Joshua.
  Sailing Alone Around the World
  The Peninsula Press, ©1995.
  Includes index, bibliography, and illustrations.
ISBN 1-883684-06-04
1. Cape Cod, Nantucket & Martha's Vineyard — Sailing.
2. Cape Cod, Nantucket & Martha's Vineyard — History and recreation.
3. Sailing — circumnavigation.
First edition
Manufactured on Cape Cod in the United States of America
2 3 4 5 6 7 8 9 0/ 03 02 01 00 99 98

To the one who said:
"The *Spray* will come back."

Chart of Captain Joshua Slocum's solo voyage
around the world aboard the sloop *Spray*:
24 April 1895 to 3 July 1898.

TABLE OF CONTENTS

A CENTENNIAL INTRODUCTION

A dream kept afloat – Boyhood in Nova Scotia to a life at sea – A wife found in Australia – Raising a family on deck – The switch from sails to steam – Sailing alone around the world – Vineyard landfall – The *Spray* does not come back.

. . . . *xi*

CHAPTER 1

A blue-nose ancestry with Yankee proclivities – Youthful fondness for the sea – Master of the ship *Northern Light* – Loss of the *Aquidneck* – Return home from Brazil in the canoe *Liberdade* – The gift of a "ship" – The rebuilding of the *Spray* – Conundrums in regard to finance and caulking – The launching of the *Spray*.

. . . . 1

CHAPTER 2

Failure as a fisherman – A voyage around the world projected – From Boston to Gloucester – Fitting out for the ocean voyage – Half of a dory for a ship's boat – The run from Gloucester to Nova Scotia – A shaking up in home waters – Among old friends.

. . . . 7

CHAPTER 3

Good-bye to the American coast – Off Sable Island in a fog – In the open sea – The man in the moon takes an interest in the voyage – The first fit of loneliness – A bottle of wine from the Spaniard – A bout of words with the captain of the *Java* – The steamship *Olympia* spoken – Arrival at the Azores.

. . . . 15

CHAPTER 4

Squally weather in the Azores – High living – Delirious from cheese and plums – The pilot of the *Pinta* – At Gibraltar – Compliments exchanged with the British Navy – A picnic on the Morocco shore.

. . . . 25

CHAPTER 5

Sailing from Gibraltar with the assistance of her Majesty's tug – The *Spray's* course changed – Chased by a pirate – A comparison with Columbus – The Cape Verde Islands – Sea life – Arrival at Pernambuco – Preparing for the stormy weather of the cape.

. . . . 35

CHAPTER 6

Departure from Rìo de Janeiro – The *Spray* ashore on the sands of Uruguay – A narrow escape from shipwreck – The boy who found a sloop – The *Spray* floated but somewhat damaged – Courtesies from the British consul – A warm greeting at Montevideo – An excursion to Buenos Aires – Shortening the mast and bowsprit.
. . . . 45

CHAPTER 7

Weighing anchor at Buenos Aires – An outburst of emotion at the mouth of the Plate – Submerged by a great wave – A stormy entrance to the strait – The happy gift of a bag of carpet-tacks – Off Cape Froward – Chased by Indians from Fortescue Bay – Taking in supplies at Three Island Cove – Animal life.
. . . . 55

CHAPTER 8

From Cape Pillar into the Pacific – Driven by a tempest toward Cape Horn – Captain Slocum's greatest sea adventure – Reaching the strait again by way of Cockburn Channel – Some savages find the carpet-tacks – Danger from firebrands – A series of fierce williwaws – Again sailing westward.
. . . . 67

CHAPTER 9

Repairing the *Spray's* sails – Savages and an obstreperous anchor – A spider-fight – An encounter with Black Pedro – A visit to the steamship *Columbia* – On the defensive against a fleet of canoes – A record of voyages through the strait – A chance cargo of tallow.
. . . . 75

CHAPTER 10

Running to Port Angosto in a snow storm – A defective sheet-rope places the *Spray* in peril – The *Spray* as a target for a Fuegian arrow – The *Spray* at Port Angosto – The island of Alan Erric – Again in the open Pacific – The run to the island of Juan Fernández – An absentee king – At Robinson Crusoe's anchorage.
. . . . 85

CHAPTER 11

The islanders entertained with Yankee doughnuts – The beauties of Robinson Crusoe's realm – The monument to Alexander Selkirk – Robinson Crusoe's cave – Westward ho! with a friendly gale – A month's free sailing with the Southern Cross and the sun for guides – Sighting the Marquesas – Experience in reckoning.
. . . . 93

CHAPTER 12

Seventy-two days without a port – Whales and birds – A peep into the *Spray's* galley – Flying-fish for breakfast – A welcome at Apia – A visit from Mrs. Robert Louis Stevenson – At Vailima – Samoan

TABLE OF CONTENTS

hospitality – Arrested for fast riding – An amusing merry-go-round – At the mercy of sea-nymphs.
. . . . 101

CHAPTER 13

Samoan royalty – King Malietoa – Good-bye to friends at Vailima – Leaving Fiji to the south – Arrival at Newcastle – The yachts of Sydney – A ducking on the *Spray* – Commodore Foy presents the sloop with a new suit of sails – A shark that proved to be valuable – A change of course – The "Rain of Blood" – In Tasmania.
. . . . 111

CHAPTER 14

A testimonial from a lady – Cruising round Tasmania – The skipper delivers his first lecture on the voyage – Abundant provisions – An inspection of the *Spray* for safety at Devonport – Again at Sydney – Northward bound for Torres Strait – An amateur shipwreck – Friends on the Australian coast – Perils of a coral sea.
. . . . 121

CHAPTER 15

Arrival at Port Denison – Reminiscences of Captain Cook – Lecturing for charity – A happy escape from a coral reef – Home Island, Sunday Island, Bird Island – An American pearl-fisherman – Jubilee at Thursday Island – A new ensign for the *Spray* – Booby Island – Across the Indian Ocean – Christmas Island.
. . . . 131

CHAPTER 16

A call for careful navigation – Three hours' steering in twenty-three days – Arrival at the Keeling Cocos Islands – A welcome from the children – Cleaning and painting the *Spray* on the beach – A blessing for a pot of jam – A risky adventure in a small boat – The governor calms the fears of the people – A convent in the hills.
. . . . 143

CHAPTER 17

A clean bill of health – Sailing the voyage over again in the opera-house – A newly discovered plant named in honor of the *Spray's* skipper – A party of young ladies – A warm reception at Durban – A friendly cross-examination by Henry M. Stanley – Three wise Boers seek proof of the flatness of the earth – Leaving South Africa.
. . . . 155

CHAPTER 18

Rounding the "Cape of Storms" in olden time – A rough Christmas – The *Spray* ties up for rest at Cape Town – A railway trip to the Transvaal – President Krüger's odd definition of the *Spray's* voyage – Cocoa-nut fiber as a padlock – Courtesies from the admiral of the Queen's navy – Land in sight.
. . . . 165

CHAPTER 19

In the isle of Napoleon's exile – Two lectures – A guest in the ghost-room at Plantation House – An excursion to historic Longwood – Coffee in the husk, and a goat to shell it – The *Spray's* ill luck with animals – A prejudice against small dogs – A rat, the Boston spider, and the cannibal cricket – Ascension Island.

· 173

CHAPTER 20

In the favoring current off Cape St. Roque, Brazil – All at sea regarding the Spanish-American War – An exchange of signals with the battle-ship *Oregon* – Off Dreyfus' prison on Devil's Island – Reappearance to the *Spray* of the north star – The light on Trinidad – A charming introduction to Grenada – Talks to friendly auditors.

· 181

CHAPTER 21

Clearing for home – In the calm belt – A sea covered with sargasso – The jibstay parts in a gale – Welcomed by a tornado off Fire Island – A change of plan – Arrival at Newport – End of a cruise of over forty-six thousand miles – The *Spray* again at Fairhaven.

· 187

APPENDIX

LINES AND SAIL-PLAN OF THE *SPRAY*

Her pedigree as known – The Lines of the *Spray* – Her self-steering qualities – Sail-plan and steering-gear – An unprecedented feat – A final word of cheer to would-be navigators.

· 195

FURTHER READING

· 205

INDEX

· 209

ACKNOWLEDGMENTS

· 216

A CENTENNIAL INTRODUCTION

A dream kept afloat — His Nova Scotia boyhood — Off to a life at sea — Sailing the South Pacific — A wife found in Australia — Raising a family on deck — Heartbreak in Buenos Aires — The world switches from sails to steam — Sailing alone around the world — The Vineyard landfall — The *Spray* does not come back.

UPON the waters of Buzzards Bay a hundred years ago, Joshua Slocum kept afloat his dream. Casting-off a line at Poverty Point, he sailed the Acushnet River south — past Popes and Crow and Palmer Islands — to the more open waters of the bay, there to shake down at last the sloop he had built up alone by hand.

For nearly a hunded years already, her name had been the *Spray* — so said the records in Noank, Connecticut — and so it still remained. But now her master was new, as was almost every other detail of her Delaware design. The *Spray's* keel he had hewn by hand from pasture oak, tempered by winds unchallenged from any quadrant of the compass; the sloop's planks and wales were of Georgia pine, sawed and planed and caulked before the curious eyes of whaling captains who had walked across the bridge from New Bedford to watch; and her mast was still very much a live spruce, straight and true, from the weathered woods of New Hampshire.

Those who had followed Joshua Slocum's progress in the Fairhaven meadow at Oxford Village — just north of the bridge — might have thought that sailing the *Spray* down the river and onto the edge of the sea most certainly would be achievement enough for a man past his own middle years.

And those who later might have watched the *Spray* pull away from the East Boston waterfront, round Deer Island, then square away for Gloucester must have recognized that — if the captain could somehow survive — sailing a thirty-seven-foot boat all the way around the world would be not only an arduous and emotional ordeal, but truly an amazing accomplishment for any man who had only himself as a crew.

And those who finally caught a glimpse of the solitary seaman bound from the Vineyard for the headwaters of the Amazon surely sensed that tracing the river's mystical flow could be the last frontier that any seafarer might possibly pioneer.

Whatever the viewpoint of those on shore, however, Slocum's view from the heeling deck of the *Spray* held true to a course that his heart had steered since his boyhood in Nova Scotia. In 1844, he was born at Wilmot during the age of sail and raised on Brier Island at the edge of the Bay of Fundy. There and then, young Joshua Slocum heard the ocean's call long before he had ever set eyes upon the wearied hulk of the *Spray*. And throughout his entire life, the world would never prove large enough to contain his love of the sea and the stars.

As a boy, he had yearned for more than just a life beside the water, and his dreams would carry him around the world at least five times in ships of his own much larger than the little sloop that carried him alone. And for years after he had brought the *Spray* safely back to the waters of Buzzards Bay and Vineyard Sound, he tried time and time again to swallow the anchor and settle on the Vineyard farm he had purchased with royalties from this book; however, he found the feat impossible. In short, Joshua Slocum possessed no great passion for *terra firma* in any sense of the phrase.

Perhaps because he was the fifth of eleven children, Slocum had felt some urge at an early age to escape the hubbub of his home life. His mother, Sarah Jane, was the daughter of the lighthouse keeper on Southwest Point in Westport on Brier Island, just off Digby Neck; his father, John, a farmer and a deacon of the church. When Joshua was eight, however, his mother's health began to fail, and his father moved the family to Westport, where he set-up a wharfside bootshop for sailors and fishermen. By the time he was ten, Josh had left school to whittle wooden pegs for leather boots and to tend the tanning vats. In what little time he had to call his own, the boy learned to sail with his friends; however, his ability to swim would remain about the same as his ability to spell.

And in other quiet moments, the boy built boats. "Next in attractiveness, after seafaring, came shipbuilding," later he would write. "I longed to be master in both professions." His father, though, the devoted deacon of the church, viewed these model ships as nothing other than toys: simple signs of idleness. But in breaking-up this handiwork, John Slocum's righteous destruction only served to strengthen his twelve-year-old's determination and skills, both of which later proved — on more than one occasion — to be the son's salvation.

As his mother's health had become increasingly frail, Joshua Slocum made his first move out onto the sea at the age of fourteen and attempted to be a cook aboard a schooner bound from St. Mary's Bay. It did not take long for him to discover, however, that there were still things other than swimming and spelling which he did not know; the captain and crew shipped the boy back home.

When Sarah Jane Slocum died some two years later at the age of forty-six, so died her son's only real reason for remaining any longer at home. At the age of sixteen, then, Joshua Slocum once again ran off to sea, this time aboard a droger for Dublin. Too young to be a man of property and too drawn by the lure of the sea, he would see no need to buy any land for yet another fifty years. Instead, he shipped out of Liverpool as an ordinary seaman aboard the *Tanjore* for China around the Cape of Good Hope. Over the next few years, he sailed aboard ships that freighted coal and grain, and twice he rounded the Horn.

By the age of eighteen, Joshua Slocum had been promoted to second mate and had made his way to the western shores of North America. With only two years of formal schooling a decade before, he had grown to be a passionate reader of his handbooks and the heavens alike. In these two years at sea Slocum not only had taught himself navigation with a sextant, but also had designed for gill-fishing a boat that was purchased at once by a cannery in British Columbia.

Slocum ran freight aboard British ships between Frisco and Seattle until he was offered full command of an American schooner out of San Francisco. That was in 1869, when he was only twenty-five, and Slocum was ready to become both an American citizen and a captain.

With the command of his second ship, Joshua Slocum's life took a decided turn outward adventure. The *Washington* was a bark built in Puget Sound, and she ran cargo from San Francisco to Sydney, Australia. On one voyage down under he met — and quickly married — Virginia Alberta Walker, who had been born in New York City on the cusp of the Gold Rush in 1849. In search of gold, her father first had brought his own family to California, then moved on to New South Wales. His daughter's natural beauty possessed a visible trace of Native American blood, and her vigorous outdoor life in Australia had nurtured skills in both horsemanship and marksmanship. With her marriage to young Captain Slocum on 31 January 1871, however, Virginia forsook all claims to that particular sort of outdoor life and willingly went wherever the winds might bear the *Washington*.

Joshua Slocum had found in his new bride a soulmate. With a deck cabin serving at once as both their honeymoon cottage and their home, the Slocums' honeymoon itself was nothing less than an unfettered run from Australia north to the waters off Alaska in search of the salmon fishery that now belonged to the United States. In fact, the *Washington* was the very first American vessel ever to enter the waters of Cooke Inlet after the Russians had sold the territory of Alaska and left. The waters were teeming with fish, but in a gale the *Washington* ran upon a bar. While a revenue cutter managed to rescue Virginia from the vessel, the industrious Captain Slocum — who had taught himself ship-building in his youth — crafted a boat to transfer his catch to some empty sealers before the ship might be lost altogether.

Though the crew and cargo were saved, the *Washington* was not. Nonetheless, its owners were so impressed with Slocum's skills and fortitude that they gave him command of the *Constitution*, a barkentine running the packet route from San Francisco to Honolulu. In the harbor of San Francisco in 1872, meanwhile, was born the Slocums' first child, a son they named Victor.

During the next year, Captain Slocum was hired away from the west coast by Aymar and Company of New York to command the square-rigger *B. Aymar*. Aboard that ship, Virginia gave birth in 1873 to their second child, Benjamin Aymar Slocum, and a pattern was emerging; so, too, was a family. In the summer of 1875, their daughter Jesse was born in the waters off the Phillipines.

While the growing Slocum family was in the islands, the captain took leave of his command to ply full time his trade as a shipbuilder. Contracted to build the hull of a steamer, he established a shipyard of sorts in a jungle village at the outskirts of Manila on the shores of Subic Bay. For nearly a year, the young family lived on land in a thatched hut.

As the project neared completion, however, Slocum's client failed; in lieu of the promised cash, he was left with the hull of a forty-five-ton schooner called the *Pato*. To this hull, the shipbuilder added a deck and a cabin, moved his family aboard, then ran freight among the islands. The children aboard ranged in age from two to five when the *Pato* headed across the South China Sea, then on to the newly-discovered codfish grounds in the North Pacific, where Slocum stated simply, "We hope to take in fish."

As had so many of his dreams, Slocum's hopes for fish came true. Unfortunately, so did some of his fears.

Only four days after Virginia had given birth to a set of twins, the *Pato* began to haul in its share of the natural wealth. The captain delivered a profitable harvest into Portland, Oregon, before concluding the 8,000-mile voyage with a run to Honolulu; however, the newborn twins could not survive. Their deaths were the fault of neither the father, nor the mother, for during the nineteenth century large families, as well as high infant mortality rates were not uncommon facts.

Slocum sold the *Pato* for some $5,000 in Hawaii, then the family steamed back to San Francisco, where the captain bought a 350-ton full-rigger, the *Amethyst*. This time with a brother as cook and with a sister aboard to assist his wife, Slocum began shipping freight throughout the Pacific. Virginia gave birth to another daughter, who died; then she gave birth in 1881 to their seventh child, James Garfield Slocum, who was born in Hong Kong Harbor.

That was also where Joshua Slocum first caught sight of the *Northern Light*, whose captain was a partial owner of the ship nearly five times larger than the *Amethyst*. Offering to buy that share and take command, Slocum became master of the *Northern Light* before he was forty and moved his family to more spacious accommodations that included a library of more than five hundred volumes. Then with a cargo of sugar, they sailed from Manila around the Cape of Good Hope and across the Atlantic to New York in 1882. So large was the *Northern Light*, infact, that portions of her rigging had to be struck so she could fit beneath the Brooklyn Bridge being built.

At this time, Joshua Slocum now had not seen his father in more than twenty years, so the captain invited him to come meet Virginia and the next generation of Slocums, as well as to witness the height of his seafaring career. John Slocum accepted the offer, but precious time had been spent in communicating and in traveling between Nova Scotia and New York, and the *Northern Light's* time in port was not particularly long. Within two months, she was bound again for the far Pacific. This voyage, however, would begin a dramatic reversal of Joshua Slocum's fortunes.

The *Northern Light* encountered the first of rudder troubles at the very outset, and while she underwent repairs in New London her crew — who, according to practice, had been paid in advance — wanted to leave altogether. But thanks to Virginia's skills with pistols, the captain was able to quell the disorder that was little short of a mutiny. The incident concluded and the ship repaired, Slocum faced the dilemma of either retaining the mutinous crew, or hiring a crew of foreigners. For better or worse, he kept loyal to his American mariners.

On the return run from Manila with a cargo of sugar

for Liverpool, the *Northern Light* barely passed Krakatau in August of 1883 when all semblance of that island was blown-up by a volcano. Then later, approaching again the Cape of Good Hope, the *Northern Light* broke her rudderhead in stormy seas. Water belowdecks ruined the cargo of sugar, and she struggled to make Port Elizabeth. There the cargo was scuttled, and an officer was discharged with sickness. Putting to sea some two months later with a repaired rudder and a new officer, Slocum soon realized that this replacement was a troublesome ex-con whom the captain was forced to put in chains for the remainder of the voyage, fifty-three days.

Home at last after eighteen months at sea, Joshua Slocum was convicted in 1884 of false and cruel imprisonment in the matter of the intractable officer. The cost of the captain's own conviction was a $500 fine, which was paid for by his underwriters; the cost for further repair of the *Northern Light*, however, was another matter altogether. The age of sail was giving way to the age of steam, and making any further repairs to his ship simply was not worth the expense. So — after the other partners bought out Slocum's share — the *Northern Light* was cut down and sold as a coal barge.

Fortunately, John and Joshua Slocum had been able to enjoy their reunion at the height of the captain's career and fortune. Suddenly without a ship for the first time in a generation, however, and facing the distinct possibility of becoming both landlocked and landless, the good captain left his own family with various other relatives in the Boston area to seek yet another command at the helm of a sailing ship.

In Baltimore, Slocum used the last of his *Pato* profit to buy the *Aquidneck*, "a little bark which of all men's handiwork," he said, was "the nearest to perfection of beauty." The *Aquidneck* — a namesake of the island at whose southernmost point sits the town of Newport, Rhode Island — was about the size of the *Amethyst*, but the Slocum family now was just a bit bigger than it had been in those days. Still, the captain summoned Virginia and their children to Baltimore, where they took on a cargo of flour and headed southward to Pernambuco, Brazil.

In Buenos Aires, Virginia took ill. Their cargo sold, Slocum anchored in Rìo de la Plata between Uruguay and Argentina, then went ashore in hopes of finding cargo that might take them to Virginia's Sydney. In the meantime, though, he spied the signal that demanded his return: the *J* — for Joshua — pennant was flying above the *Aquidneck's* rigging. On 25 July 1884, Virginia Slocum died at the age of thirty-four. Joshua's time together with her had been only sixteen years, the same the fates had allowed him with his mother. He had deeply loved each one of them both, and now the two most important women in his life were gone. Joshua Slocum was barely forty years old.

After Virginia was buried in the English Cemetery at Buenos Aires, the captain purposely ran the *Aquidneck* aground, paying dearly for his fit. He rescued his ship and sailed her back to Boston, where once again he found homes for the children with his sisters in the area. Then, for the first time since his marriage, he sailed the seas without his family on board.

During one visit to Massachusetts, Slocum was introduced to a first cousin from Nova Scotia, Henrietta Elliott, who was twenty-four. Though the lonely captain was now forty-two, he and Hettie were married in Boston on 22 February 1886. Less than a week later, the captain took Hettie, Victor and Garfield freighting along South America's eastern coast. As Slocum's luck now would have it, though, the uninsured *Aquidneck* "stranded broadside upon a bar open to the sea" off Paranaguá Bay. For nearly three days, he says, "a strong swell raked her fore and aft, the waves dashing over her groaning hull all the while till at last her back was broke and — why not add 'heart' as well! for she lay now undone."

Using the hand tools in his kit, as well as the skills he first took-up as a boy, the captain fashioned upon the beach a craft he called the *Liberdade*, which had the hull of "a Cape Ann dory with the rig of a Chinese sampan." Despite its overall length of more than thirty-five feet,

Slocum called this vessel a "canoe," and the four of them sailed it back to Washinton, D.C. in fifty-three days. Given such a maiden voyage, Hettie Slocum vowed to sail never again.

The family spent the winter in Washington, before the captain brought his brood to East Boston in the summer of '89. Gone was the mother of his children; gone, too, his money and his ships; and going quickly was the glorious age of sail. Joshua Slocum's boyhood dream of harnessing the winds and riding the waters — a dream he was certain would last as long as there were a breeze, a boat, and a breath in his body — at last was foundering and on the verge of vanishing, once and for all.

The captain was forced to face a reality that was altogether new, so he took to writing and publishing at his own expense *The Voyage of the Liberdade*. He tried selling the book for a dollar a copy, but the reception was lukewarm at best; the alternative was to take on whatever work he could find in shipyards and boatyards along the Massachusetts shore. Under these circumstances, then, on the East Boston waterfront in the winter of 1892, Joshua Slocum then met up with Eben Pierce, an old friend and retired whaling captain, and he told the whaler of his plight.

"Come to Fairhaven, and I'll give you a ship," was the almost legendary response from Captain Pierce. "But she wants some repairs."

And so, the fifty-year-old Captain Slocum found his way the next day to the coastal town of Fairhaven, where he first set his eyes upon the aged *Spray* in all of her faded splendor.

The late Walter Magnes Teller — noted historian, tireless Slocum biographer, and seasonal resident of the

Vineyard town of Chilmark — describes this encounter as no other has been able:

> A Yankee shipmaster does not wear his heart on his sleeve, and what Slocum felt at that moment he has not described. But the sight of the sloop, whose sailing days, like his own, seemed done for, stirred him deeply. The meeting on the beach of Slocum and the *Spray* was the start of one of the world's love affairs. From that hour, and for all remaining existence, Slocum and the *Spray* were never really to be parted."[1]

Meanwhile, in the course of the *Spray's* resurrection, Slocum was hired as "navigator in command" aboard the *Destroyer*, an iron gunboat bound for the Brazilian government engaged in civil war. The promise of a wartime wage — as well as the opportunity to avenge his loss of the *Aquidneck* — sidetracked Slocum from his task at hand, and he became in December of 1893 a mercenary seaman.

And though the voyage provided him with material for another book, it failed to provide him with any of the wage. So, after launching his rebuilt craft, Slocum again tried publishing a book; this time, though, he gave away the volume as he tried to create interest in chartering the *Spray* as a fishing boat.

Still somewhat luckless and not particularly wealthy, Joshua Slocum claimed that he decided to sail the *Spray* around the world in order to make money from the stories he could tell in lectures and in newspapers, not unlike two of his most admired writers: Robert Louis Stevenson and Mark Twain. Teller, on the other hand, maintains that Slocum took to the sea again alone to try to make some sense of it all of his life and of this world. In looking back from a hundred years, however, this adventure appears clearly as the further pursuit of his boyhood dream; not so much to sail around the world, but simply to live this life on the sea, alone or otherwise.

[1]Teller, Walter Magnes. "Joshua Slocum: Navigator and Writer," in *The Voyage of Joshua Slocum*. Rutgers University Press, p. 22.

INTRODUCTION

And so, Joshua Slocum set out to keep his dream afloat and to outfit the *Spray* with ample provisions and reading materials for a solo circumnavigation. After all, sailing around the world was not so wild a dream and nothing new to him. He still had his charts, his firearms, his compass and sextant, as well as all of his medicines.

But this whole idea of sailing alone was a notion heretofore unheard of.

On the day of his departure, 24 April 1895, several people had come to the East Boston wharf to see the captain off. Among them was twenty-four-year-old Mabel Wagnall, the daughter of the publisher Adam Wagnall. Already the elder Wagnall already had sent the captain a box of books for his sailing library, which included — among others — several works of Charles Darwin (whose expeditionary vessel, the *Beagle,* had also sailed the world), stories by Irving and Cervantes, poetry of Shakespeare and Tennyson, and novels from his favorites: Stevenson and Twain. The young Miss Wagnall, though, had come to deliver in person a copy of her own first book, which she asked Slocum to carry around the world and back. Then, the young lady is said to have whispered: "The *Spray* will come back." And so it is that this very book which recounts the captain's venture is dedicated "To the one who said: 'The *Spray* will come back.'"

Some three years later, in fact, Mabel Wagnall was among the first to greet Joshua Slocum upon his return at Newport Harbor — even before Hettie Slocum was able to be there and welcome her husband home.

His voyage completed, however, most people openly doubted that Slocum ever had been able to do what he was now proclaiming to have done. His running accounts had been published in several newspapers, but they had been overshadowed by reports of the ongoing Spanish-American War. As a result, some dismissed him as little more than a smuggler, or nothing other than an old sailor who refused to come to terms with the age of steam. For the time being — and in more ways than one — Joshua Slocum seemed to be right back where he had started: an aging sailor lost upon the land.

When Slocum had begun his voyage, the President of the United States was Grover Cleveland, whose summer home at Gray Gables overlooked the headwaters of Buzzards Bay, west of the Cape Cod village of Sagamore. Not long after Slocum's return, his adventure — as well as his newest book, *Sailing Alone Around the World* — gained credibility through the admiration of the new President, Teddy Roosevelt, whose summer estate at Sagamore Hill overlooked the waters of Oyster Bay on Long Island.

In addition to that sort of endorsement, this book was different from Slocum's others because there was a legitimate publisher paying the captain for his story. First it was serialized in *Century Illustrated Magazine* from September of 1899 through March of 1900, then the book was released in that final month. By then, people were willing to accept the notion that a man might be able to lash the helm and sail his vessel — night and day — over such great distances without steering it himself.

To promote his book and to earn some additional money, the captain continued to lecture, much as he had learned during the course of his voyage. TR invited Slocum to recount his tales at the White House, and the captain invited the president's young son to sail aboard the *Spray*.

Despite all the favorable publicity, though, Joshua Slocum felt no more comfortable on land than he had when he set out to circumnavigate the globe alone, and so he still sought new adventures. The Arctic was fast becoming an intriguing frontier, and Slocum considered sailing there. Then, again, the thought had occurred to him that something fascinating lurked beneath the sea. But while he contemplated those depths, he yearned to reach newer heights in the heavier-than-air machine invented by Samuel P. Langley.

To a mutual friend at the Smithsonian Institution, Slocum sent his latest book with a cover letter. "I am not the old fossil that some take me for, and I am not for old ideas when new are better," he wrote adding:

I was hoping that Professor Langley or some one else would

have launched a successful flying ship before this and that I could have a second mate's position on it, to soar. I felt sure that when you have time to scan my poor story you will find that I consider the human mind above all else that we know of in this world.

That foray into flying never met with success. Instead, Captain Slocum sailed the *Spray* up to Buffalo for the Pan American Exposition in 1901, where he became a side-show of sorts, not unlike Buffalo Bill Cody. The money that the captain had been able to earn from such appearances, from his book-selling, and from his lectures eventually enabled him to purchase the one and only piece of land he ever would own: a modest farm in the town of West Tisbury on the island of Martha's Vineyard. There he and Hettie had hoped to raise hops and fruits. But a sailor is meant to sail.

By 1905, Joshua Slocum was sailing the *Spray* alone to warmer waters in the winter, where he used his vessel to move cargo around Miami and the Caribbean. This sort of sailing he did for the next few years, returning to the island now and then. In June of 1908, the tenth anniversary of the *Spray's* return from around the world, he freighted back to the American Museum of Natural History a two-ton tree of coral discovered by scientists in the Bahamas.

The following year, Slocum turned sixty-five, an admirable age for that period, not to mention a modern-day mark for retirement. Still, the seafarer was interested in setting new goals. Back on the Vineyard for a brief stay, he was fitting-out the *Spray* for a voyage to South America: up the Orinoco River, through the Rio Negro, and on to the obscure sources of the Amazon itself. From there, he would follow its magnanimous flow back to the ocean, then home once again on the sea.

Folks on the island had been watching him make his preparations in the fishing village of Menemsha, from where he sailed east along the Vineyard Sound into the harbor at Tisbury (known now as Vineyard Haven). The move was at once both remarkable and ordinary for a man who had been so far in such a small boat. And on 14 November 1909, Joshua Slocum sailed the *Spray* away from the island's harbor.

Neither the sailor, nor his sloop was ever seen again.

Some say that the *Spray* simply fell apart, a neglected hulk whose time had come. Others believe there could have been a fire, or a storm, or a collision in the night. Of these, Slocum's oldest son, Victor, expressed belief that the *Spray* met her fate with a steamer in the shipping lanes.[2]

Without any verifiable resolution, however, Hettie Slocum finally petitioned the court in November of 1924 to declare the single-handed sailor legally dead, noting:

. . . that Joshua Slocum . . . disappeared, absconded, and absented himself on the 14th day of November A.D. 1909; . . . that said absentee . . . a Master Mariner by occupation . . . disappeared on the date above-named under the following circumstances, to wit: He sailed from Tisbury, Massachusetts in the Sloop *Spray* . . . and has never been heard from since . . . .

Thus remains without certain conclusion the story of a voyage that began a hundred years ago; thus stays afloat the dream of a boy named Joshua Slocum, as well as the dream of those who still harbor some hope that one day, "The *Spray* will come back."

Donald W. Davidson
Cape Cod, Massachusetts
24 April 1995

[2]Slocum, Victor. *Captain Joshua Slocum*, Sheridan House, p. 369.

CHAPTER 1

A blue-nose ancestry with Yankee proclivities – Youthful fondness for the sea – Master of the ship *Northern Light* – Loss of the *Aquidneck* – Return home from Brazil in the canoe *Liberdade* – The gift of a "ship" – The rebuilding of the *Spray* – Conundrums in regard to finance and caulking – The launching of the *Spray*.

I N the fair land of Nova Scotia, a maritime province, there is a ridge called North Mountain, overlooking the Bay of Fundy on one side and the fertile Annapolis valley on the other. On the northern slope of the range grows the hardy spruce-tree, well adapted for ship-timbers, of which many vessels of all classes have been built. The people of this coast, hardy, robust, and strong, are disposed to compete in the world's commerce, and it is nothing against the master mariner if the birthplace on his certificate be Nova Scotia. I was born in a cold spot, on coldest North Mountain, on a cold February 20, though I am a citizen of the United States — a naturalized Yankee, if it may be said that Nova Scotians are not Yankees in the truest sense of the word. On both sides my family were sailors; and if any Slocum should be found not seafaring, he will show at least an inclination to whittle models of boats and contemplate voyages. My father was the sort of man who — if wrecked on a desolate island — would find his way home, if he had a jack-knife and could find a tree. He was a good judge of a boat, but the old clay farm which some calamity made his was an anchor to him. He was not afraid of a capful of wind, and he never took a back seat at a camp-meeting or a good, old-fashioned revival.

As for myself, the wonderful sea charmed me from the first. At the age of eight I had already been afloat along with other boys on the bay, with chances greatly in favor of being drowned. When a lad I filled the important post of cook on a fishing-schooner. But I was not long in

1

the galley, for the crew mutinied at the appearance of my first duff, and "chucked me out" before I had a chance to shine as a culinary artist. The next step toward the goal of happiness found me before the mast in a full-rigged ship bound on a foreign voyage. Thus I came "over the bows" — and not in through the cabin windows — to the command of a ship.

My best command was that of the magnificent ship *Northern Light*, of which I was part-owner. I had a right to be proud of her, for that time — in the eighties — she was the finest American sailing-vessel afloat. Afterward I owned and sailed the *Aquidneck*, a little bark which of all man's handiwork seemed to me the nearest to perfection of beauty, and which in speed, when the wind blew, asked no favors of steamers. I had been nearly twenty years a shipmaster when I quit her deck on the coast of Brazil, where she was wrecked. My home voyage to New York with my family was made in the canoe *Liberdade*, without accident.

My voyages all were foreign. I sailed as freighter and trader principally to China, Australia, and Japan, and among the Spice Islands. Mine was not the sort of life to make one long coil up one's ropes on land, the customs and ways of which I had finally almost forgotten. And so when times for freighters got bad — as at last they did — and I tried to quit the sea, what was there for an old sailor to do? I was born in the breezes, and I had studied the sea as perhaps few men have studied it, neglecting all else. Next in attractiveness after seafaring, came ship-building. I longed to be the master in both professions, and in a small way, in time, I accomplished my desire. From the decks of stout ships in the worst gales I had made calculations as to the size and sort of ship safest for all weather and seas. Thus the voyage which I am now to narrate was a natural outcome not only of my love of adventure, but of my lifelong experience.

One midwinter day of 1892, in Boston where I had been cast up from old ocean, so to speak, a year or two before, I was cogitating whether I should apply for a command and again eat my bread and butter on the sea, or go to work at the shipyard, when I met an old acquaintance, a whaling-captain, who said: "Come to Fairhaven and I'll give you a ship. But," he added, "she wants some repairs." The captain's terms, when fully explained, were more than satisfactory to me. They included all the assistance I would require to fit the craft for sea. I was only too glad to accept, for I had already found that I could not obtain work in the shipyard without first paying fifty dollars to a society. And as for a ship to command, there were not enough ships to go round. Nearly all our tall vessels had been cut down for coal-barges and were being ignominiously towed by the nose from port to port, while many worthy captains addressed themselves to Sailors' Snug Harbor.

The next day I landed at Fairhaven, opposite New Bedford, and found that my friend had something of a joke on me. For seven years the joke had been on him. The "ship" proved to be a very antiquated sloop called the *Spray*, which the neighbors declared had been built in the year 1. She was affectionately propped up in a field some distance from salt water and was covered with canvas. The people of Fairhaven, I hardly need say they are thrifty and observant. For seven years they had asked, "I wonder what Captain Eben Pierce is going to do with the old *Spray*?" The day I appeared there was a buzz at the gossip exchange: at last some one had come and was actually at work on the old *Spray*. "Breaking her up, I s'pose?" "No; going to rebuild her." Great was the amazement. "Will it pay?" was the question which for a year or more I answered by declaring that I would make it pay.

My ax felled a stout oak-tree nearby for a keel, and Farmer Howard (for a small sum of money) hauled in this and enough timbers for the frame of the new vessel. I rigged a steam-box and a pot for a boiler. The timbers for ribs, being straight saplings, were dressed and steamed till supple, and then bent over a log, where they were secured till set. Something tangible appeared every day to show for my labor, and the neighbors made the work sociable. It was a great day in the *Spray* shipyard when her new stem was set up and fastened to the new keel. Whaling-captains came from far to survey it. With one voice they pronounced it "A1," and in their opinion "fit to smash ice." The oldest captain shook my hand warmly when the breast-hooks were put in, declaring that he could see no reason why the *Spray* should not "cut in bow-head" yet off the coast of Greenland.

The much-esteemed stem-piece was from the butt of the smartest kind of a pasture oak. It afterward split a coral patch in two at the Keeling Islands, and did not receive a blemish. Better timber for a ship than pasture white oak never grew. The breast-hooks, as well as all the ribs, were of this wood and were steamed and bent into shape as required. It was hard upon March when I began work in earnest; the weather was cold. Still, there were plenty of inspectors to back me with advice. When a whaling-captain hove in sight I just rested my adz awhile and "gammed" with him.

New Bedford, the home of whaling-captains, is connected with Fairhaven by a bridge, and the walking is good. They never "worked along up" to the shipyard too often for me. It was the charming tales about arctic whaling that inspired me to put a double set of breast-hooks in the *Spray*, that she might shunt ice.

The seasons came quickly while I worked. Hardly were the ribs of the sloop up before apple-trees were in bloom. Then the daisies and the cherries came soon after. Close by the place where the old *Spray* had now dissolved rested the ashes of John Cook, a revered Pilgrim father. So the new *Spray* rose from hallowed ground. From the deck of the new craft I could put out my hand and pick cherries that grew over the little grave. The planks for the new vessel, which I soon came to put on, were of Georgia pine an inch and a half thick. The operations of putting them on was tedious, but — when on — the caulking was easy. The outward edges stood slightly open to receive the caulking, but the inner edges were so close that I could not see daylight between them. All the butts were fastened by through bolts with screw-nuts tightening them to the timbers so that there would be no complaint from them. Many bolts with screw-nuts were used in

4

other parts of the construction, in all about a thousand. It was my purpose to make my vessel stout and strong.

Now, it is a law in Lloyd's that the *Jane* repaired all out of the old until she is entirely new is still the *Jane*. The *Spray* changed her being so gradually that it was hard to say at what point the old died or the new took birth, and it was no matter. The bulwarks I built up of white-oak stanchions fourteen inches high, and covered with seven-eighth-inch white pine. These stanchions, mortised through a two-inch covering-board, I caulked with thin cedar wedges. They have remained perfectly tight ever since.

Cross-section of the *Spray*

The deck I made of one and a half inch by three inch white pine spiked to beams, six by six inches, of yellow or Georgia pine, placed three feet apart. The deck-enclosures were one over the aperture of the main hatch — six feet by six — for a cooking-galley, and a trunk farther aft — about ten feet by twelve — for a cabin. Both of these rose about three feet above the deck and were sunk sufficiently into the hold to afford head-room. In the spaces along the sides of the cabin, under the deck, I arranged a berth to sleep in and shelves for small storage, not forgetting a place for the medicine-chest. In the midship hold — that is, the space between cabin and galley under the deck — was room for provision of water, salt beef, etc., ample for many months.

The hull of my vessel being now put together as strongly as wood and iron could make her, and the various rooms partitioned off, I set about "caulking ship." Grave fears were entertained by some that at this point I should fail. I myself gave some thought as to the

5

advisability of a "professional caulker." The very first blow I struck on the cotton with the caulking-iron — which I thought was right — many others thought wrong.

"It'll crawl!" cried a man from Marion, passing with a basket of clams on his back.

"It'll crawl!" cried another from West Island, when he saw me driving cotton into the seams.

Bruno simply wagged his tail.

Even Mr. Ben J—, a noted authority on whaling-ships, whose mind, however, was said to be totter, asked rather confidently if I did not think "it would crawl."

"How fast will it crawl?" cried my old captain friend, who had been towed by many a lively sperm-whale. "Tell us how fast," cried he, "that we may get into port in time."

However, I drove a thread of oakum on top of the cotton, as from the first I had intended to do. And Bruno again wagged his tail. The cotton never "crawled." When the caulking was finished, two coats of copper paint were slapped on the bottom, two of white lead on the topsides and bulwarks. The rudder was then shipped and painted, and on the following day the *Spray* was launched. As she rode at her ancient, rust-eaten anchor, she sat on the water like a swan.

The *Spray's* dimensions were, when finished, thirty-six feet nine inches long, over all, fourteen feet two inches wide, and four feet two inches deep in the hold, her tonnage being nine tons net and twelve and seventy-one hundredths tons gross.

Then the mast, a smart New Hampshire spruce, was fitted and likewise all the small appurtenances necessary for a short cruise. Sails were bent, and away she flew with my friend Captain Pierce and me, across Buzzard's Bay on a trial-trip — all right. The only thing that now worried my friends along the beach was, "Will she pay?" The cost of my new vessel was $553.62 for materials, and thirteen months of my own labor. I was several months more than that at Fairhaven, for I got work now and then on an occasional whale-ship fitting farther down the harbor, and that kept me the overtime.

CHAPTER 2

Failure as a fisherman – A voyage around the world projected – From Boston to Gloucester – Fitting out for the ocean voyage – Half of a dory for a ship's boat – The run from Gloucester to Nova Scotia – A shaking up in home waters – Among old friends.

I spent a season in my new craft fishing on the coast, only to find that I had not the cunning properly to bait a hook. But at last the time arrived to weigh anchor and get to sea in earnest. I had resolved on a voyage around the world, and as the wind on the morning of April 24, 1895, was fair, at noon I weighed anchor, set sail, and filled away from Boston, where the *Spray* had been moored snugly all winter. The twelve-o'clock whistles were blowing just as the sloop shot ahead under full sail. A short board was made up the harbor on the port tack, then coming about she stood seaward, with her boom well off to port, and swung past the ferries with lively heels. A photographer on the outer pier at East Boston got a picture of her as she swept by, her flag at the peak throwing its folds clear.

A thrilling pulse beat high in me. My step was light on the deck in the crisp air. I felt that there could be no turning back, and that I was engaging in an adventure the meaning of which I thoroughly understood. I had taken little advice from anyone, for I had a right to my own opinions in matters pertaining to the sea. That the next of sailors might do worse than even I alone was borne upon me not a league from Boston docks, where a great steamship — fully manned, officered, and piloted — lay stranded and broken. This was the *Venetian*. She was broken completely in two over a ledge. So in the first hour of my lone voyage I had proof that the *Spray* could at least do better than this full-handed steamship, for I was already farther on my voyage than she.

7

"Take warning, *Spray*, and have a care," I uttered aloud to my bark, passing fairylike silently down the bay.

The wind freshened, and the *Spray* rounded Deer Island light, going at the rate of seven knots. Passing it, she squared away direct of Gloucester, where she was to procure some fishermen's stores. Waves dancing joyously across Massachusetts Bay met the sloop coming out, to dash themselves instantly into the myriads of sparkling gems that hung about her breast at every surge. The day was perfect, the sunlight clear and strong. Every particle of water thrown into the air became a gem, and the *Spray* — making good her name as she dashed ahead — snatched necklace after necklace from the sea and as often threw them away. We have all seen miniature rainbows about a ship's prow, but the *Spray* flung out a bow of her own that day, such as I had never seen before. Her good angel had embarked on the voyage; I so read it in the sea.

Bold Nahant was soon abeam, then Marblehead was put astern. Other vessels were outward bound, but none of them passed the *Spray* flying along on her course. I heard the clanking of the dismal bell on Norman's Woe as we went by; and the reef where the schooner *Hesperus* struck I passed close aboard. The "bones" of a wreck tossed-up lay bleaching on the shore abreast. The wind still freshening, I settled the throat of the mainsail to ease the sloop's helm, for I could hardly hold her before it with the whole mainsail set. A schooner ahead of me lowered all sail and ran into port under bare poles, the wind being fair. As the *Spray* brushed by the stranger, I saw that some of his sails were gone, and much broken canvas hung in his rigging from the effects of a squall.

I made for the cove, a lovely branch of Gloucester's fine harbor, again to look the *Spray* over and again to weigh the voyage, and my feelings, and all that. The bay was feather-white as my little vessel tore in, smothered in foam. It was my first experience of coming into port alone with a craft of any size and in among shipping. Old fishermen ran down to the wharf for which the *Spray* was heading, apparently intent upon braining herself there. I

8

hardly know how a calamity was averted, but with my heart in my mouth, almost, I let go the wheel, stepped quickly forward, and downed the jib. The sloop naturally rounded in the wind and — just ranging ahead — laid her cheek against a mooring-pile at the windward corner of the wharf, so quietly, after all, that she would not have broken an egg. Very leisurely I passed a rope around the post, and she was moored. Then a cheer went up from the little crowd on the wharf.

"You couldn't 'a' done it better," cried an old skipper, "if you weighed a ton!"

Now, my weight was rather less than the fifteenth part of a ton, but I said nothing, only putting on a look of careless indifference to say for me, "Oh, that's nothing;" for some of the ablest sailors in the world were looking at me, and my wish was not to appear green, for I had a mind to stay in Gloucester several days. Had I uttered a word it surely would have betrayed me, for I was still quite nervous and short of breath.

I remained in Gloucester about two weeks, fitting out with the various articles for the voyage most readily obtained there. The owners of the wharf where I lay, and of the many fishing-vessels, put on board dry cod galore, also a barrel of oil to calm the waves. They were old skippers themselves and took a great interest in the voyage. They also made the *Spray* a present of a "fisherman's own" lantern, which I found would throw a light a great distance round. Indeed, a ship that would run another down having such a good light aboard would be capable of running into a light-ship. A gaff, a pugh, and a dip-net — all of which an old fisherman declared I could not sail without — were also put aboard. Then, too, from across the cove came a case of copper paint, a famous antifouling article, which stood me in good stead long after. I slapped two coats of this paint on the bottom of the *Spray* while she lay a tide or so on the hard beach.

For a boat to take along, I made shift to cut a castaway dory in two athwartships, boarding up the end where it was cut. This half-dory I could hoist in and out by the nose easily enough, by hooking the throat-halyards into a strop fitted for the purpose. A whole dory would be heavy and awkward to handle alone. Manifestly there was not room on deck for more than the half of a boat, which, after all, was better than no boat at all, and was large enough for one man. I perceived, moreover, that the newly arranged craft would answer for a washing-machine when placed athwartships and also for a bath-tub. Indeed, for the former office my razed dory gained such a reputation on the voyage that my washerwoman at Samoa would not take no for an answer. She could see with one eye that it was a new invention which beat any Yankee notion ever brought by missionaries to the islands, and she had to have it.

The want of a chronometer for the voyage was all that now worried me. In our newfangled notions of navigation it is supposed that a mariner cannot find his way without one, and I had myself drifted into this way of thinking. My old chronometer, a good one, had been long in disuse. It would cost fifteen dollars to clean and rate it. Fifteen dollars! For sufficient reasons I left that timepiece at home, where the Dutchman left his anchor. I had the great lantern, and a lady in Boston sent me the price of a large two-burner cabin lamp, which lighted the cabin at night and — by some small contriving — served for a stove through the day.

Being thus refitted, I was once more ready for sea and on May 7 again made sail. With little room in which to turn, the *Spray* in gathering headway scratched the paint off an old, fine-weather craft in the fairway, being puttied and painted for a summer voyage.

"Who'll pay for that?" growled the painters.

"I will," said I.

"With the main-sheet," echoed the captain of the *Bluebird*, close by, which was his way of saying that I was off.

There was nothing to pay for above five cents' worth of paint, maybe, but such a din was raised between the old "hooker" and the *Bluebird*, which now took up my case, that the first cause of it was forgotten altogether. Anyhow, no bill was sent after me.

The weather was mild on my day of departure from Gloucester. On the point ahead, as the *Spray* stood out of the cove, was a lively picture, for the front of a tall factory was a flutter of handkerchiefs and caps. Pretty faces peered out of the windows from the top to the bottom of the building, all smiling *bon voyage*. Some hailed me to know where away and why alone. Why? When I made as if to stand in, a hundred pairs of arms reached out and said come, but the shore was dangerous! The sloop worked out of the bay against a light southwest wind and about noon squared away off Eastern Point, receiving at the same time a hearty salute — the last of many kindnesses to her at Gloucester.

The wind freshened off the point, and skipping along smoothly, the *Spray* was soon off Thatcher's Island lights. Thence shaping her course east, by compass, to go north of Cashes Ledge and the Amen Rocks, I sat and considered the matter all over again and asked myself once more whether it were best to sail beyond the ledge and rocks at all. I had only said that I would sail round the world in the *Spray* — "dangers of the sea excepted" — but I must have said it very much in earnest. The "charter-party" with myself seemed to bind me, and so I sailed on.

Toward night I hauled the sloop to the wind and — baiting a hook — sounded for bottom-fish in thirty fathoms of water on the edge of Cashes Ledge. With fair success I hauled till dark, landing on deck three cod and two haddocks, one hake, and — best of all — a small halibut, all plump and spry. This, I thought, would be the place to take in a good stock of provisions above what I already had, so I put out a sea-anchor that would hold her head to windward. The current being southwest against the wind, I felt quite sure I would find the *Spray* still on the bank or near it in the morning. Then, "straddling" the cable and putting my great lantern in the rigging, I lay down for the first time at sea alone, not to sleep, but to doze and to dream.

I had read somewhere of a fishing-schooner hooking her anchor into a whale and being towed a long way and at great speed. This was exactly what happened to the *Spray* — in my dream! I could not shake it off entirely when I awoke and found that it was the wind blowing and the heavy sea now running that had disturbed my short rest. A scud was flying across the moon. A storm was brewing; indeed, it was already stormy. I reefed the sails, then hauled in my sea-anchor and — setting what canvas the sloop could carry — headed her away for Monhegan light, which she made before daylight on the morning of the 8th. The wind being free, I ran on into Round Pond Harbor, which is a little port east from Pemaquid. Here I rested a day, while the wind rattled among the pine trees on shore. But the following day was fine enough, and I put out to sea, first writing up my log from Cape Ann, not omitting a full account of my adventure with the whale.

The *Spray*, heading east, stretched along the coast among many islands and over a tranquil sea. At evening of this day, May 10, she came up with a considerable island, which I shall always think of as the Island of Frogs, for the *Spray* was charmed by a million voices. From the Island of Frogs we made for the Island of Birds (called Gannet Island and, sometimes, Gannet Rock), whereon is a bright, intermittent light, which flashed fitfully across the *Spray's* deck as she coasted along under its light and shade. Thence shaping a course for Briar's Island, I came among vessels the following afternoon on the western fishing-grounds, and — after speaking with a fisherman at anchor, who gave me a wrong course — the *Spray* sailed directly over the southwest ledge through the worst tide-race in the Bay of Fundy and got into Westport Harbor in Nova Scotia, where I had spent eight days of my life as a lad.

The fisherman may have said "east-southeast," the course I was steering when I hailed him; but I thought he said "east-northeast," and I accordingly changed it to that. Before he made up his mind to answer me at all, he improved the occasion of his own curiosity to know where I was from, and if I was alone, and if I didn't have "no dorg nor no cat." It was the first time in all my life at sea that I had heard a hail for information he answered by a question. I think the chap belonged to the Foreign Islands. There was one thing I was sure of, and that was that he did not belong to Briar's Island, because he dodged a sea that slopped over the rail and — stopping to brush the water from his face — lost a fine cod which he

"No dorg nor no cat."

was about to ship. My islander would not have done that. It is known that a Briar Islander — fish or no fish on his hook — never flinches from a sea. He just tends to his lines and hauls or "saws." Nay, have I not seen my old friend Deacon W. D—, a good man of the island, while listening to a sermon in the little church on the hill, reach out his hand over the door of his pew and "jig" imaginary squid in the aisle, to the intense delight of the young

13

people, who did not realize that to catch good fish one must have good bait, the thing most on the deacon's mind.

I was delighted to reach Westport. Any port at all would have been delightful after the terrible thrashing I got in the fierce sou'west rip, and to find myself among old schoolmates now was charming. It was the 13th of the month, and 13 is my lucky number — a fact registered long before Dr. Nansen sailed in search of the north pole with his crew of thirteen. Perhaps he had heard of my success in taking a most extraordinary ship successfully to Brazil with that number of crew. The very stones on Briar's Island I was glad to see again, and I knew them all. The little shop round the corner, which for thirty-five years I had not seen, was the same, except that it looked a deal smaller. It wore the same shingles — I was sure of it; for did not I know the roof where we boys night after night hunted for the skin of a black cat, to be taken on a dark night to make a plaster for a poor lame man? Lowry the tailor lived there when boys were boys. In his day he was fond of the gun. He always carried his powder loose in the tail pocket of his coat. He usually had in his mouth a short dudeen. But in an evil moment he put the dudeen, lighted, in the pocket among the powder. Mr. Lowry was an eccentric man.

At Briar's Island I overhauled the *Spray* once more and tried her seams, but found that even the test of the sou'west rip had started nothing. Bad weather and much head wind prevailing outside, I was in no hurry to round Cape Sable. I made a short excursion with some friends to St. Mary's Bay, an old cruising-ground, and back to the island. Then I sailed, putting into Yarmouth the following day on account of fog and head wind. I spend some days pleasantly enough in Yarmouth, took in some butter for the voyage, also a barrel of potatoes, filled six barrels of water, and stowed all under deck. At Yarmouth, too, I got my famous tin clock, the only timepiece I carried on the whole voyage. The price of it was a dollar and a half, but on account of the face being smashed the merchant let me have it for a dollar.

CHAPTER 3

Good-bye to the American coast – Off Sable Island in a fog – In the open sea – The man in the moon takes an interest in the voyage – The first fit of loneliness – The *Spray* encounters *La Vaguisa* – A bottle of wine from the Spaniard – A bout of words with the captain of the *Java* – The steamship *Olympia* spoken – Arrival at the Azores.

I now stowed all my goods securely, for the boisterous Atlantic was before me, and I sent the topmast down, knowing that the *Spray* would be the wholesomer with it on deck. Then I gave the lanyards a pull and hitched them afresh, and saw that the gammon was secure, also that the boat was lashed, for even in summer one may meet with bad weather in the crossing.

In fact, many weeks of bad weather had prevailed. On July 1, however, after a rude gale, the wind came out nor'west and clear, propitious for a good run. On the following day — the head sea having gone down — I sailed from Yarmouth and let go my last hold on America. The log of my first day on the Atlantic in the *Spray* reads briefly: "9:30A.M. sailed from Yarmouth. 4:30P.M. passed Cape Sable; distance, three cables from the land. The sloop making eight knots. Fresh breeze N.W." Before the sun went down I was taking my supper of strawberries and tea in smooth water under the lee of the east-coast land along which the *Spray* was now leisurely skirting.

At noon on July 3 Ironbound Island was abeam. The *Spray* was again at her best. A large schooner came out of Liverpool, Nova Scotia, this morning, steering eastward. The *Spray* put her hull down astern in five hours. At 6:45 P.M. I was in close under Chebucto Head light near Halifax Harbor. I set my flag and squared away, taking my departure from George's Island before dark to sail east of the coast.

There are many beacon lights along the coast. Sambro, the Rock of Lamentations, carries a noble light, which, however, the liner *Atlantic* — on the night of her terrible disaster — did not see. I watched light after light sink astern as I sailed into the unbounded sea, till Sambro, the last of them all, was below the horizon. The *Spray* was then alone. And sailing on, she held her course.

July 4, at 6A.M., I put in double reefs, and at 8:30A.M. turned out all reefs. At 9:40P.M. I raised the sheen only of the light on the west end of Sable Island, which may also be called the Island of Tragedies. The fog, which till this moment had held off, now lowered over the sea like a pall. I was in a world of fog, shut off from the universe. I did not see any more of the light. By the lead, which I cast often, I found that a little after midnight I was passing the east point of the island and should soon be clear of dangers of land and shoals. The wind was holding free, though it was from the foggy point, south-southwest. It is said that within a few years Sable Island has been reduced from forty miles in length to twenty, and that of three lighthouses built on it since 1880, two have been washed away and the third will soon be engulfed.

On the evening of July 5 the *Spray* — after having steered all day over a lumpy sea — took it into her head to go without the helmsman's aid. I had been steering southeast by south, but the wind hauling forward a bit, she dropped into a smooth lane, heading southeast and — making about eight knots — her very best work. I crowded on sail to cross the track of the liners without loss of time and to reach as soon as possible the friendly Gulf Stream. The fog lifting before night, I was afforded a look at the sun just as it was touching the sea. I watched it go down and out of sight. Then I turned my face eastward, and there — apparently at the very end of the bowsprit — was the smiling full moon rising out of the sea. Neptune himself coming over the bows could not have startled me more. "Good evening, sir," I cried, "I'm glad to see you." Many a long talk since then I have had with the man in the moon; he had my confidence on the voyage.

About midnight the fog shut down again denser than ever before. One could almost "stand on it." It continued so for a number of days, the wind increasing to a gale. The waves rose high, but I had a good ship. Still, in the dismal fog I felt myself drifting into loneliness, an insect on a straw in the midst of the elements. I lashed the helm,

"Good evening, sir."

and my vessel held her course. And while she sailed I slept.

During these days a feeling of awe crept over me. My memory worked with startling power. The ominous, the insignificant, the great, the small, the wonderful, the commonplace — all appeared before my mental vision in magical succession. Pages of my history were recalled which had been so long forgotten that they seemed to belong to a previous existence. I heard all the voices of the past laughing, crying, telling what I had heard them tell in many corners of the earth.

The loneliness of my state wore off when the gale was high and I found much work to do. When fine weather returned, then came the sense of solitude, which I could not shake off. I used my voice often, at first giving some order about the affairs of a ship, for I had been told that from disuse I should lose my speech. At the meridian altitude of the sun I called aloud, "Eight bells," after the custom on a ship at sea. Again from my cabin I cried to an imaginary man at the helm, "How does she head, there?" and again, "Is she on her course?" But getting no reply, I was reminded the more palpably of my condition. My voice sounded hollow on the empty air, and I dropped the practice. However, it was not long before the thought came to me that when I was a lad I used to sing; why not try that now, where it would disturb no one? My musical talent had never bred envy in others, but out on the Atlantic, to realize what it meant, you should have heard me sing. You should have seen the porpoises leap when I pitched my voice for the waves and the sea and all that was in it. Old turtles, with large eyes, poked their heads up out of the sea as I sang "Johnny Boker," and "We'll Pay Darby Doyl for his Boots," and the like. But the porpoises were, on the whole, vastly more appreciative than the turtles; they jumped a deal higher. One day when I was humming a favorite chant — I think it was "Babylon's a-Fallin" — a porpoise jumped higher than the bowsprit. Had the *Spray* been going a little faster she would have scooped him in. The sea-birds sailed around rather shy.

July 10, eight days at sea, the *Spray* was twelve hundred miles east of Cape Sable. One hundred and fifty miles a day for so small a vessel must be considered good sailing. It was the greatest run the *Spray* ever made before or since in so few days. On the evening of July 14 — in better humor than ever before — all hands cried, "Sail ho!" The sail was a barkentine, three points on the weather bow, hull down. Then came the night my ship was sailing along now without attention to the helm. The wind was south; she was heading east. Her sails were trimmed like the sails of the nautilus. They drew steadily all night. I went frequently on deck, but found all well. A merry breeze kept on from the south. Early in the morning of the 15th the *Spray* was close aboard the stranger, which proved to be *La Vaguisa* of Vigo, twenty-three days out of Philadelphia bound for Vigo. A lookout from his masthead had spied the *Spray* the evening before. The captain, when I came near enough, threw a line to me and sent a bottle of wine across slung by the neck, and very good wine it was. He also sent his card, which bore the name of Juan Gantes. I think he was a good man. But when I asked him to report me "all well" (the *Spray* passing him in a lively manner), he hauled his

shoulders much above his head. And when his mate, who knew of my expedition, told him that I was alone, he crossed himself and made for his cabin. I did not see him again. By sundown he was as far astern as he had been ahead the evening before.

There was now less and less monotony. On July 16 the wind was northwest and clear, the sea smooth, and a large bark, hull down, came in sight on the lee bow and at 2:30P.M. I spoke to the stranger. She was the bark *Java* of Glasgow, from Peru for Queenstown for orders. Her old captain was bearish, but I met a bear once in Alaska that looked pleasanter. At least, the bear seemed pleased to meet me, but this grizzly old man! Well, I supposed my hail disturbed his siesta, and my little sloop passing his great ship had

He also sent his card.

19

somewhat the effect on him that a red flag has upon a bull. I had the advantage over heavy ships, by long odds, in the light winds of this and the two previous days. The wind was light; his ship was heavy and foul, making poor headway, while the *Spray*, with a great mainsail bellying even to light winds, was just skipping along as nimbly as one could wish.

"How long has it been calm about here?" roared the captain of the *Java*, as I came within hail of him.

"Dunno, cap'n," I shouted back as loud as I could bawl. "I haven't been here long." At this the mate on the forecastle wore a broad grin. "I left Cape Sable fourteen days ago," I added. I was now well across toward the Azores.

"Mate," he roared to his chief officer, "mate, come here and listen to the Yankee's yarn. Haul down the flag, mate! Haul down the flag!" In the best of humor, after all, the *Java* surrendered to the *Spray*.

The acute pain of solitude experienced at first never returned. I had penetrated a mystery, and, by the way, I had sailed through a fog. I had met Neptune in his wrath, but he found that I had not treated him with contempt, and so he suffered me to go on and explore.

In the log for July 18 there is this entry: "Fine weather, wind south-southwest. Porpoises gamboling all about. the S.S. *Olympia* passed at 11:30A.M., long. W.34° 50′."

"It lacks now three minutes of the half-hour," shouted the captain, as he gave me the longitude and the time. I admired the businesslike air of the *Olympia*, but I have the feeling still that the captain was just a little too precise in his reckoning. That may be all well enough, however, where there is plenty of sea-room. But over-confidence, I believe, was the cause of the disaster to the liner *Atlantic*, and many more like her. The captain knew too well where he was. There were no porpoises at all skipping along with the *Olympia!* Porpoises always prefer sailing-ships. The captain was a young man, I observed, and had before him, I hope, a good record.

Land ho! On the morning of July 19 a mystic dome

like a mountain of silver stood alone in the sea ahead. Although the land was completely hidden by the white, glistening haze that shone in the sun like polished silver, I felt quite sure that it was Flores Island. At half-past four P.M. it was abeam. The haze in the meantime had disappeared. Flores is one hundred and seventy-four miles

The island of Pico.

from Fayal, and although it is a high island, it remained for many years undiscovered before the principal group of the islands had been colonized.

Early on the morning of July 20 I saw Pico looming above the clouds on the starboard bow. Lower lands burst forth as the sun burned away the morning fog, and island after island came into view. As I approached nearer, cultivated fields appeared, "and oh, how green the corn!" Only those who have seen the Azores from the deck of a vessel realize the beauty of the mid-ocean picture.

At 4:40P.M. I cast anchor at Fayal, exactly eighteen days from Cape Sable. The American consul, in a smart boat, came alongside before the *Spray* reached the breakwater, and a young naval officer, who feared for the safety of my vessel, boarded and offered his services as a pilot. The youngster, I have no good reason to doubt, could have handled a man-of-war, but the *Spray* was too small for the amount of uniform he wore. However, after fouling all the craft in port and sinking a lighter, she was moored without much damage to herself. This wonderful pilot expected a "gratification," I understood, but whether for the reason that his government — and not I — would have to pay the cost of raising the lighter, or because he did not sink the *Spray*, I could never make out. But I do forgive him.

It was the season for fruit when I arrived at the

Azores, and there was soon more of all kinds of it put on board than I knew what to do with. Islanders are always the kindest people in the world, and I met none anywhere kinder than the good hearts of this place. The people of the Azores are note a very rich community. The burden of taxes is heavy, with scant privileges in return, the air they breathe being about the only thing that is not taxed. The mother-country does not even allow them a port of entry for a foreign mail service. A packet passing never so close with mails for Horta must deliver them first in Lisbon, ostensibly to be fumigated, but really for the tariff from the packet. My own letters posted at Horta reached the United States six days behind my letter from Gibraltar, mailed thirteen days later.

The day after my arrival at Horta was the feast of a great saint. Boats loaded with people came from other islands to celebrate at Horta, the capital of the Azores. The deck of the *Spray* was crowded from morning till night with men, women, and children. On the day after the feast, a kind-hearted native harnessed a team and drove me a day over the beautiful roads all about Fayal, "because," said he in broken English, "when I was in America and couldn't speak a word of English, I found it hard till I met someone with time to listen to my story, and I promised my good saint then that if ever a stranger came to my country I would try to make him happy."

Unfortunately, this gentleman brought an interpreter, that I might "learn more of the country." The fellow was nearly the death of me, talking of ships and voyages and of the boats he had steered, the last thing in the world I wished to hear. He had sailed out of New Bedford, so he said, for "that Joe Wing they call 'John.'" My friend and host found hardly a chance to edge in a word. Before we parted, my host dined me with a cheer that would have gladdened the heart of a prince, but he was quite alone in his house.

"My wife and children all rest there," he said, pointing to the churchyard across the way. "I moved to this house from far off," he added, "to be near the spot, where I pray every morning."

Chart of the *Spray's* Atlantic voyages from Boston to Gibraltar,
thence to the Strait of Magellan in 1895,
and finally homeward from the Cape of Good Hope in 1898.

I remained four days at Fayal, and that was two more than I had intended to stay. It was the kindness of the islanders and their touching simplicity which detained me. A damsel, as innocent as an angel, came alongside one day and said she would embark on the *Spray* if I would land her at Lisbon. She could cook flying-fish, she thought, but her forte was dressing *bacalhao*. Her brother Antonio, who served as interpreter, hinted that, anyhow, he would like to make the trip. Antonio's heart went out to one John Wilson, and he was ready to sail for America by way of the two Capes to meet his friend.

"Do you know John Wilson of Boston?" he cried.

"I knew a John Wilson," I said, "but not of Boston."

"He had one daughter and one son," said Antonio, by way of identifying his friend.

If this reaches the right John Wilson, I am told to say that "Antonio of Pico remembers him."

CHAPTER 4

Squally weather in the Azores – High living – Delirious from cheese and plums – The pilot of the *Pinta* – At Gibraltar – Compliments exchanged with the British Navy – A picnic on the Morocco shore.

I set sail from Horta early on July 24. The southwest wind at the time was light, but squalls came up with the sun, and I was glad enough to get reefs in my sails before I had gone a mile. I had hardly set the mainsail, double-reefed, when a squall of wind down the mountains struck the sloop with such a violence that I thought her mast would go; however, a quick helm brought her to the wind. As it was, one of the weather lanyards was carried away, and the other was stranded. My tin basin, caught up by the wind, went flying across a French school-ship to leeward. It was more or less squally all day. Sailing along under high land, but rounding close under a bluff, I found an opportunity to mend the lanyards broken in the squall.

No sooner had I lowered my sails when a four-oared boat shot out from some gully in the rocks with a customs officer on board, who thought he had come upon a smuggler. I had some difficulty in making him comprehend the true case; however, one of his crew — a sailorly chap who understood how matters were — while we palavered jumped on board and rove off the new lanyards I had already prepared and with a friendly hand helped me "set up the rigging." This incident gave the turn in my favor. My story was then clear to all. I have found this the way of the world. Let one be without a friend, and see what will happen!

Passing the island of Pico after the rigging was mended, the *Spray* stretched across to leeward of the island of St. Michael's, which she was up with early on the morning of July 26, the wind blowing hard. Later in the day she passed the Prince of Monaco's fine steam-yacht bound to Fayal, where on a previous voyage the prince had slipped his cables to "escape a reception" which the padres of the island wished to give him. Why he so dreaded the "ovation" I could not make out. At Horta they did not know.

Since reaching the islands I had lived most luxuriously on fresh bread, butter, vegetables, and fruits of all kinds. Plums seemed the most plentiful on the *Spray*, and these I ate without stint. I had also a Pico white cheese that General Manning, the American consul-general, had given me (which I supposed was to be eaten), and of this I partook with the plums. Alas! by night-time I was doubled up with cramps.

The wind, which was already a smart breeze, was increasing somewhat with a heavy sky to the sou'west. Reefs had been turned out, and I must turn them in again somehow. Between cramps I got the mainsail down, hauled out the earings as best I could, and tied away point by point in the double reef. There being sea-room, I should in strict prudence have made all snug and gone down at once to my cabin. I am a careful man at sea, but this night in the coming storm I swayed up my sails, which (reefed though they were) were still too much in such heavy weather. And I saw to it that the sheets were securely belayed. In a word, I should have laid to, but did not. I gave her the double-reefed mainsail and whole jib instead, and set her on her course. Then I went below and threw myself upon the cabin floor in great pain. How long I lay there I could not tell, for I became delirious.

When I came to (as I thought) from my swoon, I realized that the sloop was plunging into a heavy sea, and — looking out of the companionway — to my amazement I saw a tall man at the helm. His rigid hand grasping the spokes of the wheel held them as in a vise. One may imagine my astonishment. His rig was that of a foreign sailor, and the large red cap he wore was cockbilled over his left ear, and all was set off with shaggy black whiskers. He would have been taken for a pirate in any part of the world.

While I gazed upon his threatening aspect I forgot about the storm and wondered if he had come to cut my throat. This he seemed to divine.

"Señor," said he, doffing his cap, "I have come to do you no harm." And a smile — the faintest in the world, but still a smile — played on his face, which seemed not unkind when he spoke.

"I have come to do you no harm. I have sailed free," he said, "but was never worse than a *contrabandista*. I am one of Columbus' crew," he continued. "I am the pilot of the *Pinta* come to aid you. Lie quiet, señor captain," he added, "and I will guide your ship to-night. You have a *calentura*, but you will be all right to-morrow."

I thought what a very devil he was to carry sail.

Again, as if he read my mind, he exclaimed: "Yonder is the *Pinta* ahead; we must overtake her. Give her sail; give her sail! *Vale, vale, muy vale!*" Biting off a large quid of black twist, he said: "You did wrong, captain, to mix cheese with plums. White cheese is never safe unless you know whence it comes. *Quien sabe*, it may have been from *leche de Capra* and becoming capricious —"

"Avast, there!" I cried. "I have no mind for moralizing."

I made shift to spread a mattress and lie on that instead of the hard floor, my eyes all the while fastened on my strange guest, who — remarking again that I would have "only pains and calentura" — chuckled as he chanted a wild song:

> High are the waves, fierce, gleaming,
>   High is the tempest roar!
> High the sea-bird screaming!
>   High the Azore!

I supposed I was now on the mend, for I was peevish and complained: "I detest your jingle. Your Azore should be at roost and would have been were it a respectable bird!" I begged he would tie a rope-yarn on the rest of the song, if there was any more of it. I was still in agony. Great seas were boarding the *Spray*, but in my fevered

27

brain I thought they were boats falling on deck, that careless draymen were throwing from wagons on the pier to which I imagined the *Spray* was now moored and without fenders to breast her off.

"You'll smash your boats!" I called out again and again, as the seas crashed on the cabin over my head.

The apparition at the wheel.

"You'll smash your boats, but you can't hurt the *Spray*. She is strong!" I cried.

I found, when my pains and calentura had gone, that the deck — now as white as a shark's tooth from seas washing over it — had been swept of everything movable. To my astonishment, I saw now at broad day that the *Spray* was still heading as I had left her and was going like a race-horse. Columbus himself could not have held her more exactly on her course. The sloop had made ninety miles in the night through a rough sea. I felt grateful to the old pilot, but I marveled some that he had not taken in the jib. The gale was moderating, and by noon the sun was shining. A meridian altitude and the distance on the patent log (which I always kept towing) told me that she had made a true course throughout the twenty-four hours.

I was getting much better now, but was very weak and did not turn out reefs that day or the night following, although the wind fell light. But I just put my wet clothes out in the sun when it was shining and — lying down there myself — fell asleep. Then who should visit me again but my old friend of the night before; this time, of course, in a dream.

"You did well last night to take my advice," he said, "and if you would, I should like to be with you often on the voyage, for the love of adventure alone." Finishing what he had to say, he again doffed his cap and disappeared as mysteriously as he came, returning (I suppose) to the phantom *Pinta*.

I awoke much refreshed and with the feeling that I had been in the presence of a friend and a seaman of vast experience. I gathered up my clothes (which by this time were dry), then, by inspiration, I threw overboard all the plums in the vessel.

July 28 was exceptionally fine. The wind from the northwest was light and the air balmy. I overhauled my wardrobe and bent on a white shirt against nearing some coasting-packet with genteel folk on board. I also did some washing to get the salt out of my clothes. After it all I was hungry, so I made a fire and very cautiously stewed a dish of pears and set them carefully aside till I had made a pot of delicious coffee, for both of which I could afford sugar and cream. But the crowning dish of all was a fish-hash, and there was enough of it for two. I was in good health again, and my appetite was ravenous. While I was dining I had a large onion over the double lamp stewing for luncheon later in the day. High living to-day!

In the afternoon the *Spray* came upon a large turtle asleep on the sea. He awoke with my harpoon through his neck, if he awoke at all. I had much difficulty in landing him on deck, which I finally accomplished by hooking the throat-halyards to one of his flippers, for he was about as heavy as my boat. I saw more turtles, and I rigged a burton ready with which to hoist them in; for I was obliged to lower the mainsail whenever the halyards were used for such purposes, and it was no small matter to hoist the large sail again. But the turtle-steak was good. I found no fault with the cook, and it was the rule of the voyage that the cook found no fault with me. There was never a ship's crew so well agreed. The bill of fare that evening was turtle-steak, tea and toast, fried potatoes, stewed onions; with dessert of stewed pears and cream.

Sometime in the afternoon I passed a barrel-buoy adrift, floating light on the water. It was painted red and rigged with a signal-staff about six feet high. A sudden change in the weather coming on, I got no more turtle or fish of any sort before reaching port. July 31 a gale sprang up suddenly from the north with heavy seas, and I shortened sail. The *Spray* made only fifty-one miles on her course that day. August 1 the gale continued with heavy seas. Through the night the sloop was reaching, under close-reefed main-sail and bobbed jib. At 3 P.M. the jib was washed off the bowsprit and blown to rags and ribbons. I bent the "jumbo" on a stay at the night-heads. As for the jib, let it go; I saved pieces of it, and, after all, I was in want of pot-rags.

On August 3 the gale broke, and I saw many signs of land. Bad weather having made itself felt in the galley, I was minded to try my hand at a loaf of bread, so rigging a pot of fire on deck by which to bake it, a loaf soon became an accomplished fact. One great feature about the ship's cooking is that one's appetite on the sea is always good — a fact that I realized when I cooked for the crew of fishermen in the before-mentioned boyhood days. Dinner being over, I sat for hours reading the life of

Columbus, and as the day wore on I watched the birds all flying in one direction, and said, "Land lies there."

Early the next morning, August 4, I discovered Spain. I saw fires on shore and knew that the country was inhabited. The *Spray* continued on her course till well in with the land, which was that about Trafalgar. Then keeping away a point, she passed through the Strait of Gibraltar, where she cast anchor at 3P.M. of the same day, less than twenty-nine days from Cape Sable. At the finish of this preliminary trip, I found myself in excellent health, not overworked or cramped, but as well as ever in my life, though I was as thin as a reef-point.

Two Italian barks, which had been close alongside at daylight, I saw long after I had anchored, passing up the African side of the strait. The *Spray* had sailed them both hull down before she reached Tarifa. So far as I know, the *Spray* beat everything going across the Atlantic except the steamers.

All was well, but I had forgotten to bring a bill of health from Horta, and so when the fierce old port doctor came to inspect there was a row. That, however, was the very thing needed. If you want to get on well with a true Britisher, you must first have a deuce of a row with him. I knew that well enough, and so I fired away — shot for shot — as best I could.

"Well, yes," the doctor admitted at last, "your crew are healthy enough, no doubt, but who knows the diseases of your last port?" — a reasonable enough remark.

"We ought to put you in the fort, sir!" he blustered, "but never mind. Free pratique, sir! Shove off, cockswain!" And that was the last I saw of the port doctor.

But on the following morning a steam-launch, much longer than the *Spray*, came alongside (or as much of her as could get alongside) with compliments from the senior naval officer, Admiral Bruce, saying there was a berth for the *Spray* at the arsenal. This was at the new mole. I had anchored at the old mole among the native craft, where it was rough and uncomfortable. Of course, I was glad to shift and did so as soon as possible, thinking of the great company the *Spray* would be in among battle-ships such as the *Collingwood*, *Balfleur*, and *Cormorant*, which were at that time stationed there, and on board all of which I was entertained later, most royally.

"'Put it thar!' as the Americans say," was the salute I got from Admiral Bruce when I called at the admiralty to thank him for his courtesy of the berth and for the use of the steam-launch which towed me into dock.

"About the berth, it is all right if it suits, and we'll tow you out when you are ready to go. But, say, what repairs do you want? Ahoy the *Hebe*, can you spare your sailmaker? The *Spray* wants a new jib. Construction and repair, there! will you see to the *Spray*? Say, old man, you must have knocked the devil out of her coming over alone in twenty-nine days! But we'll make it smooth for you here!" Not even her Majesty's ship the *Collingwood* was better looked after than the *Spray* at Gibraltar.

Later in the day the hail: "*Spray* ahoy! Mrs. Bruce would like to come on board and shake hands with the *Spray*. Will it be convenient to-day?"

"Very!" I joyfully shouted.

On the following day Sir F. Carrington, at the time governor of Gibraltar, with other high officers of the garrison and all the commanders of the battle-ships, came on board and signed their names in the *Spray's* logbook. Again there was a hail, "*Spray* ahoy!"

"Hello!"

"Commander Reynolds' compliments. You are invited on board H.M.S. *Collingwood*, 'at home' at 4:40P.M. Not later than 5:50P.M."

I had already hinted at the limited amount of my wardrobe and that I could never succeed as a dude.

"You are expected, sir, in a stovepipe hat and a claw-hammer coat!"

"Then I can't come."

"Dash it! Come in what you have on; that is what we mean."

"Aye, aye sir!"

The *Collingwood's* cheer was good, and had I worn a silk hat as high as the moon I could not have had a better time or been made more at home. An Englishman — even on his great battle-ship — unbends when the stranger passes his gangway, and when he says "at home" he means it.

That one should like Gibraltar would go without saying. How could one help loving so hospitable a place? Vegetables twice a week and milk every morning came from the palatial grounds of the admiralty.

"*Spray* ahoy!" would hail the admiral. "*Spray* ahoy!"

"Hello!"

"To-morrow is your vegetable day, sir."

"Aye, aye, sir!"

I rambled much about the old city, and a gunner piloted me through the galleries of the rock as far as a stranger is permitted to go. There is no excavation in the world for military purposes at all approaching these of Gibraltar in conception or execution. Viewing the stupendous works, it became hard to realize that one was within the Gibraltar of his little old Morse geography.

Before sailing, I was invited on a picnic with the governor, the officers of the garrison, and the commanders of the warships at the station. And a royal affair it was. Torpedo-boat No. 91, going twenty-two knots, carried our party to the Morocco shore and back. The day was perfect — too fine, in fact, for comfort on shore — and so no one landed at Morocco. No. 91 trembled like an aspen-leaf as she raced through the sea at top speed. Sublieutenant Boucher, apparently a mere lad, was in command and handled his ship with the skill of an older sailor.

The following day I lunched with General Carrington, the governor, at Line Wall House, which was once the Franciscan convent. In this interesting edifice are preserved relics of the fourteen sieges which Gibraltar has seen. On the next day, I supped with the admiral at his residence, the palace, which was once the convent of the Mercenaries. At each place, and all about, I felt the friendly grasp of a manly hand that lent me vital strength to pass the coming long days at sea.

I must confess that the perfect discipline, order, and

33

cheerfulness at Gibraltar were only a second wonder in the great stronghold. The vast amount of business going forward caused no more excitement than the quiet sailing of a well-appointed ship in a smooth sea. No one spoke above his natural voice, save a boatswain's mate now and then. The Hon. Horatio J. Sprague, the venerable United States consul at Gibraltar, honored the *Spray* with a visit on Sunday, August 24, and was much pleased to find that our British cousins had been so kind to her.

CHAPTER 5

Sailing from Gibraltar with the assistance of her Majesty's tug – The *Spray's* course changed – Chased by a pirate – A comparison with Columbus – The Canary Islands – The Cape Verde Islands – Sea life – Arrival at Pernambuco – A bill against the Brazilian government – Preparing for the stormy weather of the cape.

MONDAY, August 25, the *Spray* sailed from Gibraltar, well repaid for whatever deviation she had made from a direct course to reach the place. A tug belonging to her Majesty towed the sloop into the steady breeze clear of the mount, where her sails caught a volant wind, which carried her once more to the Atlantic, where it rose rapidly to a furious gale. My plan was in going down this coast to haul offshore, well clear of the land, which hereabouts is the home of pirates.

But I had hardly accomplished this when I perceived a felucca making out of the nearest port and finally following in the wake of the *Spray*. Now, my course to Gibraltar had been taken with a view to proceed up the Mediterranean Sea, through the Suez Canal, down the Red Sea, and east about, instead of a western route, which I finally adopted. By officers of vast experiences in navigating these seas, I was influenced to make the change. Longshore pirates on both coasts being numerous, I could not afford to make light of the advice. But here I was, after all, evidently in the midst of pirates and thieves! I changed my course, and the felucca did the same, both vessels sailing very fast, but the distance growing less and less between us. The *Spray* was doing nobly; she was even more than at her best. But, in spite of all I could do, she would broach now and then. She was carrying too much sail for safety. I must reef, or be dismasted and lose all, pirate or no pirate. I must reef, even if I had to grapple with him for my life.

I was not long in reefing the mainsail and sweating it

35

up — probably not more than fifteen minutes — but the felucca had in the meantime so shortened the distance between us that I now saw the tuft of hair on the heads of the crew — by which, it is said, Mohammed will pull them up into heaven — and they were coming on like the wind. From what I could clearly make out now, I felt them to be the sons of generations of pirates, and I saw by their movements that they were now preparing to strike a blow.

Chased by pirates.

The exultation on their faces, however, was changed in an instant to a look of fear and rage. Their craft, with too much sail on, broached to on the crest of a wave. This one great sea changed the aspect of affairs suddenly as the flash of a gun. Three minutes later the same wave overtook the *Spray* and shook her in every timber. At the same moment the sheet-strop parted and away went the main-boom, broken short at the rigging. Impulsively I sprang to the jib-halyards and down-haul, and instantly downed the jib. The head-sail being off and the helm put hard down, the sloop came in the wind with a bound. While shivering there — but a moment though it was — I got the mainsail down and secured inboard, broken boom and all. How I got the boom in before the sail was torn, I hardly know, but not a stitch of it was broken. The mainsail being secured, I hoisted away the jib and — without looking round — stepped quickly to the cabin and snatched down my loaded rifle and cartridges at hand, for I made mental calculations that the pirate would by this time have recovered his course and be close abroad, and that when I saw him it would be better for me to be looking at him along the barrel of a gun.

The piece was at my shoulder when I peered into the mist, but there was no pirate within a mile. The wave and squall that carried away my boom dismasted the felucca outright. I perceived his thieving crew — some dozen or more — struggling to recover their rigging from the sea.

I sailed comfortably on under the jib and forestaysail, which I now set. I fished the boom and furled the sail snug for the night, then hauled the sloop's head two points offshore to allow for the set of current and heavy rollers toward the land. This gave me the wind three points on the starboard quarter and a steady pull in the headsails. By the time I had things in this order it was dark, and a flying-fish had already fallen on my deck. I took him below for my supper, but found myself too tired to cook, or even to eat a thing already prepared. I do not remember having been more tired before or since in all my life than I was at the finish of that day.

Too fatigued to sleep, I rolled about with the motion of the vessel till near midnight, when I made shift to dress my fish and prepare a dish of tea. I fully realized now, if I had not before, that the voyage ahead would call for exertions ardent and lasting. On August 27 nothing could be seen of the Moor, or his country either, except two peaks away in the east through the clear atmosphere of morning. Soon after the sun rose, even these were obscured by haze, much to my satisfaction.

The wind, for a few days following my escape from the pirates, blew a steady but moderate gale, and the sea — though agitated into long rollers — was not uncomfortably rough or dangerous. And while sitting in my cabin, I could hardly realize that any sea was running at all, so easy was the long, swinging motion of the sloop over the

37

waves. All distracting uneasiness and excitement being now over, I was once more alone with myself in the realization that I was on the mighty sea and in the hands of the elements. I was happy and becoming more and more interested in the voyage.

Columbus, in the *Santa Maria*, sailing these seas more than four hundred years before, was not so happy as I, nor so sure of success in what he had undertaken. His first troubles at sea had already begun. His crew had managed — by foul play or otherwise — to break the ship's rudder while running before probably just such a gale as the *Spray* had passed through. And there was dissension on the *Santa Maria*, something that was unknown on the *Spray*.

After three days of squalls and shifting winds I threw myself down to rest and sleep, while — with helm lashed — the sloop sailed steadily on her course.

September 1, in the early morning, land-clouds rising ahead told of the Canary Islands not far away. A change in the weather came the next day: storm-clouds stretched their arms across the sky; from the east, to all appearances, might come a fierce harmattan, or from the south might come a fierce hurricane. Every point of the compass threatened a wild storm. My attention was turned to reefing sails, and no time was to be lost over it, either, for the sea in a moment was confusion itself, and I was glad to head the sloop three points or more away from her true course that she might ride safely over the waves. I was now scudding her for the channel between Africa and the island of Fuerteventura, the easternmost of the Canary Islands, for which I was on the lookout. At 2 P.M., the weather becoming suddenly fine, the island stood in view, already abeam to starboard and not more than seven miles off. Fuerteventura is twenty-seven hundred feet high and in fine weather is visible many leagues away.

The wind freshened in the night, and the *Spray* had a fine run through the channel. By daylight, September 3, she was twenty-five miles clear of all the islands, when a calm ensued, which was the precursor of another gale of wind that soon came on, bringing with it dust from the African shore. It howled dismally while it lasted, and though it was not the season of the harmattan, the sea in the course of an hour was discolored with a reddish-brown dust. The air remained thick with flying dust all the afternoon, but the wind — veering northwest at night — swept back to land and afforded the *Spray* once more a clear sky. Her mast now bent under a strong, steady pressure, and her bellying sail swept the sea as she rolled scuppers under, courtseying to the waves. These rolling waves thrilled me as they tossed my ship, passing quickly under her keel. This was grand sailing.

September 4, the wind, still fresh, blew from the north-northeast, and the sea surged along with the sloop. About noon a steamship — a bullock-droger from the river Plate — hove in sight, steering northeast and making bad weather of it. I signaled her, but got no answer. She was plunging into the head sea and rolling in a most astonishing manner. And from the way she yawed, one might have said that a wild steer was at the helm.

On the morning of September 6, I fund three flying-fish on deck and a fourth one down the fore-scuttle as close as possible to the frying pan. It was the best haul yet and afforded me a sumptuous breakfast and dinner.

The *Spray* had now settled down to the trade-winds and to the business of her voyage. Later in the day, another droger hove in sight, rolling as badly as her predecessor. I threw out no flag to this one, but got the worst of it for passing under her lee. She was, indeed, a stale one! And the poor cattle, how they bellowed! The time was when ships passing one another at sea backed their topsails and had a "gam," and on parting fired guns, but those good old days have gone. People have hardly time nowadays to speak even on the broad ocean, where news is news. And as for a salute of guns, they cannot afford the powder. There are no poetry-enshrined freighters on the sea now; it is a prosy life when we have no time to bid one another good morning.

My ship — running now in the full swing of the trades — left me days to myself for rest and recuperation. I employed the time in reading and writing, or in whatever I found to do about the rigging and the sails to keep them all in order. The cooking was always done quickly and was a small matter, as the bill of fare consisted mostly of flying-fish, hot biscuits and butter, potatoes, coffee and cream — dishes readily prepared.

On September 10, the *Spray* passed the island of St. Antonio, the northwesternmost of the Cape Verdes, close abroad. The landfall was wonderfully true, considering that no observations for longitude had been made. The wind, northeast, as the sloop drew by the island, was very squally, but I reefed her sails snug and steered broad from the highland of blustering St. Antonio. Then leaving the Cape Verde Islands out of sight astern, I found myself once more sailing a lonely sea and in a solitude supreme all around. When I slept, I dreamed that I was alone. This feeling never left me. But sleeping or waking, I seemed always to know the position of the sloop, and I saw my vessel moving across the chart, which became a picture before me.

One night while I sat in the cabin under this spell, the profound stillness all about was broken by human voices alongside! I sprang instantly to the deck, startled beyond my power to tell. Passing close under lee, like an apparition, was a white bark under full sail. The sailors on board of her were hauling ropes to brace the yards, which just cleared the sloop's mast as she swept by. No one hailed from the white-winged flier, but I heard some one on board say that he saw lights on the sloop and that he made her out to be a fisherman. I sat long on the starlit deck that night, thinking of ships and watching the constellations on their voyage.

On the following day, September 13, a large four-masted ship passed some distance to windward, heading north. The sloop was now rapidly drawing toward the region of doldrums, and the forces of the trade-winds was lessening. I could see by the ripples that a counter-current had set in. This I estimated to be about sixteen miles a day. In the heart of the counter-stream the rate was more than that setting eastward.

September 14 a lofty three-masted ship heading north was seen from the masthead. Neither this ship, nor the one seen yesterday was within signal distance, yet it was good even to see them. On the following day, heavy rain-clouds rose in the south, obscuring the sun; this was ominous of doldrums. On the 16th, the *Spray* entered this gloomy region to battle with squalls and to be harassed by fitful calms, for this is the state of the elements between the northeast and the southeast trades, where each wind — struggling in turn for mastery — expends its force whirling about in all directions. Making this still more trying to one's nerve and patience, the sea was tossed into confused cross-lumps and fretted by eddying currents. As if something more were needed to complete a sailor's discomfort in this state, the rain poured down in torrents day and night. The *Spray* struggled and tossed for ten days, making only three hundred miles on her course in all that time. I didn't say anything!

On September 23, the fine schooner *Nantasket* of Boston (from Bear River for the River Plate), lumber-laden and just through the doldrums, came up with the *Spray*, and her captain passing a few words, she sailed on. Being much fouled on the bottom by shell-fish, she drew along with her fishes which had been following the *Spray*, which was less provided with that sort of food. Fishes will always follow a foul ship. A barnacle-grown log adrift has the same attraction for deep-sea fishes.

One of this little school of deserters was a dolphin that had followed the *Spray* a thousand miles and had been content to eat scraps of food thrown overboard from my table; for, having been wounded, it could not dart through the sea to prey on other fishes. I had become accustomed to seeing the dolphin (which I knew by its scars) and missed it whenever it took occasional excursions away from the sloop. One day after it had been off for some hours, it returned in company with three yellowtails, a sort of cousin to the dolphin. This little school kept together, except when in danger and when foraging about the sea. Their lives were often threatened by hungry sharks that came round the vessel, and more than once they had narrow escapes. Their mode of escape interested me greatly, and I passed hours watching them. They would dart away, each in a different direction, so that the wolf of the sea — the shark — pursuing one, would be led away from the others; then, after a while they would all return and rendezvous under one side or the other of the sloop. Twice their pursuers were diverted by a tin pan, which I towed astern of the sloop and which was mistaken for a bright fish. And while turning in the peculiar way that sharks have when about to devour their prey, I shot them through the head.

Their precarious life seemed to concern the yellow-tails little, if at all. All living beings, without doubt, are afraid of death. Nevertheless, some of the species I saw huddle together as though they knew they were created for the larger fishes and wished to give the least possible trouble to their captors. I have seen, on the other hand, whales swimming in a circle around a school of herrings, and with mighty exertion "bunching" them together in a whirlpool set in motion by their flukes. And when the small fry were all whirled nicely together, one or the other of the leviathans, lunging through the center with open jaws, would take in a boat-load or so at a single mouthful. Off the Cape of Good Hope I saw schools of sardines or other small fish being treated in this way by great numbers of cavally-fish. There was not the slightest chance of escape for the sardines, while the cavally circled round and round, feeding from the edge of the mass. It was interesting to note how rapidly the small fry disappeared, and though it was repeated before my eyes over and over, I could hardly perceive the capture of a single sardine, so dexterously was it done.

Along the equatorial limit of the southeast trade-winds, the air was heavily charged with electricity, and there was much thunder and lightning. It was hereabout I remembered that, a few years before, the American ship *Alert* was destroyed by lightning. Her people, by wonderful good fortune, were rescued on the same day and brought to Pernambuco, where I then met them.

On September 25, in the latitude of 5° N., longitude

26° 30′ W., I spoke with the ship *North Star* of London. The great ship was out forty-eight days from Norfolk, Virginia, and was bound for Rìo, where we met again about two months later. The *Spray* was now thirty days from Gibraltar.

The *Spray's* next companion of the voyage was a swordfish that swam alongside, showing its tall fin out of the water till I made a stir for my harpoon, when it hauled its black flag down and disappeared. September 30, at half-past eleven in the morning, the *Spray* crossed the equator in longitude 29° 30′ W. At noon, she was two miles south of the line. The southeast trade-winds, met rather light in about 4° N., gave her sails now a stiff full sending he handsomely over the sea toward the coast of Brazil, where on October 5 just north of Olinda Point, without further incident, she made the land, casting anchor in Pernambuco Harbor about noon: forty days from Gibraltar and all well on board. Did I tire of the voyage in all that time? Not a bit of it! I was never in better trim in all my life and was eager for the more perilous experience of rounding the Horn.

It was not at all strange in a life common to sailors that — having already crossed the Atlantic twice and being now half-way from Boston to the Horn — I should find myself still among friends. My determination to sail westward from Gibraltar not only enabled me to escape the pirates of the Red Sea, but (in bringing me to Pernambuco) landed me on familiar shores. I had made many voyages to this and other ports in Brazil. In 1893, I was employed as master to take the famous Ericsson ship *Destroyer* from New York to Brazil to go against the rebel Mello and his party. The *Destroyer*, by the way, carried a submarine cannon of enormous length.

In the same expedition went the *Nictheroy*, the ship purchased by the United States government during the Spanish war and renamed the *Buffalo*. The *Destroyer* was in many ways the better ship of the two, but the Brazilians in their curious war sank her themselves at Bahia. With her sank my hope of recovering wages due me. Still, I could but try to recover, for to me it meant a great deal. But now — within two years — the whirligig of time had brought the Mello party into power, and although it was the legal government which had employed me, the so-called "rebels" felt under less obligation to me than I could have wished.

CHAPTER 6

Departure from Rìo de Janeiro – The *Spray* ashore on the sands of
Uruguay – A narrow escape from shipwreck – The boy who found a
sloop – The *Spray* floated but somewhat damaged – Courtesies
from the British consul – A warm greeting at Montevideo – An
excursion to Buenos Aires – Shortening the mast and bowsprit.

O N November 28, the *Spray* sailed from Rìo de
Janeiro, and first of all ran into a gale of wind, which
tore up things generally along the coast, doing considerable damage to shipping. It was well for her, perhaps, that
she was clear of the land. Coasting along on this part of
the voyage, I observed that while some of the small
vessels I fell in with were able to outsail the *Spray* by day,
they fell astern of her by night. To the *Spray*, day and
night were the same; to the others, clearly there was a
difference. On one of the very fine days experienced after
leaving Rìo, the steamship *South Wales* spoke the *Spray*
and unsolicited gave the longitude by chronometer as 48°
W., "as near as I can make it," the captain said. The
Spray, with her tin clock, had exactly the same reckoning.
I was feeling at ease in my primitive method of
navigation, but it startled me not a little to find my
position by account verified by the ship's chronometer.

On December 5, a barkentine hove in sight, and for
several days the two sailed along the coast together. Right
here a current was experienced setting north, making it
necessary to hug the shore, with which the *Spray* became
rather familiar. Here I confess a weakness: I hugged the
shore entirely too close. In a word, at daybreak on the
morning of December 11, the *Spray* ran hard and fast on
the beach. This was annoying, but I soon found that the
sloop was in no great danger. The false appearance of the
sand-hills under a bright moon had deceived me, and I
lamented now that I had trusted to appearances at all.

The sea, though moderately smooth, still carried a

swell which broke with some force on the shore. I managed to launch my small dory from the deck and ran out a kedge-anchor and warp. But it was too late to kedge the sloop off, for the tide was falling, and she had already sewed a foot.

Then I went about "laying out" the larger anchor, which was no easy matter, for my only life-boat (the frail dory), when the anchor and cable were in it, was swamped at once in the surf, the load being too great for her. Then I cut the cable and made two loads of it instead of one. The anchor — with forty fathoms bent and already buoyed — I now took and succeeded in getting through the surf, but my dory was leaking fast, and by the time I had rowed far enough to drop the anchor she was full to the gunwale and sinking. There was not a moment to spare, and I saw clearly that if I failed now all might be lost.

I sprang from the oars to my feet and — lifting the anchor above my head — threw it clear just as she was turning over. I grasped her gunwale and held on as she turned bottom up, for I suddenly remembered that I could not swim. Then I tried to right her, but with too much eagerness, for she rolled clean over and left me as before, clinging to her gunwale while my body was still in the water.

Giving a moment to cool reflection, I found that — although the wind was blowing moderately toward the land — the current was carrying me to sea and that something would have to be done. Three times I had been under water trying to right the dory, and I was just saying, "Now I lay me," when I was seized by a determination to try yet once more, so that no one of the prophets of evil I had left behind could say, "I told you so." Whatever the danger may have been — much or little — I can truly say that the moment was the most serene of my life.

After righting the dory for the fourth time, I finally succeeded by the utmost care in keeping her upright while I hauled myself into her and with one of the oars, which I had recovered, paddled to the shore, somewhat the worse for wear and pretty full of salt water. The

46

position of my vessel, now high and dry, gave me anxiety. To get her afloat again was all I thought of or cared for. I had little difficulty in carrying the second part of my cable out and securing it to the first, which I had taken the precaution to buoy before I put it into the boat. To bring the end back to the sloop was a smaller matter still, and I believe I chuckled above my sorrows when I found that in all the haphazard my judgment or my good genius had faithfully stood by me.

The cable reached from the anchor in deep water to the sloop's windlass by just enough to secure a turn and no more. The anchor had been dropped at the right distance from the vessel. To heave all taut now and wait for the coming tide was all I could do.

I suddenly remembered that I could not swim.

I had already done enough work to tire a stouter man and was only too glad to throw myself on the sand above the tide and rest, for the sun was already up and pouring a generous warmth over the land. While my state could have been worse, I was on the wild coast of a foreign country and not entirely secure in my property, as I soon found out. I had not been long on the shore when I heard the patter, patter of a horse's feet approaching along the hard beach, which ceased as it came abreast of the sand-ridge where I lay sheltered from the wind. Looking up cautiously, I saw mounted on a nag probably the most astonished boy on the whole coast. He had found a sloop!

"It must be mine," he thought, "for am I not the first to see it on the beach?"

Sure enough, there it was all high and dry and painted white. He trotted his horse around it and — finding no owner — hitched the nag to the sloop's bobstay and hauled as though he would take her home. But, of course, she was too heavy for one horse to move. With my skiff,

47

however, it was different; this he hauled some distance and concealed behind a dune in a bunch of tall grass. He had made up his mind, I dare say, to bring more horses and drag his bigger prize away, anyhow, and was starting off for the settlement a mile or so away for the reinforcement when I discovered myself to him, at which he seemed displeased and disappointed.

A double surprise.

"Buenos dias, muchacho," I said.

He grunted a reply and eyed me keenly from head to foot. Then bursting into a volley of questions (more than six Yankees could ask), he wanted to know, first, where my ship was from and how many days she had been coming. Then he asked what I was doing here ashore so early in the morning.

"Your questions are easily answered," I replied. "My ship is from the moon, it has taken her a month to come, and she is here for a cargo of boys."

But the intimation of this enterprise — had I not been on the alert — might have cost me dearly; for while I spoke, this child of the campo coiled his lariat ready to throw, and — instead of being himself carried to the moon — he was apparently thinking of towing me home by the neck, astern of his wild cayuse, over the fields of Uruguay.

The exact spot where I was stranded was at the

Castillo Chicos, about seven miles south of the dividing-line of Uruguay and Brazil, and of course the natives there speak Spanish. To reconcile my early visitor, I told him that I had on my ship biscuits and that I wished to trade them for butter and milk. On hearing this, a broad grin lighted up his face and showed that he was greatly interested, and that even in Uruguay a ship's biscuit will cheer the heart of a boy and make him your bosom friend. The lad almost flew home and returned quickly with butter, milk, and eggs. I was, after all, in a land of plenty. With the boy came others, old and young, from neighboring ranches, among them a German settler who was of great assistance to me in many ways.

A coast-guard from Fort Teresa, a few miles away, also came, "to protect your property from the natives of the plains," he said. I took occasion to tell him, however, that if he would look after the people of his own village, I would take care of those from the plains, pointing, as I spoke, to the nondescript "merchant" who had already stolen my revolver and several small articles from my cabin, which by a bold front I had recovered. The chap was not a native Uruguayan. Here, as in many other places that I visited, the natives themselves were not the ones discreditable to the country.

Early in the day a dispatch came from the port captain of Montevideo, commanding the coast-guards to render the *Spray* every assistance. This, however, was not necessary, for a guard was already on the alert and making all the ado that would become the wreck of a steamer with a thousand emigrants aboard. The same messenger brought word from the captain that he would dispatch a steam-tug to tow the *Spray* to Montevideo. The officer was as good as his word; a powerful tug arrived on the following day, but — to make a long story short — with the help of the German and one soldier and one Italian (called "Angel of Milan"), I had already floated the sloop and was sailing for port with the boom off before a fair wind. The adventure cost the *Spray* no small amount of pounding on the hard sand; she lost her shoe and part of her false keel, and received other damage, which, however, was readily mended afterward in the nearby dock.

On the following day, I anchored at Maldonado. The British consul, his daughter, and another young lady came on board, bringing with them a basket of fresh eggs, strawberries, bottles of milk, and a great loaf of sweet bread. This was a good landfall and better cheer than I had found at Maldonado once upon a time when I entered the port with a stricken crew in my bark, the *Aquidneck*.

In the waters of Maldonado Bay a variety of fishes abound, and fur-seals in their season haul out on the island abreast the bay to breed. Currents on this coast are greatly affected by the prevailing winds, and a tidal wave higher than that ordinarily produced by the moon is sent up the whole shore of Uruguay before a southwest gale, or lowered by a northeaster, as may happen. One of these waves — having just receded before the northeast wind which brought the *Spray* in — left the tide now at low ebb with oyster-rocks laid bare for some distance along the shore. Other shellfish of good flavor were also plentiful, though in small size. I gathered a mess of oysters and mussels here, while a native with hook and line, and with mussels for bait, fished from a point of detached rocks for bream, landing several good-sized ones.

The fisherman's nephew, a lad about seven years old, deserves mention as the tallest blasphemer (for a short boy) that I met on the voyage. He called his old uncle all the vile names under the sun for not helping him across the gully. While he swore roundly in all the moods and tenses of the Spanish language, his uncle fished on, now and then congratulating his hopeful nephew on his accomplishment. At the end of his rich vocabulary, the urchin sauntered off into the fields and shortly returned with a bunch of flowers, and with all smiles handed them to me with the innocence of an angel. I remembered having seen the same flower on the banks of the river farther up some years before. I asked the young pirate why he had brought them to me.

Said he, "I don't know; I only wished to do so."

Whatever the influence was that put so amiable a wish

in this wild pampa boy, it must be far-reaching, thought I, and potent, seas over.

Shortly after, the *Spray* sailed for Montevideo, where she arrived on the following day and was greeted by steam-whistles till I felt embarrassed and wished that I had arrived unobserved. The voyage so far alone may have seemed to the Uruguayans a feat worthy of some recognition; but there was so much of it yet ahead — and of such an arduous nature — that any demonstration at this point seemed, somehow, like boasting prematurely.

The *Spray* had barely come to anchor at Montevideo when the agents of the Royal Mail Steamship Company, Messrs. Humphreys & Co., sent word that they would dock and repair her free of expense and give me twenty pounds sterling — which they did to the letter — and more besides. The caulkers paid very careful attention to the work of making the sloop tight. Carpenters mended the keel and also the life-boat (the dory), painting it till I hardly knew it from a butterfly.

Christmas of 1895 found the *Spray* refitted even to a wonderful makeshift stove, which was contrived from a large iron drum of some sort punched full of holes to give it a draft; the pipe reached straight up through the top of the forecastle. Now, this was not a stove by mere courtesy. It was always hungry, even for green wood. And in cold, wet days off the coast of Tierra del Fuego it stood me in good stead. Its one door swung on copper hinges, which one of the yard apprentices with laudable pride polished till the whole thing blushed like the brass binnacle of a P. & O. steamer.

The *Spray* was now ready for sea. Instead of proceeding at once on her voyage, however, she made an excursion up the river, sailing December 29. An old friend of mine, Captain Howard of Cape Cod and of River Plate fame, took the trip in her to Buenos Aires, where she arrived early on the following day with a gale of wind and a current so much in her favor that she outdid herself. I was glad to have a sailor of Howard's experience on board to witness her performance of sailing with no living being at the helm. Howard sat near the binnacle and watched the compass while the sloop held her course so steadily that one would have declared that the card was nailed fast. Not a quarter of a point did she deviate from her course. My old friend had owned and sailed a pilot-sloop on the river for many years, but this feat took the wind out of his sails at last, and he cried, "I'll be stranded on Chico Bank if ever I saw the like of it!"

Perhaps he had never given his sloop a chance to show what she could do. The point I make for the *Spray* here — above all other points — is that she sailed in shoal water and in a strong current with other difficult and unusual conditions. Captain Howard took all this into account.

In all the years away from his native home, Howard had not forgotten the art of making fish chowders. And to prove this he brought along some fine rockfish and prepared a mess fit for kings. When the savory chowder was done — chocking the pot securely between two boxes on the cabin floor so that it could not roll over — we helped ourselves and swapped yarns over it while the *Spray* made her own way through the darkness on the river. Howard told me about the Fuegian cannibals as she reeled along, and I told him about the pilot of the *Pinta* steering my vessel through the storm off the coast of the Azores, and that I looked for him at the helm in a gale such as this. I do not charge Howard with superstition — we are none of us superstitious — but when I spoke about his returning to Montevideo on the *Spray*, he shook his head and took a steam-packet instead.

I had not been in Buenos Aires for a number of years. The place where I had once landed from packets in a cart was now built up with magnificent docks. Vast fortunes had been spent in remodeling the harbor; London bankers could tell you that. The port captain — after assigning the *Spray* a safe berth with his compliments — sent me word to call on him for anything I might want while in port, and I felt quite sure that his friendship was sincere. The sloop was well cared for at Buenos Aires; her dockage and tonnage dues were all free, and the yachting fraternity of the city welcomed her with a good will. In town I found things not so greatly changed as about the docks, and I soon felt myself more at home.

From Montevideo I had forwarded a letter from Sir Edward Hairby to the owner of the *Standard*, Mr. Mulhall, and in reply to it was assured of a warm welcome to the warmest heart, I think, outside of Ireland. Mr. Mulhall, with a prancing team, came down to the docks as soon as the *Spray* was berthed and would have me go to his house at once, where a room was waiting. And it was New Year's day, 1896. The course of the *Spray* had been followed in the columns of the *Standard*.

Mr. Mulhall kindly drove me to see many improvements about the city, and we went in search of some of the old landmarks. The man who sold "lemonade" on the plaza when I first visited this wonderful city I found selling lemonade still at two cents a glass; he had made a fortune by it. His stock in trade was a wash-tub and a neighboring hydrant, a moderate supply of brown sugar, and about six lemons that floated on the sweetened water. The water from time to time was renewed from the friendly pump, but the lemon "went on forever," and all at two cents a glass.

But we looked in vain for the man who once sold whisky and coffins in Buenos Aires; the march of civilization had crushed him — memory only clung to his name. Enterprising man that he was, I fain would have looked him up. I remember the tiers of whisky-barrels ranged on end on one side of the store, while on the other side — and divided by a thin partition — were the coffins in the same order, of all sizes and in great numbers. The unique arrangement seemed in order, for as a cask was emptied a coffin might be filled. Besides cheap whisky and many other liquors, he sold "cider," which he manufactured from damaged Malaga raisins. Within the scope of his enterprise was also the sale of mineral waters, not entirely blameless of the germs of disease. This man surely catered to all the tastes, wants, and conditions of his customers.

Farther along in the city, however, survived the good man who wrote on the side of his store, where thoughtful men might read and learn: "This wicked world will be destroyed by a comet! The owner of this store is therefore bound to sell out at any price and avoid the catastrophe." My friend Mr. Mulhall drove me round to view the fearful comet with streaming tail pictured large on the trembling merchant's walls.

I unshipped the sloop's mast at Buenos Aires and shortened it by seven feet. I reduced the length of the bowsprit by about five feet, and even then I found it reaching far enough from home. And more than once, when on the end of it reefing the jib, I regretted that I had not shortened it another foot.

CHAPTER 7

Weighing anchor at Buenos Aires – An outburst of emotion at the mouth of the Plate – Submerged by a great wave – A stormy entrance to the strait – The happy gift of a bag of carpet-tacks – Off Cape Froward – Chased by Indians from Fortescue Bay – Taking in supplies at Three Island Cove – Animal life.

O N January 26, 1896, the *Spray*, being refitted and well provisioned in every way, sailed from Buenos Aires. There was little wind at the start; the surface of the great river was like a silver disk, and I was glad of a tow from a harbor tug to clear the port entrance. But a gale came up soon after and caused an ugly sea, and instead of being all silver, as before, the river was now all mud. The Plate is a treacherous place for storms. One sailing there should always be on alert for squalls. I cast anchor before dark in the best lee I could find near the land, but was tossed miserably all night, heartsore of choppy seas. On the following morning I got the sloop under way and — with reefed sails — worked her down the river against a head wind. Standing in that night to the place where pilot Howard joined me for the up-river sail, I took a departure, shaping my course to clear Point Indio on the one hand and the English Bank on the other.

I had not for many years been south of these regions. I will not say that I expected all fine sailing on the course for Cape Horn direct, but while I worked at the sails and rigging I thought only of onward and forward. It was when I anchored in the lonely places that a feeling of awe crept over me. At the last anchorage on the monotonous and muddy river, weak as it may seem, I gave way to my feelings. I resolved then that I would anchor no more north of the Strait of Magellan.

On the 28th of January, the *Spray* was clear of Point Indio, English Bank, and all the other dangers of the River Plate. With a fair wind she then bore away for the

Strait of Magellan, under all sail, pressing farther and farther toward the wonderland of the South, till I forgot the blessings of our milder North.

My ship passed in safety Bahia Blanca, also the Gulf of St. Matias and the mighty Gulf of St. George. Hoping that she might go clear of the destructive tide-races — the dread of big craft or little along this coast — I gave all the capes a berth of about fifty miles, for these dangers extend many miles from the land. But where the sloop avoided one danger she encountered another. For, one day well off the Patagonian coast while the sloop was reaching under short sail, a tremendous wave — the culmination, it seemed, of many waves — rolled down upon her in a storm, roaring as it came. I had only a moment to get all sail down and myself up on the peak halyards, out of danger, when I saw the mighty crest towering masthead-high above me.

The mountain of water submerged my vessel. She shook in every timber and reeled under the weight of the sea, but rose quickly out of it and rode grandly over the rollers that followed. It may have been a minute that from my hold in the rigging I could see no part of the *Spray's* hull. Perhaps it was even less time than that, but it seemed a long while, for under great excitement one lives fast, and in a few seconds one may think a great deal of one's life past. Not only did the past with electric speed flash before me, but I had time while in my hazardous position for resolutions for the future that would take a long time to fulfill. The first one was, I remember, that if the *Spray* came through this danger I would dedicate my best energies to building a larger ship on her lines, which I hope yet to do. Other promises less easily kept I should have made under protest; however, the incident — which filled me with fear — was only one more test of the *Spray's* seaworthiness. It reassured me against the rude Cape Horn.

From the time the great wave swept over the *Spray* until she reached Cape Virgins nothing occurred to move a pulse and set blood in motion. On the contrary, the weather became fine and the sea smooth and life tranquil.

The phenomenon of mirage frequently occurred. An albatross sitting on the water one day loomed up like a large ship; two fur-seals asleep on the surface of the sea appeared like great whales; and a bank of haze I could have sworn was high land. The kaleidoscope then changed, and on the following day I sailed in a world peopled by dwarfs.

On February 11, the *Spray* rounded Cape Virgins and entered the Strait of Magellan. The scene was again real and gloomy; the wind, northeast, and blowing a gale, sent feather-white spumes along the coast; such a sea ran as would swamp an ill-appointed ship. As the sloop neared the entrance to the strait I observed that two great tide-races made ahead, one very close to the point of the land and one farther offshore. Between the two — in a sort of channel through combers — went the *Spray* with close-reefed sails. But a rolling sea followed her a long way in, and a fierce current swept around the cape against her. But this she stemmed and was soon chirruping under the lee of Cape Virgins and running every minute into smoother water; however, long trailing kelp from sunken rocks waved forebodingly under her keel, and the wreck of a great steamship smashed on the beach abreast gave a gloomy aspect to the scene.

I was not to be let off easy. The Virgins would collect tribute even from the *Spray* passing their promontory. Fitful rain-squalls from the northwest followed the northeast gale. I reefed the sloop's sails, and — sitting in the cabin to rest my eyes — I was so strongly impressed with what in all nature I might expect that as I dozed the very air I breathed seemed to warn me of danger. My senses heard "*Spray* ahoy!" shouted in warning.

I sprang to the deck, wondering who could be there that knew the *Spray* so well as to call out her name passing in the dark, for it was now the blackest of nights all around, except away in the southwest, where the old familiar white arch — the terror of Cape Horn — rapidly pushed up by a southwest gale. I had only a moment to douse sail and lash all solid when it struck like a shot from a cannon, and for the first half-hour it was something to be remembered by way of a gale. For thirty hours it kept on blowing hard. The sloop could carry no more than a three-reefed mainsail and forestaysail; with these she held on stoutly and was not blown out of the strait. In the height of the squalls in this gale she doused all sail, and this occurred often enough.

After this gale followed only a smart breeze, and the *Spray*, passing through the narrows without mishap, cast anchor at Sandy Point on February 14, 1896.

Sandy Point (Punta Arenas) is a Chilean coaling-station and boasts about two thousand inhabitants of mixed nationality, but mostly Chileans. What with sheep-farming, gold-mining, and hunting, the settlers in this dreary land seemed not the worst off in the world. But the natives — Patagonian and Fuegian — on the other hand, were as squalid as contact with unscrupulous traders could make them. A large percentage of the business there was traffic in "fire-water." If there was a law against selling the poisonous stuff to the natives, it was not enforced. Fine specimens of the Patagonian race, looking smart in the morning when they came into town, had repented before night of ever having seen a white man, so beastly drunk were they, to say nothing about the peltry of which they had been robbed.

The port at that time was free, but a custom-house was in course of construction, and when it is finished, port and tariff dues are to be collected. A soldier police guarded the place, and a sort of vigilante force besides took down its guns now and then. But as a general thing, to my mind, whenever an execution was made they killed the wrong man. Just previous to my arrival, the governor — himself of a jovial turn of mind — had sent a party of young bloods to foray a Fuegian settlement and wipe out what they could of it on account of the recent massacre of a schooner's crew somewhere else.

Altogether the place was quite newsy and supported two papers — dailies, I think. The port captain, a Chilean naval officer, advised me to ship hands to fight Indians in the strait farther west and spoke of my stopping until a gunboat should be going through, which would give me a tow. After canvassing the place, however, I found only one man willing to embark, and he on condition that I should ship another "mon and a doog." But as no one else was willing to come along and as I drew the line at dogs, I said no more about the matter, but simply loaded my guns.

At this point in my dilemma, Captain Pedro Samblich — a good Austrian of large experience — coming along gave me a bag of carpet-tacks worth more than all the fighting men and dogs of Tierra del Fuego. I protested that I had no use for carpet-tacks on board. Samblich smiled at my want of experience and maintained stoutly that I would have use for them.

"You must use them with discretion," he said. "That is to say, don't step on them yourself."

With this remote hint about the use of the tacks I got on all right and saw the way to maintain clear decks at night without the care of watching.

Samblich was greatly interested in my voyage, and after giving me the tacks he put on board bags of biscuits and a large quantity of smoked venison. He declared that my bread — which was ordinary sea-biscuits and easily broken — was not nutritious as his, which was so hard that I could break it only with a stout blow from a maul. Then he gave me from his own sloop a compass, which was certainly better than mine, and offered to unbend her mainsail for me if I would accept it. Last of all, this large-hearted man brought out a bottle of Fuegian gold-dust from a place where it had been *cached* and begged me to help myself from it, for use farther along on the voyage. But I felt sure of success without this draft on a friend, and I was right. Samblich's tacks, as it turned out, were of more value than gold.

The port captain finding that I was resolved to go even alone — since there was no help for it — set up no further objections, but advised me — in case the savages tried to surround me with their canoes — to shoot straight and begin to do it in time, but to avoid killing them if possible, which I heartily agreed to do. With these simple instructions the officer gave me my port clearance free of charge, and I sailed on the same day, February 19, 1896. It was not without thoughts of strange and stirring adventure beyond all I had yet encountered that I now sailed into the country and very core of the savage Fuegians.

A fair wind from Sandy Point brought me on the first day to St. Nicholas Bay, where (so I was told) I might expect to meet savages. But seeing no signs of life, I came to anchor in eight fathoms of water, where I lay all night under a high mountain. Here I had my first experience with the terrific squalls, called williwaws, which extended from this point on through the strait to the Pacific. They were compressed gales of wind that Boreas handed down over the hills in chunks. A full-blown williwaw will throw a ship — even without sail on — over on her beam ends; but, like other gales, they cease now and then, if only for a short time.

February 20 was my birthday, and I found myself alone with hardly so much as a bird in sight off Cape Froward, the southernmost point of the continent of America. By daylight in the morning I was getting my ship underway for the bout ahead.

The sloop held the wind fair while she ran thirty miles farther on her course, which brought her to Fortescue Bay and at once among the natives' signal-fires, which blazed up now on all sides. Clouds flew over the mountain from the west all day; at night my good east wind failed, and in its stead a gale from the west soon came on. I gained anchorage at twelve o'clock that night, under the lee of a little island and then prepared myself a cup of coffee, of which I was sorely in need; for (to tell the truth) hard beating in the heavy squalls and against the current had told on my strength. Finding that the anchor held, I drank my beverage and named the place Coffee Island. It lies to the south of Charles Island with only a narrow channel between.

By daylight the next morning the *Spray* was again under way, beating hard, but she came to in a cove in Charles Island, two and a half miles along in her course. Here she remained undisturbed two days with both anchors down in a bed of kelp. Indeed, she might have remained undisturbed indefinitely had not the wind moderated; for during these two days it blew so hard that no boat could venture out on the strait, and — the natives being away to other hunting-grounds — the island anchorage was safe. But at the end of the fierce wind-storm fair weather came; then I got my anchors and again sailed out upon the strait.

Canoes manned by savages from Fortescue now came in pursuit. The wind falling light, they gained on me rapidly till coming within hail, when they ceased paddling, and a bow-legged savage stood up and called, "Yammer-schooner! Yammerschooner!" which is their begging term.

I said, "No!"

Now, I was not for letting on that I was alone, and so I stepped into the cabin, and — passing through the hold — came out at the fore-scuttle, changing my clothes as I went along. That made two men. Then the piece of bowsprit — which I had sawed off at Buenos Aires and which I had still on board — I arranged forward on the lookout, dressed as a seaman, attaching a line by which I could pull it into motion. That made three of us, and we didn't want to "yammerschooner."

But for all that, the savages came on faster than before. I saw that — besides four at the paddles in the canoe nearest to me — there were others in the bottom and that they were shifting hands often. At eighty yards, I fired a shot across the bow of the nearest canoe, at which they all stopped, but only for a moment. Seeing that they persisted in coming nearer, I fired the second shot so close to the chap who wanted to "yammerschooner" that he changed his mind quickly enough and bellowed with fear, "Bueno jo via Isla," and sitting down in his canoe, he rubbed his starboard cat-head for some time.

I was thinking of the good port captain's advice when I pulled the trigger and must have aimed pretty straight; however, a miss was as good as a mile for Mr. "Black Pedro," as he it was, and no other, a leader in several bloody massacres. He made for the island now, and the others followed him. I knew by his Spanish lingo and by his full beard that he was the villain I have named, a renegade mongrel, and the worst murderer in Tierra del Fuego. The authorities had been in search of him for two years. The Fuegians are not bearded.

So much for the first day among the savages. I came to anchor at midnight in Three Island Cove, about twenty miles along from Fortescue Bay. I saw on the opposite side of the strait signal-fires and heard the barking of

A brush with Fuegians.

dogs, but where I lay it was quite deserted by natives. I have always taken it as a sign that where I found birds sitting about, or seals on the rocks, I should not find savage Indians. Seals are never plentiful in these waters, but in Three Island Cove I saw one on the rocks, and other signs of the absences of savage men.

On the next day the wind was again blowing a gale, and although she was in the lee of the land, the sloop dragged her anchors, so that I had to get her under way and beat farther into the cove, where I came to in a landlocked pool. At another time or place this would have been a rash thing to do, and it was safe now only from the fact that the gale which drove me to shelter would keep the Indians from crossing the strait. Seeing this was the case, I went ashore with gun and ax on an island where I could not in any event be surprised and there felled trees and split about a cord of fire-wood, which loaded my small boat several times.

While I carried the wood — though I was morally sure there were no savages near — I never once went to or from the skiff without my gun. While I had that and a clear field of over eighty yards about me I felt safe.

The trees on the island, very scattering, were a sort of beech and a stunted cedar, both of which made good fuel. Even the green limbs of the beech, which seemed to possess a resinous quality, burned readily in my great drum-stove. I have described my methods of wooding up in detail so that the reader who has kindly borne with me so far may see that in this (as in all other particulars of my voyage) I took great care against all kinds of surprises, whether by animals or by the elements. In the Strait of Magellan the greatest vigilance was necessary. In this instance I reasoned that I had all about me the greatest danger of the whole voyage — the treachery of cunning savages, for which I must be particularly on the alert.

The *Spray* sailed from Three Island Cove in the morning after the gale went down, but was glad to return for shelter from another sudden gale. Sailing again on the following day, she fetched Borgia Bay, a few miles on her course, where vessels had anchored from time to time and had nailed boards on the trees ashore with name and date of harboring carved or painted. Nothing else could I see to indicate that civilized man had ever been there. I had taken a survey of the gloomy place with my spy-glass and was getting my boat out to land and to take notes, when the Chilean gunboat *Huemel* came in, and officers coming on board advised me to leave the place at once, a thing that required little eloquence to persuade me to do. I accepted the captain's kind offer of a tow to the next anchorage, at the place called Notch Cove — eight miles farther along — where I should be clear of the worst Fuegians.

We made anchorage at the cove about dark that night, while the wind came down in fierce williwaws from the mountains. An instance of Magellan weather was afforded when the *Huemel*, a well-appointed gunboat of great power — after attempting on the following day to proceed on the voyage — was obliged by sheer force of the wind to return and take up anchorage again and remain till the gale abated. And lucky she was to get back!

Meeting this vessel was a little godsend. She was commanded and officered by high-class sailors and educated gentlemen. An entertainment that was gotten up on her, impromptu, at the Notch would be hard to beat anywhere. One of her midshipmen sang popular songs in French, German, and Spanish, and one (so he said) in Russian. If the audience did not know the lingo of one song from another, it was no drawback to the merriment.

I was left alone the next day, for then the *Huemel* put out on her voyage the gale having abated. I spent a day taking in wood and water; by the end of that time, the weather was fine. Then I sailed from the desolate place.

There is little more to be said concerning the *Spray's* first passage through the strait that would differ from what I have already recorded. She anchored and weighed many more times and beat many days against the current — with now and then a "slant" for a few miles — till finally she gained anchorage and shelter for the night at Port Tamar with Cape Pillar in sight to the west. Here I felt the throb of the great ocean that lay before me. I knew now that I had put another world behind me and that I was opening out another world ahead. I had passed the haunts of savages. Great piles of granite mountains of bleak and lifeless aspect were now astern; on some of them not even a speck of moss had ever grown. There was an unfinished newness all about the land. On the hill back of Port Tamar a small beacon had been thrown up, showing that some man had been there. But how could one tell but that he had died of loneliness and grief? In a bleak land is not the place to enjoy solitude.

Throughout the whole of the strait west of Cape Froward I saw no animals except dogs owned by savages.

These I saw often enough and heard them yelping night and day. Birds were not plentiful. The scream of a wild fowl (which I took for a loon) sometimes startled me with its piercing cry. The steamboat duck, so called because it propels itself over the sea with its wings and resembles a miniature side-wheel steamer in its motion, was sometimes seen scurrying on out of danger. It never flies, but — hitting the water instead of the air with its wings — it moves faster than a rowboat or a canoe. The few fur-seals I saw were very shy; and of fishes I saw next to none at all. I did not catch one; indeed, I seldom or never put a hook over during the whole voyage. Here in the strait I found great abundance of mussels of an excellent quality. I fared sumptuously on them. There was a sort of swan, smaller than a Muscovy duck, which might have been brought down with the gun, but in the loneliness of life about the dreary country, I found myself in no mood to make one life less, except in self-defense.

CHAPTER 8

From Cape Pillar into the Pacific – Driven by a tempest toward Cape Horn – Captain Slocum's greatest sea adventure – Reaching the strait again by way of Cockburn Channel – Some savages find the carpet-tacks – Danger from firebrands – A series of fierce williwaws – Again sailing westward.

IT was the 3rd of March when the *Spray* sailed from Port Tamar direct for Cape Pillar, with the wind from the northeast, which I fervently hoped might hold till she cleared the land. But there was no such good luck in store. It soon began to rain and thicken in the northwest, boding no good. The *Spray* neared Cape Pillar rapidly and, nothing loath, plunged into the Pacific Ocean at once, taking her first bath of it in the gathering storm. There was no turning back even had I wished to do so, for the land was now shut out by the darkness of night. The wind freshened, and I took in a third reef. The sea was confused and treacherous. In such a time as this the old fisherman prayed, "Remember, Lord, my ship is small and thy sea is so wide!" I saw now only the gleaming crests of the waves. They showed white teeth while the sloop balanced over them. "Everything for an offing," I cried, and to this end I carried all the sail she would bear.

She ran all night with a free sheet, but on the morning of March 4 the wind shifted to southwest, then back suddenly to northwest and blew with terrific force. The *Spray*, stripped of her sails, then bore off under bare poles. No ship in the world could have stood up against so violent a gale. Knowing that this storm might continue for many days and that it would be impossible to work back to the westward along the coast outside of Tierra del Fuego, there seemed nothing to do but to keep on and go east about, after all. Anyhow, for my present safety the only course lay in keeping her before the wind. And so she drove southeast, as though about to round the Horn, while the waves rose and fell and bellowed their never-ending story of the sea, but the Hand that held these held also the *Spray*. She was running now with a reefed forestaysail, the sheets flat amidship. I paid out two long ropes to steady her course and to break combing seas astern, and I lashed the helm amidship. In this trim she ran before it, shipping never a sea. Even while the storm raged at its worst, my ship was wholesome and noble. My mind as to her seaworthiness was put at ease for aye.

When all had been done that I could do for the safety of the vessel, I got to the fore-scuttle between seas and prepared a pot of coffee over a wood fire and made a good Irish stew. Then, as before and afterward on the *Spray*, I insisted on warm meals. In the tide-race off Cape Pillar, however, where the sea was marvelously high, uneven, and crooked, my appetite was slim, and for a time I postponed cooking. (Confidentially, I was seasick!)

The first day of the storm gave the *Spray* her actual test in the worst sea that Cape Horn or its wild regions could afford, and in no part of the world could a rougher sea be found than at this particular point, namely off Cape Pillar, the grim sentinel of the Horn.

Farther offshore, while the sea was majestic, there was less apprehension of danger. There the *Spray* rode, now like a bird on the crest of a wave, and now like a waif deep down in the hollow between seas; and so she drove on. Whole days passed, counted as other days, but with always a thrill — yes, of delight.

On the fourth day of the gale, rapidly nearing the pitch of Cape Horn, I inspected my chart and pricked off the course and distance to Port Stanley in the Falkland Islands, where I might find my way and refit, when I saw through a rift in the clouds a high mountain, about seven leagues away on the port beam. The fierce edge of the gale by this time had blown off, and I had already bent a squaresail on the boom in the place of the mainsail, which was torn to rages. I hauled in the trailing ropes, hoisted this awkward sail reefed, the forestaysail being already set, and under this sail brought her at once on the wind heading for the land, which appeared as an island in the sea. So it turned out to be, though not the one I had supposed.

I was exultant over the prospect of once more entering the Strait of Magellan and beating through again into the Pacific, for it was more than rough on the outside coast of Tierra del Fuego. It was indeed a mountainous sea. When the sloop was in the fiercest squalls, with only the reefed forestaysail set, even that small sail shook her from keelson to truck when it shivered by the leech. Had I harbored the shadow of a doubt for her safety, it would have been that she might spring a leak in the garboard at the heel of the mast, but she never called me once to the pump. Under pressure of the smallest sail I could set, she made for the land like a race-horse, and steering her over the crests of the waves so that she might not trip was nice work. I stood at the helm now and made the most of it.

Night closed in before the sloop reached the land, leaving her feeling the way in pitchy darkness. I saw breakers ahead before long. At this I wore ship and stood offshore, but was immediately startled by the tremendous roaring of breakers again ahead and on the lee bow. This puzzled me, for there should have been no broken water where I supposed myself to be. I kept off a good bit, then wore round, but finding broken water also there, threw her head again offshore. In this way, among dangers, I spent the rest of the night. Hail and sleet in the fierce squalls cut my flesh till the blood trickled over my face, but what of that? It was daylight, and the sloop was in the midst of the Milky Way of the sea, which is northwest of Cape Horn, and it was the white breakers of a huge sea over sunken rocks which had threatened to engulf her through the night. It was Fury Island I had sighted and steered for, and what a panorama was before me now and all around! It was not the time to complain of a broken skin. What could I do but fill away among the breakers and find a channel between them, now that it was day? Since she had escaped the rocks through the night, surely she would find her way by daylight. This was the greatest sea adventure of my life. God knows how my vessel escaped.

The sloop at last reached inside of small islands that sheltered her in smooth water. Then I climbed the mast to survey the wild scene astern. The great naturalist Darwin looked over this seascape from the deck of the *Beagle*, and wrote in his journal, "Any landsman seeing the Milky Way would have a nightmare for a week." He might have added, "or seaman" as well.

The *Spray's* good luck followed fast. I discovered, as she sailed along through a labyrinth of islands, that she was in the Cockburn Channel, which leads into the Strait of Magellan at a point opposite Cape Froward, and that she was already passing Thieves' Bay, suggestively named. And at night, March 8, behold, she was at anchor in a snug cove at the Turn! Every heart-beat on the *Spray* now counted thanks.

Here I pondered on the events of the last few days, and strangely enough, instead of feeling rested from sitting or lying down, I now began to feel jaded and worn, but a hot meal of venison stew soon put me right so that I could sleep. As drowsiness came on, I sprinkled the deck with tacks, and then I turned in, bearing in mind the advice of my old friend Samblich that I was not to step on them myself. I saw to it that not a few of them stood "business end" up, for when the *Spray* passed Thieves' Bay two canoes had put out and followed in her wake, and there was no disguising the fact any longer that I was alone.

Now, it is well known that one cannot step on a tack without saying something about it. A pretty good Christian will whistle when he steps on the "commercial end" of a carpet-tack; a savage will howl and claw the air, and that was just what happened that night about twelve o'clock, while I was asleep in the cabin, where the savages thought they "had me," sloop and all, but changed their minds when they stepped on deck, for then they thought that I or somebody else had them. I had no need of a dog; they howled like a pack of hounds. I had hardly use for a gun. They jumped pell-mell — some into their canoes and some into the sea — to cool off, I suppose, and there was a deal of free language over it as they went. I fired several guns when I came on deck to let the rascals know that I was home, and then I turned in again, feeling sure I should not be disturbed any more by people who left in so great a hurry.

The Fuegians, being cruel, are naturally cowards; they regard a rifle with superstitious fear. The only real danger one could see that might come from their quarter would be from allowing them to surround one within bow-shot, or to anchor within range where they might lie in ambush. As for their coming on deck at night, even had I not put tacks about, I could have cleared them off by shots from the cabin and hold. I always kept a quantity of ammunition within reach in the hold and in the cabin and in the forepeak, so that retreating to any of these places I could "hold the fort" simply by shooting up through the deck.

Perhaps the greatest danger to be apprehended was from the use of fire. Every canoe carries fire; nothing is thought of that, for it is their custom to communicate by smoke-signals. The harmless brand that lies smoldering in the bottom of one of their canoes might be ablaze in one's cabin if he were not on the alert. The port captain of Sandy Point warned me particularly of this danger. Only a short time before they had fired a Chilean gunboat by throwing brands in through the stern windows of the cabin. The *Spray* had no openings in the cabin or deck, except two scuttles, and these were guarded by fastenings which could not be undone without waking me if I were asleep.

On the morning of the 9th, after a refreshing rest and a warm breakfast, and after I had swept the deck of tacks, I got out what spare canvas there was on board and began to sew the pieces together in the shape of a peak for my square-mainsail, the tarpaulin. The day to all appearances promised fine weather and light winds, but appearances in Tierra del Fuego do not always count. While I was wondering why no trees grew on the slope abreast of the anchorage — half minded to lay by the sail-making and land with my gun for some game and to inspect a white boulder on the beach near the brook — a williwaw came down with such terrific force as to carry the *Spray* — with

71

two anchors down — like a feather out of the cover and away into the deep water. No wonder trees did not grow on the side of that hill! Great Boreas! a tree would need to be all roots to hold on against such a furious wind.

From the cove to the nearest land to leeward was a long drift, however, and I had ample time to weigh both anchors before the sloop came near any danger, and so no harm came of it. I saw no more savages that day or the next. They probably had some sign by which they knew of the coming williwaw; at least, they were wise in not being afloat on the second day, for I had no sooner gotten to work at sail-making after the anchor was down than the wind (as on the day before) picked us up and flung us seaward with a vengeance — anchor and all — as before.

This fierce wind, usual to the Magellan country, continued on through the day and swept the sloop by several miles of steep bluffs and precipices overhanging a bold shore of wild and uninviting appearance. I was not sorry to get away from it, though in doing so it was no Elysian shore to which I shaped my course. I kept on sailing in hope — since I had no choice but to go on — heading across for St. Nicholas Bay, where I had cast anchor February 19. It was now the 10th of March!

Upon reaching the bay the second time, I had circumnavigated the wildest part of desolate Tierra del Fuego. But the *Spray* had not yet arrived at St. Nicholas, and by the merest accident her bones were saved from resting there when she did arrive. The parting of a staysail-sheet in a williwaw — when the sea was turbulent and she was plunging into the storm — brought me forward to see instantly a cliff ahead and breakers so close under the bows that I felt surely lost, and in my thoughts cried, "Is the hand of fate against me, after all, leading me in the end to this dark spot?" I sprang aft again — unheeding the flapping sail — and threw the wheel over, expecting as the sloop came down into the hollow of a wave to feel her timbers smash under me on the rocks. But at the touch of her helm she swung clear of the danger, and in the next moment she was in the lee of the land.

It was the small island in the middle of the bay for which the sloop had been steering and which she made with such unerring aim as nearly to run it down. Farther along in the bay was the anchorage, which I managed to reach, but before I could get the anchor down another squall caught the sloop and whirled her round like a top and carried her away, altogether to leeward of the bay. Still farther to leeward was a great headland, and I bore off for that. This was retracing my course toward Sandy Point, for the gale was from the southwest.

I had the sloop soon under good control, however, and in a short time rounded to under the lee of a mountain, where the sea was as smooth as a mill-pond, and the sails flapped and hung limp while she carried her way close in. Here I thought I would anchor and rest till morning, the depth being eight fathoms very close to the shore. But it was interesting to see, as I let go the anchor, that it did not reach the bottom before another williwaw struck down from this mountain and carried the sloop off faster than I could pay out cable. Instead of resting, I had to "man the windlass" and heave up the anchor and fifty fathoms of cable hanging up and down in the deep water. This was in that part of the strait called Famine Reach. I could have wished it Jericho! On that little crab-windlass I worked the rest of the night, thinking how much easier it was for me when I could say, "Do that thing or the other," than to do it myself. But I hove away on the windlass and sang the old chants that I had sung when I was a sailor, from "Blow, Boys, Blow for Californy, O" to "Sweet By and By."

It was daybreak when the anchor was at the hawse. By this time the wind had gone down, and cat's-paws took the place of williwaws. The sloop was then drifting slowly toward Sandy Point. She came within sight of ships at anchor in the roads, and I was more than half minded to put in for new sails, but the wind coming out from the northeast — which was fair for the other direction — I turned the prow of the *Spray* westward once more for the Pacific, to traverse a second time the second half of my first course through the strait.

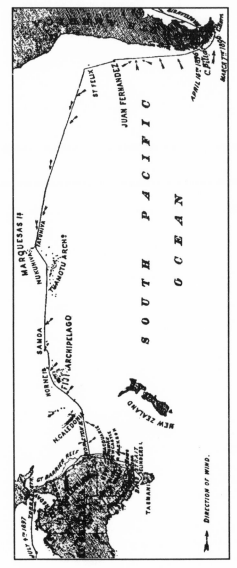

The *Spray's* course from the Strait of Magellan to Torres Strait.

CHAPTER 9

Repairing the *Spray's* sails – Savages and an obstreperous anchor – A spider-fight – An encounter with Black Pedro – A visit to the steamship *Columbia* – On the defensive against a fleet of canoes – A record of voyages through the strait – A chance cargo of tallow.

I was determined to rely on my own small resources to repair the damages of the great gale which drove me southward toward the Horn after I had passed from the Strait of Magellan out into the Pacific. So when I had got back into the strait by way of Cockburn Channel, I did not proceed eastward for help at the Sandy Point settlement, but — turning again into the northwestward reach of the strait — set to work with my palm and needle at every opportunity, when at anchor and when sailing. It was slow work, but little by little the squaresail on the boom expanded to the dimensions of a serviceable mainsail with a peak to it and a leech besides. If it was not the best-setting sail afloat, it was at least very strongly made and would stand a hard blow. A ship meeting the *Spray* long afterward reported her as wearing a mainsail of some improved design and patent reefer, but that was not the case.

The *Spray* for a few days after the storm enjoyed fine weather and made fair time through the strait for the distance of twenty miles, which — in these days of many adversities — I called a long run. The weather, I say, was fine for a few days, but it brought little rest. Care for the safety of my vessel — and even for my own life — was in no wise lessened by the absence of heavy weather. Indeed, the peril was even greater, inasmuch as the savages on comparatively fine days ventured forth on their marauding excursions and in boisterous weather disappeared from sight, their wretched canoes being frail and undeserving the name of craft at all.

This being so, I now enjoyed gales of wind as never before, and the *Spray* was never long without them during her struggle about Cape Horn. I became in a measure inured to the life and began to think that one more trip through the strait — if perchance the sloop should be blown off again — would make me the aggressor and put the Fuegians entirely on the defensive. This feeling was forcibly borne in on me at Snug Bay, where I anchored at one gray morning after passing Cape Froward, to find when broad day appeared that two canoes which I had eluded by sailing all night were now entering the same bay stealthily under the shadow of the high headland. They were well manned, and the savages were well armed with spears and bows. At a shot from my rifle across the bows, both turned aside into a small creek out of range.

In danger now of being flanked by the savages in the bush close aboard, I was obliged to hoist the sails — which I had barely lowered — and make across to the opposite side of the strait, a distance of six miles. But now I was put to my wit's end as to how I should weigh anchor, for through an accident to the windlass right here I could not budge it; however, I set sail and filled away, first hauling short by hand. The sloop carried her anchor away as though it was meant to be always towed in this way underfoot, and with it she towed a ton or more of kelp from a reef in the bay, the wind blowing a wholesale breeze.

Meanwhile, I worked till blood started from my fingers and — with one eye over my shoulder for savages — I watched at the same time and sent a bullet whistling whenever I saw a limb or twig move; for I kept a gun always at hand, and an Indian appearing then within range would have been taken as a declaration of war. As it was, however, my own blood was all that was spilt — and from the trifling accident of sometimes breaking the flesh against a cleat or a pin which came in the way when I was in haste. Sea-cuts in my hands from pulling on hard, wet ropes were sometimes painful and often bled freely, but these healed when I finally got away from the strait into fine weather.

After clearing Snug Bay, I hauled the sloop to the wind, repaired the windlass, and hove the anchor to the hawse, catted it, and then stretched across to a port of refuge under a high mountain about six miles away, and came to in nine fathoms close under the face of a perpendicular cliff. Here my own voice answered back, and I named the place "Echo Mountain." Seeing dead trees farther along where the shore was broken, I made a landing for fuel, taking — besides my ax — a rifle, which on these days I never left far from hand.

But I saw no living thing here, except a small spider, which had nested in a dry log that I boated to the sloop. The conduct of this insect interested me now more than anything else around the wild place. In my cabin it met, oddly enough, a spider of its own size and species that had come all the way from Boston — a very civil little chap, too, but mighty spry. Well, the Fuegian threw up its antennae for a fight, but my little Bostonian downed it at once, then broke its legs and pulled them off, one by one, so dexterously that in less than three minutes from the time the battle began the Fuegian spider didn't know itself from a fly.

I made haste the following morning to be under way after a night of wakefulness on the weird shore. Before weighing anchor, however, I prepared a cup of warm coffee over a smart wood fire in my great Montevideo stove. In the same fire was cremated the Fuegian spider, slain the day before by the little warrior from Boston, which a Scots lady at Cape Town long after named "Bruce" upon hearing of its prowess at Echo Mountain. The *Spray* now reached away for Coffee Island, which I sighted on my birthday, February 20, 1896.

There she encountered another gale that brought her in the lee of great Charles Island for shelter. On a bluff point on Charles were signal-fires, and a tribe of savages — mustered here since my first trip through the strait — manned their canoes to put off for the sloop. It was not prudent to come to — the anchorage being within bow-shot of the shore, which was thickly wooded — but I made signs that one canoe might come alongside, while

77

the sloop ranged about under sail in the lee of the land. The others I motioned to keep off and incidentally laid a smart Martini-Henry rifle in sight, close at hand, on the top of the cabin.

In the canoe that came alongside, crying their never-ending begging word "yammerschooner," were two squaws and one Indian, the hardest specimens of humanity I had ever seen in any of my travels. "Yammerschooner" was their plaint when they pushed off from the shore, and "yammerschooner" it was when they got alongside. The squaws beckoned for food, while the Indian — a black-visaged savage — stood sulkily as if he took no interest at all in the matter, but on my turning my back for some biscuits and jerked beef for the squaws, the "buck" sprang on deck and confronted me, saying in Spanish jargon that we had met before. I thought I recognized the tone of his "yammerschooner," and his full beard identified him as the Black Pedro whom, it was true, I had met before.

"Where are the rest of the crew?" he asked, as he looked uneasily around, expecting hands, maybe, to come out of the fore-scuttle and deal him his just desserts for many murders. "About three weeks ago," said he, "when you passed up here, I saw three men on board. Where are the other two?"

I answered him briefly that the same crew was still on board.

"But," said he, "I see you are doing all the work," and with a leer he added as he glanced at the mainsail, "hombre valiente."

I explained that I did all the work in the day, while the rest of the crew slept, so that they would be fresh to watch for Indians at night. I was interested in the subtle cunning of this savage, knowing him, as I did, better perhaps than he was aware. Even had I not been advised before I sailed from Sandy Point, I should have measured him for an arch-villain now. Moreover, one of the squaws — with that spark of kindliness which is somehow found in the breast of even the lowest savage — warned me by a sign to be on my guard, or Black Pedro would do me harm. There was no need of the warning, however, for I was on my guard from the first and at that moment held a smart revolver in my hand ready for instant service.

"When you sailed through before," he said, "you fired a shot at me," adding with some warmth that it was "muy malo."

I affected not to understand and said, "You have lived at Sandy Point, have you not?"

He answered frankly, "Yes," and appeared delighted to meet one who had come from the dear old place.

"At the mission?" I queried.

"Why, yes," he replied, stepping forward as if to embrace an old friend.

I motioned him back, for I did not share his flattering humor." And you know Captain Samblich?" continued I.

"Yes," said the villain, who had killed a kinsman of Samblich — "Yes, indeed; he is a great friend of mine."

"I know it," said I. Samblich had told me to shoot him on sight.

Pointing to my rifle on the cabin, he wanted to know how many times it fired. "Cuantos?" said he.

When I explained to him that the gun kept right on shooting, his jaw fell, and he spoke of getting away. I did not hinder him from going. I gave the squaws biscuits and beef, and one of them gave me several lumps of tallow in exchange, and I think it worth mentioning that she did not offer me the smallest pieces, but with some extra trouble handed me the largest of all the pieces in the canoe. No Christian could have done more.

Before pushing off from the sloop, the cunning savage asked for matches and made as if to reach with the end of his spear the box I was about to give him, but I held it toward him on the muzzle of my rifle, the one that "kept on shooting." The chap picked the box off the gun gingerly enough, to be sure, but he jumped when I said, "Quedao [Look out]," at which the squaws laughed and seemed not at all displeased. Perhaps the wretch had clubbed them that morning for not gathering mussels enough for his breakfast. There was a good understanding among us all.

From Charles Island the *Spray* crossed over to Fortescue Bay, where she anchored and spent a comfortable night under the lee of high land, while the wind howled outside. The bay was deserted now. They were Fortescue Indians whom I had seen at the island, and I felt quite sure they could not follow the *Spray* in the present hard blow. Not to neglect precaution, however, I sprinkled tacks on deck before I turned in.

On the following day, the loneliness of the place was broken by the appearance of a great steamship making for the anchorage with a lofty bearing. She was no Diego craft. I knew the sheer, the model, and the poise. I threw out my flag and directly saw the Stars and Stripes flung to the breeze from the great ship.

The wind had then abated, and toward night the savages made their appearance from the island, going direct to the steamer to "yammerschooner." Then they came to the *Spray* to beg more — or to steal all — declaring that they got nothing from the steamer. Black Pedro here came alongside again. My own brother could not have been more delighted to see me, and he begged me to lend him my rifle to shoot a guanaco for me in the morning. I assured the fellow that if I remained there another day I would lend him the gun, but I had no mind to remain. I gave him a cooper's draw-knife and some other small implements which would be of service in canoe-making and bade him be off.

Under the cover of darkness that night I went to the steamer, which I found to be the *Colombia*, and Captain Henderson, from New York bound for San Francisco. I carried all my guns along with me in case it should be necessary to fight my way back. In the chief mate of the *Colombia*, Mr. Hannibal, I found an old friend, and he referred affectionately to the days in Manila when we were there together; he in the *Southern Cross* and I in the *Northern Light*, both ships as beautiful as their names.

The *Colombia* had an abundance of fresh stores on board. The captain gave his steward some order, and I remember that the guileless young man asked me if I could manage — besides other things — a few cans of milk and cheese. When I offered my Montevideo gold for the supplies, the captain roared like a lion and told me to put my money up. It was a glorious outfit of provisions of all kinds that I got.

Returning to the *Spray*, where I fond all secure, I prepared for an early start in the morning. It was agreed that the steamer should blow her whistle for me if first on the move. I watched the steamer, off and on, through the night for the pleasure alone of seeing her electric lights, a pleasing sight in contrast to the ordinary Fuegian canoe with a brand of fire in it. The sloop was the first under way, but the *Colombia* — soon following — passed and saluted as she went by. Had the captain given me his steamer, his company would have been no worse off than they were two or three months later. I read afterward in a late California paper, "The *Colombia* will be a total loss." On her second trip to Panama, she was wrecked on the rocks of the California coast.

The *Spray* was then beating against the wind and current, as usual in the strait. At this point, the tides from the Atlantic and the Pacific meet, and in the strait — as on the outside coast — their meeting makes a commotion of whirlpools and combers that in a gale of wind is dangerous to canoes and other frail craft.

A few miles farther along was a large steamer ashore, bottom up. Passing this place, the sloop ran into a streak of light wind, and then — a most remarkable condition for strait weather — it fell entirely calm. Signal-fires sprang up at once on all sides, and then more than twenty canoes hove in sight, all heading for the *Spray*. As they came within hail, their savage crews cried, "Amigo yammerschooner," "Anclas aqui," "Bueno puerto aqui," and like scraps of Spanish mixed with their own jargon. I had no thought of anchoring in their "good port." I hoisted the sloop's flag and fired a gun, all of which they might construe as a friendly salute or an invitation to come on. They drew up in a semicircle, but kept outside of eighty yards, which in self-defense would have been the death-line.

In this mosquito fleet was a ship's boat stolen

probably from a murdered crew. Six savages paddled this rather awkwardly with the blades of oars which had been broken off. Two of the savages standing erect wore sea-boots, and this sustained the suspicion that they had fallen upon some luckless ship's crew, and also added a hint that they had already visited the *Spray's* deck, and would now — if they could — try her again. Their sea-boots, I have no doubt, would have protected their feet and rendered carpet-tacks harmless.

Paddling clumsily, they passed down the strait at a distance of a hundred yards from the sloop, in an offhand manner and as if bound to Fortescue Bay. This I judged to be a piece of strategy and so kept a sharp lookout over a small island which soon came in range between them and the sloop — completely hiding them from view — and toward which the *Spray* was now drifting helplessly with the tide and with every prospect of going on the rocks, for there was no anchorage, at least, none that my cables would reach.

And, sure enough, I soon saw a movement in the grass just on top of the island, which is called Bonet Island and is one hundred and thirty-six feet high. I fired several shots over the place, but saw no other sign of the savages. It was they that had moved the grass, for as the sloop swept past the island — the rebound of the tide carrying her clear — there on the other side was the boat, surely enough exposing their cunning and treachery. A stiff breeze, coming up suddenly, now scattered the canoes while it extricated the sloop from a dangerous position, albeit the wind, though friendly, was still ahead.

The *Spray*, flogging against current and wind, made Borgia Bay on the following afternoon, and now cast anchor there for the second time. I would now, if I could, describe the moonlit scene on the strait at midnight after I had cleared the savages and Bonet Island. A heavy cloud-bank that had swept across the sky then cleared away, and the night became suddenly as light as day, or nearly so. A high mountain was mirrored in the channel ahead, and the *Spray* sailing along with her shadow was as two sloops on the sea.

The sloop being moored, I threw out my skiff and with ax and gun landed at the head of the cove, and filled a barrel of water from a stream. Then, as before, there was no sign of Indians at the place. Finding it quite deserted, I rambled about near the beach for an hour or more. The fine weather seemed somehow to add loneliness to the place, and when I came upon a spot where a grave was marked, I went no further. Returning to the head of the cove, I came to a sort of Calvary, it appeared to me, where navigators carrying their cross had each set one up as a beacon to others coming after. They had anchored here and gone on, all except the one under the little mound. One of the simple marks, curiously enough, had been left there by the steamship *Colimbia*, sister ship to the *Colombia*, my neighbor of that morning.

I read the names of many other vessels; some of them I copied in my journal, others were illegible. Many of the crosses had decayed and fallen, and many a hand that put them there I had known, many a hand now still. The air of depression was about the place, and I hurried back to the sloop to forget myself again in the voyage.

Early next morning I stood out from Borgia Bay, and off Cape Quod, where the wind fell light, I moored the sloop by kelp in twenty fathoms of water and held her there a few hours against a three-knot current. That night I anchored in Langara Cove, a few miles farther along, where on the following day I discovered wreckage and goods washed up from the sea. I worked all day now, salving and boating off a cargo to the sloop. The bulk of goods was tallow in casks and in lumps from which the casks had broken away. And embedded in the seaweed was a barrel of wine, which I also towed alongside. I hoisted them all in with the throat-halyards, which I took to the windlass. The weight of some of the casks was a little over eight hundred pounds.

There were no Indians about Langara; evidently there had not been any since the great gale which had washed the wreckage on shore. Probably it was the same gale that drove the *Spray* off Cape Horn from March 3 to 8. Hundreds of tons of kelp had been torn from beds in deep water and rolled up into ridges on the beach. A specimen stalk which I found entire — roots, leaves, and all — measured one hundred and thirty-one feet in length. At this place, I filled a barrel of water at night, and the following day sailed with a fair wind at last.

Salving wreckage.

I had not sailed far, however, when I came abreast of more tallow in a small cove, where I anchored and boated off as before. It rained and snowed hard all that day, and it was no light work carrying tallow in my arms over the boulders on the beach. But I worked on till the *Spray* was leaded with a full cargo. I was happy then in the prospect of doing a good business farther along on the voyage, for the habits of an old trader would come to the surface. I sailed from the cove about noon, greased from top to toe, while my vessel was tallowed from keelson to truck. My cabin — as well as the hold and deck — was stowed full of tallow, and all were thoroughly smeared.

CHAPTER 10

Running to Port Angosto in a snow storm – A defective sheet-rope places the *Spray* in peril – The *Spray* as a target for a Fuegian arrow – The *Spray* at Port Angosto – The island of Alan Erric – Again in the open Pacific – The run to the island of Juan Fernández – An absentee king – At Robinson Crusoe's anchorage.

A NOTHER gale had then sprung up, but the wind was still fair, and I had only twenty-six miles to run for Port Angosto — a dreary enough place — where, however, I would find a safe harbor in which to refit and stow cargo. I carried on sail to make the harbor before dark, and she fairly flew along all covered with snow, which fell thick and fast, till she looked like a white winter bird. Between the storm-bursts I saw the headland of my port and was steering for it when a flaw of wind caught the mainsail by the lee, jibed it over, and dear! dear! how nearly was this the cause of disaster, for the sheet parted and the boom unshipped, and it was then close upon night. I worked till the perspiration poured from my body to get things adjusted and in working order before dark and — above all — to get it done before the sloop drove to leeward of the port of refuge. Even then I did not get the boom shipped in its saddle. I was at the entrance of the harbor before I could get this done, and it was time to haul her to or lose the port. But in that condition — like a bird with a broken wing — she made the haven. The accident which so jeopardized my vessel and cargo came of a defective sheet-rope, one made from sisal, a treacherous fiber which has caused a deal of strong language among sailors.

I did not run the *Spray* into the inner harbor of Port Angosto, but came to inside a bed of kelp under a steep bluff on the port hand going in. It was an exceedingly snug nook, and — to make doubly sure of holding on here against all williwaws — I moored her with two anchors and secured her, besides, by cables to trees; however, no wind ever reached there except back flaws from the mountains on the opposite side of the harbor. There, as elsewhere in that region, the country was made up of mountains. This was the place where I was to refit and whence I was to sail direct, once more, for Cape Pillar and the Pacific.

I remained at Port Angosto some days, busily employed about the sloop. I stowed the tallow from the deck to the hold, arranged my cabin in better order, and took in a good supply of wood and water. I also mended the sloop's sails and rigging and fitted a jigger, which changed the rig to a yawl — though I called the boat a sloop just the same — the jigger being merely a temporary affair.

I never forgot, even at the busiest time of my work there, to have my rifle by me ready for instant use, for I was of necessity within range of savages, and I had seen Fuegian canoes at this place when I anchored in the port farther down the reach on the first trip through the strait. I think it was on the second day, while I was busily employed about the decks, that I heard the swish of something through the air close by my ear and heard a "zip"-like sound in the water, but saw nothing. Presently, however, I suspected that it was an arrow of some sort, for just then one passing not far from me struck the mainmast, where it stuck fast, vibrating from the shock — a Fuegian autograph.

A savage was somewhere near; there could be no doubt about that. I did not know but he might be shooting at me with a view to getting my sloop and her cargo. And so I threw up my old Martini-Henry (the rifle that kept on shooting), and the first shot uncovered three Fuegians, who scampered from a clump of bushes where they had been concealed and made over the hills. I fired away a good many cartridges, aiming under their feet to encourage their climbing. My dear old gun woke up the hills, and at every report all three of the savages jumped as if shot. But they kept on and put Fuegian real estate between themselves and the *Spray* as fast as their legs could carry them. I took care then — more than ever before — that all my firearms should be in order and that a supply of ammunition should always be ready at hand. But the savages did not return, and — although I put tacks on deck every night — I never discovered that any more visitors came, and I had only to sweep the deck of tacks carefully every morning after.

As the days went by, the season became more favorable for a chance to clear the strait with a fair wind, and so I made up my mind after six attempts — being driven back each time — to be in no further haste to sail. The bad weather on my last return to Port Angosto for shelter brought the Chilean gunboat *Condor* and the Argentine cruiser *Azopardo* into port. As soon as the latter came to anchor, Captain Mascarella sent a boat to the *Spray* with the message that he would take me in tow for Sandy Point if I would give up the voyage and return — the farthest thing from my mind.

The officers of the *Azopardo* told me that — coming up the strait after the *Spray* on her first passage through — they saw Black Pedro and learned that he had visited me. The *Azopardo*, being a foreign man-of-war, had no right to arrest the Fuegian outlaw, but her captain blamed me for not shooting the rascal when he came to my sloop.

I procured some cordage and other small supplies from these vessels, and the officers of each of them mustered a supply of warm flannels, of which I was most in need. With these additions to my outfit and with the vessel in good trim (though somewhat deeply laden), I was well prepared for another bout with the Southern — misnamed *Pacific* — Ocean.

In the first week in April, southeast winds — such as appear about Cape Horn in the fall and winter, bringing better weather than that experienced in the summer — began to disturb the upper clouds; a little more patience, and the time would come for sailing with a fair wind.

At Port Angosto, I met Professor Dusen of the Swedish scientific expedition to South America and the Pacific Islands. The professor was camped by the side of a brook at the head of the harbor, where there were many varieties of moss in which he was interested and where the water was — as his Argentine cook said — "muy rico." The professor had three well-armed Argentines along in his camp to fight savages. They seemed disgusted when I filled water at a small stream near the vessel, slighting their advice to go farther up to the greater brook, where it was "muy rico." But they were all fine fellows, though it was a wonder that they did not all die of rheumatic pains from living on the wet ground.

Of all the little haps and mishaps on the *Spray* at Port Angosto, of the many attempts to put to sea, and of each return for shelter, it is not my purpose to speak. Of hindrances, there were many to keep her back. But on the seventh and last time, she weighed anchor from that port. Difficulties, however, multiplied all about in so strange a manner that I had been given to superstitious fears I should not have persisted in sailing on a thirteenth day, notwithstanding that a fair wind blew in the offing.

Many of the incidents were ludicrous. When I found myself, for instance, disentangling the sloop's mast from the branches of a tree after she had drifted three times around a small island against my will, it seemed more than one's nerves could bear, and I had to speak about it (so I thought), or die of lockjaw, and I apostrophized the *Spray* as an impatient farmer might his horse or ox.

"Didn't you know," cried I — "didn't you know that you couldn't climb a tree?"

But the poor old *Spray* had essayed — and successfully too — nearly everything else in the Strait of Magellan, and my heart softened toward her when I thought of what she had gone through. Moreover, she had discovered an island. On the charts this one that she had sailed around was traced as a point of land. I named it Alan Erric Island, after a worthy literary friend I had met in strange by-places, and I put up a sign ("Keep off the grass"), which as discoverer was within my rights.

Now at last the *Spray* carried me free of Tierra del Fuego. If by a close shave only, still she carried me clear, though her boom actually hit the beacon rocks to leeward as she lugged on sail to clear the point. The thing was done on the 13th of April, 1896. But a close shave and a narrow escape were nothing new to the *Spray*.

The waves doffed their white caps beautifully to her in the strait that day before the southeast wind, the first true winter breeze of the season from that quarter, and here she was out on the first of it, with every prospect of clearing Cape Pillar before it should shift. So it turned out; the wind blew hard, as it always blows about Cape Horn, but she had cleared the great tide-race off Cape Pillar and the Evangelistas — the outermost rocks of all — before the change came. I remained at the helm, humoring my vessel in the cross seas, for it was rough, and I did not dare to let her take a straight course. It was necessary to change her course in the combing seas, to meet them with what skill I could when they rolled up ahead, and to keep them off when they came abeam.

On the following morning, April 14, only the tops of the highest mountains were in sight, and the *Spray* — making good headway on a northwest course — soon sank these out of sight.

"Hurrah for the *Spray!*" I shouted to seals, sea-gulls, and penguins, for there were no other living creatures about, and she had weathered all the dangers of Cape Horn. Moreover, she had on her voyage around the Horn salved a cargo of which she had not jettisoned a pound. And why should not one rejoice also in the main chance coming so of itself?

I shook out a reef and set the whole jib, for — having sea-room — I could square away two points. This brought the sea more on her quarter, and she was wholesomer under a press of sail. Occasionally an old southwest sea, rolling up, combed athwart her, but did no harm. The wind freshened as the sun rose half-mast or more, and the air, a bit chilly in the morning, softened later in the day, but I gave little thought to such things as these.

One wave in the evening, larger than the others that had threatened all day, — one such as sailors call "fine-weather seas" — broke over the sloop fore and aft. It washed over me at the helm, the last that swept over the *Spray* off Cape Horn. It seemed to wash away old regrets. All my troubles were now astern; summer was ahead; all the world was again before me. The wind was even literally fair. My "trick" at the wheel was now up, and it was 5P.M. I had stood at the helm since eleven o'clock the morning before, or thirty hours.

Then was the time to uncover my head, for I sailed alone with God. The vast ocean was again around me, and the horizon was unbroken by land. A few days later the *Spray* was under full sail, and I saw her for the first time with a jigger spread. This was indeed, a small incident, but it was the incident following a triumph. The wind was still southwest, but it had moderated, and roaring seas had turned to gossiping waves that rippled and pattered against her sides as she rolled among them, delighted with their story. Rapid changes went on those days in things all about while she headed for the tropics. New species of birds came around; albatrosses fell back and became scarcer and scarcer; lighter gulls came in their stead, and pecked for crumbs in the sloop's wake.

On the tenth day from Cape Pillar a shark came along, the first of its kind on this part of the voyage to get into trouble. I harpooned him and took out his ugly jaws. I had not till then felt inclined to take the life of any animal, but when John Shark hove in sight my sympathy flew to the winds. It is a fact that in Magellan I let pass many ducks that would have made a good stew, for I had no mind in the lonesome strait to take the life of any living thing.

From Cape Pillar I steered for Juan Fernández and on the 26th of April, fifteen days out, made that historic island right ahead. The blue hills of Juan Fernández high among the clouds could be seen about thirty miles off. A thousand emotions thrilled me when I saw the island, and I bowed my head to the deck. We may mock the Oriental salaam, but for my part I could find no other way of expressing myself.

The wind being light through the day, the *Spray* did not reach the island till night. With what wind there was to fill her sails she stood close in to shore on the northeast side, where it fell calm and remained so all night. I saw the twinkling of a small light farther along in a cove and fired a gun, but got no answer, and soon the light disappeared altogether. I heard the sea booming against the cliffs all night and realized that the ocean swell was still great, although from the deck of my little ship it was apparently small. From the cry of animals in the hills — which sounded fainter and fainter through the night — I judged that a light current was drifting the

sloop from the land, though she seemed all night dangerously near the shore, for (the land being very high) appearances were deceptive.

Soon after daylight I saw a boat putting out toward me. As it pulled near, it so happened that I picked up my gun — which was on the deck — meaning only to put it below. But the people in the boat, seeing the piece in my hands, quickly turned

The *Spray* approaches Juan Fernández, Robinson Crusoe's island.

and pulled back for shore, which was about four miles distant. There were six rowers in her, and I observed that they pulled with oars in oar-locks, after the manner of trained seamen, and so I knew they belonged to a civilized race.

But their opinion of me must have been anything but flattering when they mistook my purpose with the gun and pulled away with all their might. I made them understand by signs — but not without difficulty — that I did not intend to shoot, that I was simply putting the piece in the cabin, and that I wished them to return. When they understood my meaning they came back and were soon on board.

91

One of the party, whom the rest called "king," spoke English; the others spoke Spanish. They had all heard of the voyage of the *Spray* through the papers of Valparaiso, and were hungry for news concerning it. They told me of a war between Chile and the Argentine, which I had not heard of when I was there. I had just visited both countries, and I told them that — according to the latest reports while I was in Chile — their own island was sunk. (This same report that Juan Fernández had sunk was current in Australia when I arrived there three months later.)

I had already prepared a pot of coffee and a plate of doughnuts, which — after some words of civility — the islanders stood up to and discussed with a will, after which they took the *Spray* in tow of their boat and made toward the island with her at the rate of a good three knots. The man they called king took the helm, and with whirling it up and down he so rattled the *Spray* that I thought she would never carry herself straight again. The others pulled away lustily with their oars.

The king, I soon learned, was only king by courtesy. Having lived longer on the island than any other man in the world — thirty years — he was so dubbed. Juan Fernández was then under the administration of a governor of Swedish nobility, so I was told. I was also told that his daughter could ride the wildest goat on the island. The governor at the time of my visit was away at Valparaiso with his family to place his children at school. The king had been away once for a year or two, and in Rìo de Janeiro had married a Brazilian woman who followed his fortunes to the far-off island. He was himself a Portuguese and a native of the Azores. He had sailed in New Bedford whale-ships and had steered a boat. All this I learned — and more too — before we reached the anchorage. The sea-breeze, coming in before long, filled the *Spray's* sails, and the experienced Portuguese mariner piloted her to a safe berth in the bay, where she was moored to a buoy abreast the settlement.

CHAPTER 11

The islanders entertained with Yankee doughnuts – The beauties of
Robinson Crusoe's realm – The monument to Alexander Selkirk –
Robinson Crusoe's cave – Westward ho! with a friendly gale – A
month's free sailing with the Southern Cross and the sun for
guides – Sighting the Marquesas – Experience in reckoning.

THE *Spray* being secured, the islanders returned to
the coffee and doughnuts, and I was more than
flattered when they did not slight my buns, as the
professor had done in the Strait of Magellan. Between
buns and doughnuts there was little difference except in
name. Both had been fried in tallow — which was the
strong point in both — for there was nothing on the
island fatter than a goat, and a goat is a lean beast, to
make the best of it. So with a view to business, I hooked
my steel-yards to the boom at once, ready to weigh out
tallow (there being no customs officer to say, "Why do
you do so?") and before the sun went down the islanders
had learned the art of making buns and doughnuts.

I did not charge a high price for what I sold, but the
ancient and curious coins I got in payment — some of
them from the wreck of a galleon sunk in the bay no one
knows when — I sold afterward to antiquarians for more
than face-value. In this way I made a reasonable profit. I
brought away money of all denominations from the island
and nearly all there was, so far as I could find out.

Juan Fernández, as a place of call, is a lovely spot.
The hills are well wooded, the valleys fertile, and pouring
down through many ravines are streams of pure water.
There are no serpents on the island and no wild beasts
other than pigs and goats — of which I saw a number —
with possibly a dog or two. The people lived without the
use of rum or beer of any sort. There was not a police
officer or a lawyer among them. The domestic economy of
the island was simplicity itself. The fashions of Paris did

not affect the inhabitants; each dressed according to his own taste.

Although there was no doctor, the people were all healthy, and the children were all beautiful. There were about forty-five souls on the island all told. The adults were mostly from the mainland of South America. One lady there from Chile — who made a flying-jib for the *Spray*, taking her pay in tallow — would be called a belle at Newport.

Blessed island of Juan Fernández! Why Alexander

The house of the king.

Selkirk ever left you was more than I could make out.

A large ship which had arrived some time before — on fire — had been stranded at the head of the bay, and as the sea smashed her to pieces on the rocks after the fire was drowned, the islanders picked up the timbers and utilized them in the construction of houses, which naturally presented a ship-like appearance. The house of the king of Juan Fernández — Manuel Carroza by name — besides resembling the ark, wore a polished brass knocker on its only door, which was painted green. In front of this gorgeous entrance was a flag-mast all ataunto and near it a smart whale-boat painted red and blue, the delight of the king's old age.

MONUMENT TO ALEXANDER SELKIRK

I of course made a pilgrimage to the old lookout place at the top of the mountain, where Selkirk spent many days peering into the distance for a ship which came at last. From a tablet fixed into the face of the rock I copied these words, inscribed in Arabic capitals:

IN MEMORY
OF
ALEXANDER SELKIRK,
MARINER,
A native of Largo, in the county of Fife, Scotland,
who lived on this island in complete solitude
for four years and four months.
He was landed from the *Cinque Ports* galley, 96 tons, 18 guns,
A.D. 1704,
and was taken off in the *Duke*, privateer,
12th February, 1709.
He died Lieutenant of H.M.S. *Weymouth*,
A.D. 1723[1],
aged 47.
This tablet is erected near Selkirk's lookout,
by Commodore Powell and the officers of H.M.S. *Topaze*,
A.D. 1868.

The cave in which Selkirk dwelt while on the island is at the head of the bay now called Robinson Crusoe Bay. It is around a bold headland west of the present anchorage and landing. Ships have anchored there, but it affords a very indifferent berth. Both of these anchorages are exposed to north winds, which, however, do not reach home with much violence. The holding-ground being good in the first-named bay to the eastward, the anchorage there may be considered safe, although the undertow at times makes it wild riding.

I visited Robinson Crusoe Bay in a boat and with some difficulty landed through the surf near the cave, which I entered. I found it dry and inhabitable. It is located in a beautiful nook sheltered by high mountains

[1] Mr. J. Cuthbert Hadden, in the *Century Magazine* for July, 1899, shows that the tablet is in error as to the year of Selkirk's death. It should be 1721.

from all the severe storms that sweep over the island, which are not many, for it lies near the limits of the trade-wind regions, being in latitude 35½° S. The island is about fourteen miles in length, east and west, and eight miles in width; its height is over three thousand feet. Its distance from Chile — to which country it belongs — is about three hundred and forty miles.

Juan Fernández was once a convict station. A number of caves in which the prisoners were kept — damp, unwholesome dens — are no longer in use, and no more prisoners are sent to the island.

The pleasantest day I spent on the island — if not the pleasantest day on my whole voyage — was my last day on shore (but by no means because it was the last) when the children of the little community, one and all, went out with me to gather wild fruits for the voyage. We found quinces, peaches, and figs, and the children gathered a basket of each. It takes very little to please children, and these little ones — never hearing a word in their lives except Spanish — made the hills ring with mirth at the sound of words in English. They asked me the names of all manner of things on the island. We came to a wild fig-tree loaded with fruit, of which I gave them the English name.

"Figgies, figgies!" they cried, while they picked till their baskets were full.

But when I told them that the *cabra* they pointed out was only a goat, they screamed with laughter and rolled on the grass in wild delight to think that a man had come to their island who would call a cabra a goat.

The first child born on Juan Fernandez, I was told, had become a beautiful woman and was now a mother. Manuel Carroza and the good soul who followed him here from Brazil had laid away their only child, a girl, at the age of seven, in the little churchyard on the point. In the same half-acre were other mounds among the rough lava rocks, some marking the burial-place of native-born children, some of the resting-places of seamen from passing ships, landed here to end days of sickness and get into a sailors' heaven.

The greatest drawback I saw in the island was the want of a school. A class there would necessarily be small, but to some kind soul who loved teaching and quietude life would for a limited time be one of delight.

On the morning of May 5, 1896, I sailed from Juan Fernández, having feasted on many things, but on nothing sweeter than the adventure itself of a visit to the home and to the very cave of Robinson Crusoe. From the island, the *Spray* bore away to the north, passing the island of St. Felix before she gained the trade-winds, which seemed slow in reaching their limits.

If the trades were tardy, however, when they did come they came with a bang and made up for lost time. And the *Spray*, under reefs — sometimes one, sometimes two — flew before a gale for a great many days with a bone in her mouth toward the Marquesas in the west — which she made on the forty-third day out — and still kept on sailing. My time was all taken up those days — not by standing at the helm; no man, I think, could stand or sit and steer a vessel round the world. I did better than that, for I sat and read my books, mended my clothes, or cooked my meals and ate them in peace. I had already found that it was not good to be alone, and so I made companionship with what there was around me, sometimes with the universe and sometimes with my own insignificant self. But my books were always my friends, let fail all else. Nothing could be easier or more restful than my voyage in the trade-winds.

I sailed with a free wind day after day, marking the position of my ship on the chart with considerable precision, but this was done by intuition (I think) more than by slavish calculations. For one whole month my vessel held her course true; I had not, the while, so much as a light in the binnacle. The Southern Cross I saw every night abeam. The sun every morning came up astern; every evening it went down ahead. I wished for no other compass to guide me, for these were true. If I doubted my reckoning after a long time at sea, I verified it by reading the clock aloft made by the Great Architect, and it was right.

There was no denying that the comical side of the strange life appeared. I awoke sometimes to find the sun already shining into my cabin. I heard water rushing by with only a thin plank between me and the depths, and I said, "How is this?" But it was all right. It was my ship on her course, sailing as no other ship had ever sailed before in the world. The rushing water along her side told me that she was sailing at full speed. I knew that no human hand was at the helm; I knew that all was well with "the hands" forward, and that there was no mutiny on board.

The phenomena of ocean meteorology were interesting studies even here in the trade-winds. I observed that about every seven days the winds freshened and drew several points farther than usual from the direction of the pole; that is, it went round from east-southeast to the south-southeast, while at the same time a heavy swell rolled up from the southwest. All this indicated that gales were going on in the anti-trades. The wind then hauled day after day as it moderated, till it stood again at the normal point, east-southeast. This is more or less the constant state of the winter trades in latitude 12° S., where I "ran down the longitude" for weeks. The sun, we all know, is the creator of the trade-winds and of the wind system all over the earth. But ocean meteorology is, I think, the most fascinating of all. From Juan Fernández to the Marquesas, I experienced six changes of the great palpitations of sea-winds and of the sea itself, the effect of far-off gales. To know the laws that govern the winds — and to know that you know them — will give you an easy mind on your voyage round the world; otherwise, you may tremble at the appearance of every cloud. What is true of this in the trade-winds is much more so in the variables, where changes run more to extremes.

To cross the Pacific Ocean — even under the most favorable circumstances — brings you for many days close to nature, and you realize the vastness of the sea. Slowly but surely, the mark of my little ship's course on the track-chart reached out on the ocean and across it, while at her utmost speed she marked with her keel still slowly the sea that carried her. On the forty-third day from land

— a long time to be at sea alone — the sky being
beautifully clear and the moon being "in distance" with
the sun, I threw up my sextant for sights. I found from
the result of three observations — after long wrestling
with lunar tables — that her longitude by observation
agreed within five miles of that by dead reckoning.

This was wonderful; both, however, might be in error,
but somehow I felt confident that both were nearly true,
and that in a few hours more I should see land. And so it
happened, for then I made the island of Nukahiva, the
southernmost of the Marquesas group, clear-cut and
lofty. The verified longitude when abreast was somewhere
between the two reckonings; this was extraordinary. All
navigators will tell you that from one day to another a
ship may lose or gain more than five miles in her
sailing-account, and again — in the matter of lunars —
even expert lunarians are considered as doing clever work
when they average within eight miles of the truth.

I hope I am making it clear that I do not lay claim to
cleverness or to slavish calculations in my reckonings. I
think I have already stated that I kept my longitude, at
least, mostly by intuitions. A rotator log always towed
astern, but so much has to be allowed for currents and for
drift, which the log never shows, that it is only an
approximation, after all, to be corrected by one's own
judgment from data of a thousand voyages. And even then
the master of the ship — if he be wise — cries out for the
lead and the lookout.

Unique was my experience in nautical astronomy
from the deck of the *Spray* — so much so that I feel
justified in briefly telling it here. The first set of sights,
just spoken of, put her many hundred miles west of my
reckoning by account. I knew that this could not be
correct. In about an hour's time I took another set of
observations with the utmost care; the mean result of
these was about the same as that of the first set. I asked
myself why, with my boasted self-dependence, I had not
done at least better than this. Then I went in search of a
discrepancy in the tables, and I found it. In the tables I
found that the column of figures from which I had got an

important logarithm was in error. It was a matter I could prove beyond a doubt, and it made the difference as already stated.

The tables being corrected, I sailed on with self-reliance unshaken and with my tin clock fast asleep. The result of these observations naturally tickled my vanity, for I knew that it was something to stand on a great ship's deck and with two assistants take lunar observations approximately near the truth. As one of the poorest of American sailors, I was proud of the little achievement alone on the sloop, even by chance though it may have been.

I was *en rapport* now with my surroundings and was carried on a vast stream where I felt the buoyancy of His hand who made all the worlds. I realized the mathematical truth of their motions, so well known that astronomers compile tables of their positions through the years and the days, and the minutes of the day, with such precision that one coming along over the sea even five years later may by their aid find the standard time of any given meridian on the earth.

To find local time is a simpler matter. The difference between local and standard time is longitude expressed in time — four minutes, we all know, representing one degree. This, briefly, is the principle on which longitude is found independent of chronometers. The work of the lunarian — though seldom practiced in these days of chronometers — is beautifully edifying, and there is nothing in the realm of navigation that lifts one's heart up more in adoration.

CHAPTER 12

Seventy-two days without a port – Whales and birds – A peep into the *Spray's* galley – Flying-fish for breakfast – A welcome at Apia – A visit from Mrs. Robert Louis Stevenson – At Vailima – Samoan hospitality – Arrested for fast riding – An amusing merry-go-round – At the mercy of sea-nymphs.

TO be alone forty-three days would seem a long time, but in reality, even here, winged moments flew lightly by, and instead of my hauling in for Nukahiva — which I could have made as well as not — I kept on for Samoa, where I wished to make my next landing. This occupied twenty-nine days more, making seventy-two days in all. I was not distressed in any way during that time. There was no end of companionship; the very coral reefs kept me company, or gave me no time to feel lonely, which is the same thing, and there were many of them now in my course to Samoa.

First among the incidents of the voyage from Juan Fernández to Samoa — which were not many — was a narrow escape from collisions with a great whale that was absent-mindedly plowing the ocean at night while I was below. The noise from his startled snort and the commotion he made in the sea as he turned to clear my vessel brought me on deck in time to catch a wetting from the water he threw up with his flukes. The monster was apparently frightened. He headed quickly for the east; I kept on going west. Soon another whale passed — evidently a companion — following in its wake. I saw no more on this part of the voyage, nor did I wish to.

Hungry sharks came about the vessel often when she neared islands or coral reefs. I own to a satisfaction in shooting them as one would a tiger. Sharks, after all, are the tigers of the sea. Nothing is more dreadful to the mind of a sailor, I think, than a possible encounter with a hungry shark.

101

A number of birds were always about; occasionally one poised on the mast to look the *Spray* over, wondering, perhaps, at her odd wings, for she now wore her Fuego mainsail, which — like Joseph's coat — was made of many pieces. Ships are less common on the Southern seas than formerly. I saw not one in the many days crossing the Pacific.

My diet on these long passages usually consisted of potatoes and salt cod and biscuits, which I made two or three times a week. I had always plenty of coffee, tea, sugar, and flour. I carried usually a good supply of potatoes, but before reaching Samoa I had a mishap which left me destitute of this highly prized sailors' luxury. Through meeting at Juan Fernández the Yankee Portuguese name Manuel Carroza — who nearly traded me out of my boots — I ran out of potatoes in mid-ocean and was wretched thereafter. I prided myself on being something of a trader, but this Portuguese from the Azores by way of New Bedford, who gave me new potatoes for the older ones I had got from the *Colombia*, a bushel or more of the best, left me no ground for boasting. He wanted mine, he said, "for changee the seed." When I got to sea I found that his tubers were rank and unedible, and full of fine yellow streaks of repulsive appearance. I tied the sack up and returned to the few left of my old stock, thinking that maybe when I got right hungry the island potatoes would improve in flavor. Three weeks later, I opened the bag again and out flew millions of winged insects! Manuel's potatoes had all turned to moths. I tied them up quickly and threw all into the sea.

Manuel had a large crop of potatoes on hand, and as a hint to whalemen, who are always eager to buy vegetables, he wished me to report whales off the island of Juan Fernández, which I have already done — and big ones at that — but they were a long way off.

Taking things by and large (as sailors say), I got on fairly well in the matter of provisions even on the long voyage across the Pacific. I found always some small stores to help the fare of luxuries; what I lacked of fresh meat was made up in fresh fish, at least while in the trade-winds, where flying-fish crossing on the wing at night would hit the sails and fall on deck, sometimes two or three of them, sometimes a dozen. Every morning — except when the moon was large — I got a bountiful supply by merely picking them up from the lee scuppers. All tinned meats went begging.

First exchange of courtesies in Samoa.

On the 16th of July, after considerable care and some skill and hard work, the *Spray* cast anchor at Apia in the kingdom of Samoa about noon. My vessel being moored, I spread an awning sat till late in the evening, listening to the musical voices of the Samoan men and women.

A canoe coming down the harbor with three young women in it rested her paddles abreast the sloop. One of the fair crew, hailing with the native salutation, "Talofa lee" ("Love to you, chief"), asked:

"Schoon come Melike?"

"Love to you," I answered and said, "Yes."

"You man come 'lone?"

Again I answered, "Yes."

"I don't believe that. You had other mans, and you eat 'em."

At this sally the others laughed: "What for you come long way?" they asked.

"To hear you ladies sing," I replied.

"Oh, talofa lee!" they all cried and sang on. Their voices filled the air with music that rolled across to the grove of tall palms on the other side of the harbor and back. Soon after this, six young men came down in the United States consul-general's boat, singing in parts and beating time with their oars. In my interview with them I came off better than with the damsels in the canoe. They bore an invitation from General Churchill for me to come and dine at the consulate. There was a lady's hand in things about the consulate at Samoa. Mrs. Churchill picked the crew for the general's boat and saw to it that they wore a smart uniform and that they could sing the Samoan boatsong, which in the first week Mrs. Churchill herself could sing like a native girl.

Next morning bright and early Mrs. Robert Louis Stevenson came to the *Spray* and invited me to Vailima the following day. I was, of course, thrilled when I found myself, after so many days of adventure, face to face with this bright woman, so lately the companion of the author who had delighted me on the voyage. The kindly eyes, that looked me through and through, sparkled when we compared notes of adventure. I marveled at some of her experiences and escapes. She told me that — along with her husband — she had voyaged in all manner of rickety craft among the islands of the Pacific, reflectively adding, "Our tastes were similar."

Following the subject of voyages, she gave me the four beautiful volumes of sailing directories for the Mediterranean, writing on the fly-leaf of the first:

TO CAPTAIN SLOCUM. These volumes have been read and re-read many times by my husband, and I am very sure that he would be pleased that they should be passed on to the sort of seafaring man that he like above all others.

FANNY V. DE G. STEVENSON.

Mrs. Stevenson also gave me a great directory of the Indian Ocean. It was not without a feeling of reverential awe that I received the books so nearly direct from the hand of Tusitala, "who sleeps in the forest." Aolele, the *Spray* will cherish your gift.

The novelist's stepson, Mr. Lloyd Osbourne, walked through the Vailima mansion with me and bade me write my letters at the old desk. I thought it would be presumptuous to do that; it was sufficient for me to enter the hall on the floor of which the "Writer of Tales," according to the Samoan custom, was wont to sit.

Coming through the main street of Apia one day with my hosts all bound for the *Spray* — Mrs. Stevenson on horseback, I walking by her side, and Mr. and Mrs. Osbourne close in our wake on bicycles — at a sudden turn in the road we found ourselves mixed with a remarkable native procession with a somewhat primitive band of music in front of us, while behind was a festival or funeral, we could not tell which. Several of the stoutest men carried bales and bundles on poles. Some were evidently bales of tapa-cloth. The burden of one set of poles, heavier than the rest, however, was not so easily made out. My curiosity was whetted to know whether it was a roast pig or something of a gruesome nature, and I inquired about it.

"I don't know," said Mrs. Stevenson, "whether this is a wedding or a funeral. Whatever it is, though, captain, our place seems to be at the head of it."

The *Spray* being in the stream, we boarded her from the beach abreast in the little razeed Gloucester dory, which had been painted a smart green. Our combined weight loaded it gunwale to the water, and I was obliged to steer with great care to avoid swamping. The adventure pleased Mrs. Stevenson greatly, and as we paddled along she sang, "They went to sea in a pea-green boat." I could understand her saying of her husband and herself, "Our tastes were similar."

As I sailed farther from the center of civilization, I heard less and less of what would and what would not pay. Mrs. Stevenson — in speaking of my voyage — did not once ask me what I would make out of it. When I came to a Samoan village, the chief did not ask the price of gin, or say, "How much will you pay for roast pig?" but, "Dollar, dollar," said he. "White man know only dollar."

"Never mind dollar. The *tapo* has prepared ava; let us drink and rejoice." The tapo is the virgin hostess of the village; in this instance it was Taloa, daughter of the chief.

"Our taro is good; let us eat. On the tree there is fruit. Let the day go by; why should we mourn over that? There are millions of days coming. The breadfruit is yellow in the sun, and from the cloth-tree is Taloa's gown. Our house, which is good, cost but the labor of building it, and there is no lock on the door."

While the days go thus in these Southern islands, we at the North are struggling for the bare necessities of life.

For food the islanders have only to put out their hand and take what nature has provided for them; if they plant a banana-tree, their only care afterward is to see that too many trees do not grow. They have great reason to love their country and to fear the white man's yoke, for — once harnessed to the plow — their life would no longer be a poem.

The chief of the village of Caini, who was a tall and dignified Tonga man, could be approached only through an interpreter and talking man. It was perfectly natural for him to inquire the object of my visit, and I was sincere when I told him that my reason for casting anchor in Samoa was to see their fine men, and fine women, too. After a considerable pause the chief said: "The captain has come a long way to see so little, but," he added, "the tapo must sit nearer the captain."

"Yack," said Taloa, who had so nearly learned to say *yes* in English and suiting the action to the word, she hitched a peg nearer, all hands sitting in a circle upon mats.

I was no less taken with the chief's eloquence than delighted with the simplicity of all he said. About him there was nothing pompous; he might have been taken for a great scholar or statesman, the least assuming of the men I met on the voyage. As for Taloa — a sort of Queen of the May — and the other tapo girls, well, it is wise to learn as soon as possible the manners and customs of these hospitable people and meanwhile not to mistake for overfamiliarity that which is intended as honor to a guest. I was fortunate in my travels in the islands and saw nothing to shake one's faith in native virtue.

To the unconventional mind the punctilious etiquette of Samoa is perhaps a little painful. For instance, I found that in partaking of ava (the social bowl), I was supposed to toss a little of the beverage over my shoulder — or pretend to do so — and say, "Let the gods drink," and then drink it all myself. And the dish (invariably a cocoanut-shell) being empty, I might not pass it politely as we would do, but politely throw it twirling across the mats at the tapo.

My most grievous mistake while at the islands was made on a nag, which — inspired by a bit of good road — must needs break into a smart trot through a village. I was instantly hailed by the chief's deputy, who in an angry voice brought me to a halt. Perceiving that I was in trouble, I made signs for pardon — the safest thing to do — though I did not know what offense I had committed. My interpreter coming up, however, put me right, but not until a long palaver had ensured.

The deputy's hail, liberally translated, was: "Ahoy, there, on the frantic steed! Know you not that it is against the law to ride this through the village of our fathers?"

I made what apologies I could and offered to dismount and, like my servant, lead my nag by the bridle. This, the interpreter told me, would also be a grievous wrong, and so I again begged for pardon. I was summoned to appear before a chief, but my interpreter — being a wit as well as a bit of a rogue — explained that I was myself something of a chief and should not be detained, being on a most important mission. In my own behalf I could only say that I was a stranger, but pleading all this, I knew I still deserved to be roasted, at which the chief showed a fine row of teeth and seemed pleased, but allowed me to pass on.

The chief of the Tongas and his family at Caini, returning my visit, brought presents of tapa-cloth and fruits. Taloa, the princess, brought a bottle of cocoanut-oil for my hair, which another man might have regarded as coming late.

It was impossible to entertain on the *Spray* after the royal manner in which I had been received by the chief. His fare had included all that the land could afford: fruits, fowl, fishes, and flesh, a hog having been roasted whole. I set before them boiled salt pork and salt beef — with which I was well supplied — and in the evening took them all to a new amusement in the town, a rocking-horse merry-go-round, which they called a "kee-kee," meaning *theater*. And in a spirit of justice, they pulled off the horses' tails, for the proprietors of the show — two hard-fisted countrymen of mine, I grieve to say — unceremoniously hustled them off for a new set, almost at the first spin. I was not a little proud of my Tonga friends; the chief, finest of them all, carried a portentous club. As for the theater, through the greed of the proprietors it was becoming unpopular, and the representatives of the three great powers — in want of laws which they could enforce — adopted a vigorous foreign policy, taxing it twenty-five per cent on the gate money. This was considered a great stroke of legislative reform!

It was the fashion of the native visitors to the *Spray* to come over the bows, where they could reach the head-gear and climb aboard with ease, and on going ashore to jump off the stern and swim away; nothing could have been more delightfully simple. The modest natives wore *lava-lava* bathing-dresses, a native cloth from the bark of the mulberry-tree, and they did no harm to the *Spray*. In summer-land Samoa their coming and going was only a merry every-day scene.

One day the head teachers of Papauta College, Miss Schultze and Miss Moore, came on board with their ninety-seven young women students. They were all dressed in white, and each wore a red rose, and of course came in boats or canoes in the cold-climate style. A merrier bevy of girls it would be difficult to find. As soon as they got on deck, by request of one of the teachers, they sang, "The Watch on the Rhine," which I had never heard before.

"And now," said they all, "let's up anchor and away."

But I had no inclination to sail from Samoa so soon. On leaving the *Spray*, these accomplished young women each seized a palm-branch or paddle (or whatever else would serve the purpose) and literally paddled her own canoe. Each could have swum as readily and would have done so, I dare say, had it not been for the holiday muslin.

It was not uncommon at Apia to see a young woman swimming alongside a small canoe with a passenger for the *Spray*. Mr. Trood, an old Eton boy, came in this manner to see me, and he exclaimed, "Was ever a king ferried in such state?" Then, suiting his action to the sentiment, he gave the damsel pieces of silver till the natives on shore yelled with envy. My own canoe, a small dugout, one day when it had rolled over with me, was seized by a party of fair bathers and — before I could get my breath almost — was towed around and around the *Spray*, while I sat in the bottom of it, wondering what they would do next. But in this case there were six of them, three on a side, and I could not help myself. One of the sprites, I remember, was a young English lady, who made more sport of it than any of the others.

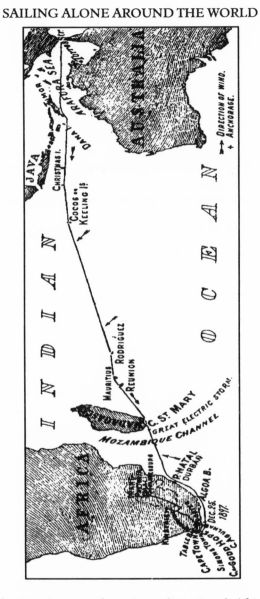

The *Spray's* course from Australia to South Africa.

CHAPTER 13

Samoan royalty – King Malietoa – Good-bye to friends at Vailima – Leaving Fiji to the south – Arrival at Newcastle – The yachts of Sydney – A ducking on the *Spray* – Commodore Foy presents the sloop with a new suit of sails – A shark that proved to be valuable – A change of course – The "Rain of Blood" – In Tasmania.

A T Apia I had the pleasure of meeting Mr. A. Young, the father of the late Queen Margaret, who was Queen of Manua from 1891 to 1895. Her grandfather was an English sailor who married a princess. Mr. Young is now the only survivor of the family, two of his children — the last of them all — having been lost in an island trader which a few months before had sailed, never to return. Mr. Young was a Christian gentleman, and his daughter Margaret was accomplished in graces that would become any lady. It was with pain that I saw in the newspapers a sensational account of her life and death — taken evidently from a paper in the supposed interest of a benevolent society — but without foundation in fact. And the startling headlines saying, "Queen Margaret of Manua is dead," could hardly be called news in 1898, the queen having then been dead three years.

While hobnobbing — as it were — with royalty, I called on the king himself, the late Malietoa. King Malietoa was a great ruler; he never got less than forty-five dollars a month for the job — as he told me himself — and this amount had lately been raised so that he could live on the fat of the land and no longer be called "Tin-of-salmon Malietoa" by graceless beach-combers.

As my interpreter and I entered the front door of the palace, the king's brother, who was viceroy, sneaked in through a taro-patch by the back way and sat cowering by the door while I told my story to the king. Mr. W— of New York — a gentleman interested in missionary work — had charged me, when I sailed, to give his remembrance to the king of the Cannibal Islands, other islands of course being meant. But good King Malietoa — notwithstanding that his people have not eaten a missionary in a hundred years — received the message himself and seemed greatly pleased to hear so directly from the publishers of the *Missionary Review*, and wished me to make his compliments in return. His Majesty then excused himself, while I talked with his daughter, the beautiful Faamu-Sami (a name signifying "To make the sea burn"), and soon reappeared in the full-dress uniform of the German commander-in-chief, Emperor William himself; for — stupidly enough — I had not sent my credentials ahead that the king might be in full regalia to receive me. Calling a few days later to say good-bye to Faamu-Sami, I saw King Malietoa for the last time.

Of the landmarks in the pleasant town of Apia, my memory rests first on the little school just back of the London Missionary Society coffee-house and reading-rooms, where Mrs. Bell taught English to about a hundred native children, boys and girls. Brighter children you will not find anywhere.

"Now, children," said Mrs. Bell, when I called one day, "let us show the captain that we know something about the Cape Horn he passed in the *Spray*," at which a lad of nine or ten years stepped nimbly forward and read Basil Hall's fine description of the great cape and read it well. He afterward copied the essay for me in a clear hand.

Calling to say good-bye to my friends at Vailima, I met Mrs. Stevenson in her Panama hat and went over the estate with her. Men were at work clearing the land, and to one of them she gave an order to cut a couple of bamboo-trees for the *Spray* from a clump she had planted four years before and which had grown to the height of sixty feet. I used them for spare spars, and the butt of one made a serviceable jib-boom on the homeward voyage. I had then only to take ava with the family and be ready for the sea.

This ceremony — important among Samoans — was conducted after the native fashion. A Triton horn was sounded to let us know when the beverage was ready, and in response we all clapped hands. The bout being in honor of the *Spray*, it was my turn first — after the custom of the country — to spill a little over my shoulder. But having forgotten the Samoan for "Let the gods drink," I repeated the equivalent in Russian and Chinook — as I remembered a word in each — whereupon Mr. Osbourne pronounced me a confirmed Samoan.

Then I said "Tofah!" to my good friends of Samoa, and — all wishing the *Spray bon voyage* — she stood out of the harbor August 20, 1896, and continued on her course. A sense of loneliness seized upon me as the islands faded astern, and as a remedy for it I crowded on sail for lovely Australia, which was not a strange land to me. But for long days in my dreams Vailima stood before the prow.

The *Spray* had barely cleared the islands when a sudden burst of trades brought her down to close reefs, and she reeled off one hundred and eighty-four miles the first day, of which I counted forty miles of current in her favor. Finding a rough sea, I swung her off free and sailed north of the Horn Islands, also north of Fiji instead of south — as I had intended — and coasted down the west side of the archipelago. Thence I sailed direct for New South Wales, passing south of New Caledonia, and arrived at Newcastle after a passage of forty-two days, mostly of storms and gales.

One particularly severe gale encountered near New Caledonia foundered the American clipper-ship *Patrician* farther south. Again, nearer the coast of Australia, when, however, I was not aware that the gale was extraordinary, a French mail-steamer from New Caledonia for Sydney — blown considerably out of her course — on her arrival reported it an awful storm and to inquiring friends said: "Oh, my! we don't know what has become of the little sloop *Spray*. We saw her in the thick of the storm."

The *Spray* was all right, lying to like a duck. She was under a goose's wing mainsail and had had a dry deck while the passengers on the steamer, I heard later, were up to their knees in water in the saloon. When their ship arrived at Sydney, they gave the captain a purse of gold for his skill and seamanship in bringing them safe into port. The captain of the *Spray* got nothing of this sort. In this gale, I made the land about Seal Rocks, where the steamship *Catherton* (with many lives) was lost a short time before. I was many hours off the rocks, beating back and forth, but weathered them at last.

I arrived at Newcastle in the teeth of a gale of wind. It was a stormy season. The government pilot, Captain Cumming, met me at the harbor bar and with the assistance of a steamer carried my vessel to a safe berth. Many visitors came on board, the first being the United States consul, Mr. Brown. Nothing was too good for the *Spray* here. All government dues with remitted, and — after I had rested a few days — a port pilot with a tug carried her to sea again, and she made along the coast toward the harbor of Sydney, where she arrived on the following day, October 10, 1896.

I came to in a snug cove near Manly for the night, the Sydney harbor police-boat giving me a pluck into the anchorage while they gathered data from an old scrap-book of mine, which seemed to interest them. Nothing escapes the vigilance of the New South Wales police; their reputation is known the world over. They made a shrewd guess that I could give them some useful information, and they were the first to meet me. Someone said they came to arrest me, and — well, let it go at that.

Summer was approaching, and the harbor of Sydney was blooming with yachts. Some of them came down to the weather-beaten *Spray* and sailed round her at Shelcote, where she took a berth for a few days. At Sydney, I was at once among friends. The *Spray* remained at the various water-places in the great port for several weeks and was visited by many agreeable people, frequently by officers of the H.M.S. *Orlando* and their friends.

Captain Fisher, the commander, with a party of young ladies from the city and gentlemen belonging to his ship, came one day to pay me a visit in the midst of a deluge of rain. I never saw it rain harder even in Australia. But they were out for fun, and rain could not dampen their feelings, however hard it poured. But, as ill luck would have it, a young gentleman of another party on board — in the full uniform of a very great yacht club with brass buttons enough to sink him — stepping quickly to get out of the wet, tumbled holus-bolus, head and heels, into a barrel of water I had been coopering and — being a short man — was soon out of sight and nearly drowned before he was rescued. It was the nearest to a casualty on the *Spray* in her whole course, so far as I know. The young man having come on board with compliments made the mishap most embarrassing. It had been decided by his club that the *Spray* could not be officially recognized for the reason that she brought no letters from yacht-clubs in America, and so I say it seemed all the more embarrassing and strange that I should have caught at least one of the members in a barrel and, too, when I was not fishing for yachtsmen.

The typical Sydney boat is a handy sloop of great beam and enormous sail-carrying power, but a capsize is not uncommon, for they carry sail like Vikings. In Sydney, I saw all manner of craft, from the smart steam-launch and sailing-cutter to the smaller sloop and canoe pleasuring on the bay. Everybody owned a boat. If a boy in Australia has not the means to buy him a boat, he builds one. And it is usually one not to be ashamed of. The *Spray* shed her Joseph's coat — the Fuego mainsail — in Sydney, and wearing a new suit — the handsome present of Commodore Foy — she was flagship of the Johnstone's Bay Flying Squadron when the circumnavigators of Sydney harbor sailed in their annual regatta. They "recognized" the *Spray* as belonging to "a club of her own," and with more Australian sentiment than fastidiousness gave her credit for her record.

Time flew fast those days in Australia, and it was December 6, 1896, when the *Spray* sailed from Sydney. My intention was now to sail around Cape Leeuwin direct for Mauritius on my way home, and so I coasted along toward Bass Strait in that direction.

There was little to report on this part of the voyage, except changeable winds — "busters" — and rough seas.

115

The 12th of December, however, was an exceptional day, with a fine coast wind, northeast. The *Spray* early in the morning passed Twofold Bay and later Cape Bundooro in a smooth sea with land close aboard. The lighthouse on the cape dipped a flag to the *Spray's* flag, and children on the balconies of a cottage near the shore waved handker- chiefs as she passed by. There were only a few people on the shore, but the scene was a happy one. I saw festoons of evergreen in token of Christmas near at hand. I saluted the merrymakers, wishing them a "Merry Christmas," and could hear them say, "I wish you the same."

From Cape Bundooro, I passed by Cliff Island in Bass Strait and exchanged signals with the light-keepers while the *Spray* worked up under the island. The wind howled that day while the sea broke over their rocky home.

A few days later, December 17, the *Spray* came in close under Wilson's Promontory, again seeking shelter. The keeper of the light at that station, Mr. J. Clark, came on board and gave me directions for Waterloo Bay, about three miles to leeward, for which I bore up at once, finding good anchorage there in a sandy cove protected from all westerly and northerly winds.

Anchored here was the ketch *Secret*, a fisherman, and the *Mary* of Sydney, a steam ferry-boat fitted for whaling. The captain of the *Mary* was a genius — and an Australian genius at that — and smart. His crew, from a sawmill up the coast, had not one of them seen a live whale when they shipped. But they were boatmen after an Australian's own heart, and the captain had told them that to kill a whale was no more than to kill a rabbit. They believed him, and that settled that. As luck would have it, the very first one they saw on their cruise — although an ugly humpback — was a dead whale in no time, Captain Young, the master of the *Mary*, killing the monster at a single thrust of a harpoon. It was taken in tow for Sydney, where they put it on exhibition. Nothing but whales interested the crew of the gallant *Mary*, and they spent most of their time here gathering fuel along shore for a cruise on the grounds off Tasmania. Whenever the word "whale" was mentioned in the hearing of these men, their eyes glistened with excitement.

We spent three days in the quite cove, listening to the wind outside. Meanwhile Captain Young and I explored the shores, visited abandoned miners' pits, and prospected for gold ourselves.

Captain Slocum working the *Spray* out of the Yarrow River, a part of Melbourne Harbor.

Our vessels, parting company the morning they sailed, stood away like sea-birds each on its own course. The wind for a few days was moderate, and with unusual luck of fine weather the *Spray* made Melbourne Heads on the 22d of December, and — taken in tow by the steam-tug *Racer* — was brought into port.

Christmas day was spent at a berth in the river Yarrow, but I lost little time in shifting to St. Kilda, where I spent nearly a month.

117

The *Spray* paid no port charges in Australia or anywhere else on the voyage, except at Pernambuco, till she poked her nose into the custom-house at Melbourne, where she was charged tonnage dues; in this instance, sixpence a ton on the gross. The collector exacted six shillings and sixpence, taking off nothing for the fraction under thirteen tons, her exact gross being 12.70 tons. I squared the matter by charging people sixpence each for coming on board, and — when this business got dull — I caught a shark and charged them sixpence each to look at that.

The shark was twelve feet six inches in length and carried a progeny of twenty-six, not one of them less than two feet in length. A slit of a knife let them come out in a canoe full of water, which (changed constantly) kept them alive one whole day. In less than an hour from the time I heard of the ugly brute, it was on deck and on exhibition with rather more than the amount of the *Spray's* tonnage dues already collected. Then I hired a good Irishman, Tom Howard by name — who knew all about sharks, both on the land and in the sea, and could talk about them — to answer questions and lecture. When I found that I could not keep abreast of the questions, I turned the responsibility over to him.

Returning from the bank, where I had been to deposit money early in the day, I found Howard in the midst of a very excited crowd, telling imaginary habits of the fish. It was a good show; the people wished to see it, and it was my wish that they should. But owing to his over-stimulated enthusiasm, I was obliged to let Howard resign. The income from the show and the proceeds of the tallow I had gathered in the Strait of Magellan (the last of which I had disposed of to a German soap-boiler at Samoa) put me in ample funds.

January 24, 1897, found the *Spray* again in tow of the tug *Racer*, leaving Hobson's Bay after a pleasant time in Melbourne and St. Kilda, which had been protracted by a succession of southwest winds that seemed never-ending.

In the summer months — that is, December, January, February, and sometimes March — east winds are

118

prevalent through Bass Strait and round Cape Leeuwin. But owing to a vast amount of ice drifting up from the Antarctic, this was all changed now and emphasized with much bad weather; so much so, that I considered it impracticable to pursue the course farther. Therefore, instead of thrashing round cold and stormy Cape Leeuwin, I decided to spend a pleasanter and more profitable time in Tasmania, waiting for the season for favorable winds through Torres Strait by way of the Great Barrier Reef, the route I finally decided on. To sail this course would be taking advantage of anticyclones, which never fail. And besides, it would give me the chance to put foot on the shores of Tasmania, round which I had sailed years before.

I should mention that while I was at Melbourne there occurred one of those extraordinary storms sometimes called "rain of blood," the first of the kind in many years about Australia. The "blood" came from a fine brick-dust matter afloat in the air from the deserts. A rain-storm setting in brought down this dust simply as mud; it fell in such quantities that a bucketful was collected from the sloop's awnings, which were spread at the time. When the wind blew hard and I was obliged to furl awnings, her sails — unprotected on the booms — got mud-stained from clue to earing.

The phenomena of dust-storms, well understood by scientists, are not uncommon on the coast of Africa. Reaching some distance out over the sea, they frequently cover the track of ships, as in the case of the one through which the *Spray* passed in the earlier part of her voyage. Sailors no longer regard them with superstitious fear, but our credulous brothers on the land cry out "Rain of blood!" at the first splash of the awful mud.

The rip off Port Heads, a wild place, was rough when the *Spray* entered Hobson's Bay from the sea and was rougher when she stood out. But, with sea-room and under sail, she made good weather immediately after passing it. It was only a few hours' sail to Tasmania across the strait, the wind being fair and blowing hard. I carried the St. Kilda shark along — stuffed with hay — and

119

disposed of it to Professor Porter, the curator of the Victoria Museum of Launceston, which is at the head of the Tamar. For many a long day to come may be seen there the shark of St. Kilda. Alas! the good but mistaken people of St. Kilda, when the illustrated journals with pictures of my shark reached their news-stands, flew into a passion and swept all papers containing mention of fish into the fire, for St. Kilda was a watering-place — and the idea of a shark *there!* But my show went on.

The *Spray* was berthed on the beach at a small jetty at Launceston while the tide driven in by the gale that brought her up the river was unusually high. And she lay there hard and fast, with not enough water around her at any time after to wet one's feet till she was ready to sail; then, to float her, the ground was dug from under her keel.

In this snug place I left her in charge of three children, while I made journeys among the hills and rested my bones for the coming voyage on the moss-covered rocks at the gorge hard by and among the ferns I found wherever I went. My vessel was well taken care of. I never returned without finding that the decks had been washed and that one of the children — my nearest neighbor's little girl from across the road — was at the gangway attending to visitors, while the others — a brother and sister — sold marine curios (such as were in the cargo) on "ship's account." They were a bright, cheerful crew, and people came a long way to hear them tell the story of the voyage and of the monsters of the deep "the captain had slain." I had only to keep myself away to be a hero of the first water. And it suited me very well to do so and to rusticate in the forests and among the streams.

CHAPTER 14

A testimonial from a lady – Cruising round Tasmania – The skipper
delivers his first lecture on the voyage – Abundant provisions – An
inspection of the *Spray* for safety at Devonport – Again at Sydney –
Northward bound for Torres Strait – An amateur shipwreck –
Friends on the Australian coast – Perils of a coral sea.

FEBRUARY 1, 1897, on returning to my vessel I
found waiting for me the letter of sympathy which I
subjoin:

A lady sends Mr. Slocum the enclosed five-pound note as a
token of her appreciation of his bravery in crossing the wide
seas on so small a boat, and all alone, without human sympathy
to help when danger threatened. All success to you.

To this day I do not know who wrote it or to whom I
am indebted for the generous gift it contained. I could not
refuse a thing so kindly meant, but promised myself to
pass it on with interest at the first opportunity, and this I
did before leaving Australia.

The season of fair weather around the north of
Australia being yet a long way off, I sailed to other ports
in Tasmania — where it is fine the year round — the first
of these being Beauty Point, near which are Beaconsfield
and the great Tasmania gold-mine, which I visited in turn.
I saw much gray, uninteresting rock being hoisted out of
the mine there and hundreds of stamps crushing it into
powder. People told me there was gold in it, and I
believed what they said.

I remember Beauty Point for its shady forest and for
the road among the tall gum-trees. While there, the
governor of New South Wales, Lord Hampden, and his
family came in on a steam-yacht sight-seeing. The *Spray*,
anchored near the landing-pier, threw her bunting out, of
course, and probably a more insignificant craft bearing
the Stars and Stripes was never seen in those waters;

however, the governor's party seemed to know why it floated there and all about the *Spray*, and when I heard his Excellency say, "Introduce me to the captain," or "Introduce the captain to me," (whichever it was) I found myself at once in the presence of a gentleman and a friend and one greatly interested in my voyage. If any one of the party was more interested than the governor himself, it was the Honorable Margaret, his daughter. On leaving, Lord and Lady Hampden promised to rendezvous with me on board the *Spray* at the Paris Exposition in 1900. "If we live," they said, and I added for my part, "Dangers of the sea excepted."

From Beauty Point, the *Spray* visited Georgetown, near the mouth of the river Tamar. This little settlement, I believe, marks the place where the first footprints were made by whites in Tasmania, though it never grew to be more than a hamlet.

Considering that I had seen something of the world and finding people here interested in adventure, I talked the matter over before my first audience in a little hall by the country road. A piano having been brought in from a neighbor's, I was helped out by the severe thumping it got and by a "Tommy Atkins" song from a strolling comedian. People came from a great distance, and the attendance all told netted the house about three pounds sterling. The owner of the hall, a kind lady from Scotland, would take no rent, and so my lecture from the start was a success.

From this snug little place I made sail for Devonport, a thriving place on the river Mersey, a few hours' sail westward along the coast and fast becoming the most important port in Tasmania. Large steamers enter there now and carry away great cargoes of farm produce, but the *Spray* was the first vessel to bring the Stars and Stripes to the port, the harbor-master, Captain Murray, told me, and so it is written in the port records. For the great distinction the *Spray* enjoyed many civilities while she rode comfortably at anchor in her port-duster awning that covered her from stem to stern.

From the magistrate's house, "Mulannah" — on the point — she was saluted by the Jack both on coming in and going out, and dear Mrs. Aikenhead, the mistress of Malunnah, supplied the *Spray* with jams and jellies of all sorts (by the case) prepared from the fruits of her own rich garden — enough to last all the way home and to spare. Mrs. Wood, farther up the harbor, put up bottles of

The *Spray* in her port duster at Devonport, Tasmania, February 22, 1897.

raspberry wine for me. At this point, more than ever before, I was in the land of good cheer. Mrs. Powell sent on board chutney prepared "as we prepare it in India." Fish and game were plentiful here; the voice of the gobbler was heard; and from Pardo, farther up the country, came an enormous cheese. And yet, people inquire: "What did you live on? What did you eat?"

I was haunted by the beauty of the landscape all about, of the natural ferneries then disappearing, and of the domed forest-trees on the slopes, and was fortunate in meeting a gentleman intent on preserving in art the beauties of his country. He presented me with many reproductions from his collection of pictures, also many originals to show to my friends.

By another gentleman I was charged to tell the glories of Tasmania in every land and on every occasion. This was Dr. McCall, M.L.C. The doctor gave me useful hints on lecturing. It was not without misgivings, however, that I filled away on this new course, and I am free to say that it is only by the kindness of sympathetic audiences that my oratorical bark was held on even keel. Soon after my first talk, the kind doctor came to me with words of approval. As in many other enterprises, I had gone about it at once and without second thought.

"Man, man," said he, "a great nervousness is only a sign of brain, and the more brain a man has the longer it takes him to get over the affliction. But," he added reflectively, "you will get over it."

However, in my own behalf I think it only fair to say that I am not yet entirely cured.

The *Spray* was hauled out on the marine railway at Devonport and examined carefully top and bottom, but was found absolutely free from the destructive teredo and sound in all respects. To protect her further against the ravage of these insects, the bottom was coated once more with copper paint, for she would have to sail through the Coral and Arafura Seas before refitting again. Everything was done to fit her for all the known dangers, but it was not without regret that I looked forward to the day of sailing from a country of so many pleasant associations. If there was a moment in my voyage when I could have given it up, it was there and then. But no vacancies for a better post being open, I weighed anchor April 16th, 1897, and again put out to sea.

The season of summer was then over; winter was rolling up from the south, with fair winds for the north. A foretaste of winter wind sent the *Spray* flying round Cape Howe and as far as Cape Bundooro farther along, which she passed on the following day, retracing her course northward. This was a fine run and boded good for the long voyage home from the antipodes. My old Christmas friends on Bundooro seemed to be up and moving when I came the second time by their cape, and we exchanged signals again, while the sloop sailed along as before in a smooth sea and close to the shore.

The weather was fine, with clear sky the rest of the passage to Port Jackson (Sydney), where the *Spray* arrived April 22, 1897, and anchored in Watson's Bay, near the heads in eight fathoms of water. The harbor from the heads to Parramatta up the river was more than ever alive with boats and yachts of every class. It was, indeed, a scene of animation, hardly equaled in any other part of the world.

A few days later the bay was flecked with tempestuous waves, and none but stout ships carried sail. I was in a neighboring hotel then — nursing a neuralgia which I had picked up alongshore — and had only that moment got a glance of just the stern of a large, unmanageable steamship passing the range of my window as she forged in by the point, when the bell-boy burst into my room shouting that the *Spray* had "gone bung."

I tumbled out quickly to learn that "bung" meant that a large steamship had run into her and that it was the one of which I saw the stern, the other end of her having hit the *Spray*. It turned out, however, that no damage was done beyond the loss of an anchor and chain, which from the shock of the collision had parted at the hawse. I had nothing at all to complain of though in the end, for the captain — after he clubbed his ship — took the *Spray* in tow up the harbor — clear of all dangers — and sent her back again in charge of an officer and three men to her anchorage in the bay, with a polite note saying that he would repair any damages done.

But what yawing about she made of it when she came with a stranger at the helm! Her old friend the pilot of the *Pinta* would not have been guilty of such lubberly work. But to my delight they got her into a berth, and the neuralgia left me then (or was forgotten). The captain of the steamer — like a true seaman — kept his word, and his agent, Mr. Collishaw handed me on the very next day the price of the lost anchor and chain, with something over for anxiety of mind. I remember that he offered me twelve pounds at once. But my lucky number being thirteen, we made the account thirteen pounds, which squared all accounts.

I sailed again, May 9, before a strong southwest wind, which sent the *Spray* gallantly on as far as Port Stevens, where it fell calm and then came up ahead; but the weather was fine, and so remained for many days, which was a great change from the state of weather experienced here some months before.

Having a full set of admiralty sheet-charts of the coast and the Barrier Reef, I felt easy in mind. Captain Fisher, R.N., who had steamed through the Barrier passages in H.M.S. *Orlando*, advised me from the first to take this route, and I did not regret coming back to it now.

The wind, for a few days after passing Port Stevens, Seal Rocks, and Cape Hawk, was light and dead ahead, but these points are photographed on my memory from the trial of beating round them some months before when bound the other way. But now with a good stock of books on board, I fell to reading day and night, leaving this pleasant occupation merely to trim sails or tack, or to lie down and rest while the *Spray* nibbled at the miles.

I tried to compare my state with that of the old circumnavigators, who sailed exactly over the route which I took from the Cape Verde Islands or farther back to this point and beyond, but there was no comparison so far as I had got. Their hardships and romantic escapes — those of them who escaped death and worse sufferings — did not enter into my experience sailing all alone around the world. For me is left to tell only of pleasant experiences, till finally my adventures are prosy and tame.

I had just finished reading some of the most interesting of the old voyages in woe-begone ships and was already near Port Macquarie on my own cruise, when I made out, May 13, a modern dandy craft in distress, anchored on the coast. Standing in for her, I found that she was the cutter-yacht *Akbar*[1] which had sailed from Watson's Bay about three days ahead of the *Spray* and

[1] *Akbar* was not her registered name, which need not be told.

that she had run at once into trouble. No wonder she did so. It was a case of babes in the wood or butterflies at sea. Her owner, on his maiden voyage, was all duck trousers; the captain, distinguished for the enormous yachtsman's cap he wore, was a Murrumbidgee[1] whaler before he took command of the *Akbar*; and the navigating office — poor fellow — was almost as deaf as a post and nearly as stiff and immovable as a post in the ground. These three jolly tars comprised the crew. None of them knew more about the sea or about a vessel than a newly born babe knows about another world. They were bound for New Guinea, so they said; perhaps it was as well that three tenderfeet so tender as those never reached that destination.

The owner, whom I had met before he sailed, wanted to race the poor old *Spray* to Thursday Island en route. I declined the challenge, naturally, on the ground of the unfairness of three young yachtsmen in a clipper against an old sailor all alone in a craft of coarse build. Besides that, I would not on any account race in the Coral Sea.

"*Spray* ahoy!" they all hailed now. "'What's the weather goin' t'be? Is it a-goin' to blow? And don't you think we'd better go back t' r-r-refit?"

I thought, "If ever you get back, don't refit," but I said: "Give me the end of a rope, and I'll tow you into yon port farther along. And on your lives," I urged, "do not go back round Cape Hawk, for it's winter to the south of it."

They purposed making for Newcastle under jury-sails, for their mainsail had been blown to ribbons. Even the jigger had been blown away, and her rigging flew at loose ends. The *Akbar*, in a word, was a wreck.

"Up anchor," I shouted, "up anchor, and let me tow you into Port Macquerie, twelve miles north of this."

"No," cried the owner, "we'll go back to Newcastle. We missed Newcastle on the way coming; we didn't see the light, and it was not thick, either." This he shouted very loud, ostensibly for my hearing, but closer even than necessary, I thought, to the ear of the navigating officer.

[1]The Murrumbidgee is a small river winding among the mountains of Australia, and would be the last place to look for a whale.

Again, I tried to persuade them to be towed into the port of refuge so near at hand. It would have cost them only the trouble of weighing their anchor and passing me a rope; of this I assured them, but they declined even this, in sheer ignorance of a rational course.

"What is your depth of water?" I asked.

"Don't know; we lost our lead. All the chain is out. We sounded with the anchor."

"Send your dinghy over, and I'll give you a lead."

"We've lost our dinghy, too," they cried.

"God is good, else you would have lost yourselves," and "Farewell" was all I could say.

The trifling service proffered by the *Spray* would have saved their vessel.

"Is it a-goin' to blow?"

"Report us," they cried, as I stood on — "report us with sails blown away, and that we don't care a dash and are not afraid."

"Then there is no hope for you," and again "Farewell."

I promised I would report them and did so at the first opportunity. And out of humane reasons I do so again. On the following day, I spoke the steamship *Sherman*, bound down the coast, and reported the yacht in distress and that it would be an act of humanity to tow her somewhere away from her exposed position on an open

128

coast. That she did not get a tow from the steamer was from no lack of funds to pay the bill, for the owner — lately heir to a few hundred pounds — had the money with him. The proposed voyage to New Guinea was to look that island over with a view to its purchase. It was about eighteen days before I heard of the *Akbar* again, which was on the 31st of May, when I reached Cooktown on the Endeavor River, where I found this news:

May 31, the yacht *Akbar*, from Sydney for New Guinea, three hands on board, lost at Crescent Head; the crew saved.

So it took them several days to lose the yacht, after all.

After speaking the distressed *Akbar* and the *Sherman*, the voyage for many days was uneventful, save in the pleasant incident on May 16 of a chat by signal with the people on South Solitary Island, a dreary stone heap in the ocean just off the coast of New South Wales, in latitude 30° 12′ south.

"What vessel is that?" they asked, as the sloop came abreast of their island. For answer, I tried them with the Stars and Stripes at the peak. Down came their signals at once, and up went the British ensign instead, which they dipped heartily. I understood from this that they made out my vessel and knew all about her, for they asked no more questions. They didn't even ask if the "voyage would pay," but they threw out this friendly message, "Wishing you a pleasant voyage," which at that very moment I was having.

May 19, the *Spray* — passing the Tweed River — was signaled from Danger Point, where those on shore seemed most anxious for the state of my health, for they asked if "all hands" were well, to which I could say, "Yes."

On the following day, the *Spray* rounded Great Sandy Cape and — what is a notable event in every voyage — picked up the trade-winds, and these winds followed her now for many thousands of miles, never ceasing to blow from a moderate gale to a mild summer breeze, except at rare intervals.

From the pitch of the cape was a noble light seen twenty-seven miles; passing from this to Lady Elliott Light — which stands on an island as a sentinel at the gateway of the Barrier Reef — the *Spray* was at once in the fairway leading north. Poets have sung of beacon-light and of pharos, but did ever poet behold a great light flash up before his path on a dark night in the midst of a coral sea? If so, he knew the meaning of his song.

The *Spray* had sailed for hours in suspense, evidently stemming a current. Almost mad with doubt, I grasped at the helm to throw her head off shore, when — blazing out of the sea — was the light ahead. "Excalibur!" I cried "all hands," and rejoiced and sailed on. The *Spray* was now in a protected sea and smooth water — the first she had dipped her keel into since leaving Gibraltar — and a change it was from the heaving of the misnamed "Pacific" Ocean.

The Pacific is perhaps — upon the whole — no more boisterous than other oceans, though I feel quite safe in saying that it is not more pacific except in name. It is often wild enough in one part or another. I once knew a writer who — after saying beautiful things about the sea — passed through a Pacific hurricane, and he became a changed man. But where, after all, would be the poetry of the sea were there no wild waves?

At last here was the *Spray* in the midst of a sea of coral. The sea itself might be called smooth indeed, but coral rocks are always rough, sharp, and dangerous. I trusted now to the mercies of the Maker of all reefs, keeping a good lookout at the same time for perils on every hand.

Lo! the Barrier Reef and the waters of many colors studded all about with enchanted islands! I behold among them after all many safe harbors, else my vision is astray. On the 24th of May, the sloop — having made one hundred and ten miles a day from Danger Point — now entered Whitsunday Pass and that night sailed through among the islands. When the sun rose next morning, I looked back and regretted having gone by while it was dark, for the scenery far astern was varied and charming.

CHAPTER 15

Arrival at Port Denison – Reminiscences of Captain Cook – Lecturing for charity – A happy escape from a coral reef – Home Island, Sunday Island, Bird Island – An American pearl-fisherman – Jubilee at Thursday Island – A new ensign for the *Spray* – Booby Island – Across the Indian Ocean – Christmas Island.

ON the morning of the 26th, Gloucester Island was close aboard, and the *Spray* anchored in the evening at Port Denison, where rests on a hill the sweet little town of Bowen, the future watering place and health-resort of Queensland. The country all about here had a healthful appearance.

The harbor was easy of approach, spacious and safe, and afforded excellent holding-ground. It was quiet in Bowen when the *Spray* arrived, and the good people with an hour to throw away on the second evening of her arrival came down to the School of Arts to talk about the voyage, it being the latest event. It was duly advertised in the two little papers, *Boomerang* and *Nully Nully*; in the one the day before the affair came off and in the other the day after — which was all the same to the editor, and (for that matter) it was the same to me.

Besides this, circulars were distributed with a flourish, and the "best bellman" in Australia was employed. But I could have keelhauled the wretch, bell and all, when he came to the door of the little hotel where my prospective audience and I were dining and — with his clattering bell and fiendish yell — made noises that would awake the dead, all over the voyage of the *Spray* from "Boston to Bowen, the two Hubs in the cart-wheels of creation," as the *Boomerang* afterward said.

Mr. Myles (magistrate, harbor-master, land commissioner, &c.) was chairman and introduced me — for what reason I never knew, except to embarrass me with a sense of vain ostentation and embitter my life — for Heaven

131

knows I had met every person in town the first hour ashore. I knew them all by name now, and they all knew me; however, Mr. Myles was a good talker. Indeed, I tried to induce him to go on and tell the story while I showed the pictures, but this he refused to do. I may explain that it was a talk illustrated by stereopticon. The views were good, but the lantern — a thirty-shilling affair — was wretched and had only an oil-lamp in it.

I sailed early the next morning before the papers came out, thinking it best to do so. They each appeared with a favorable column, however, of what they called a lecture — so I learned afterward — and they had a kind word for the bellman besides.

From Port Denison, the sloop ran before the constant trade-wind and made no stop at all — night or day — till she reached Cooktown on the Endeavor River, where she arrived Monday, May 31, 1897, before a furious blast of wind encountered that day fifty miles down the coast. On this parallel of latitude is the high ridge and backbone of the tradewinds, which about Cooktown amount often to a hard gale.

I had been charged to navigate the route with extra care and to feel my way over the ground. The skilled officer of the royal navy who advised me to take the Barrier Reef passage wrote me that H.M.S. *Orlando* steamed nights as well as days through it, but that I — under sail — would jeopardize my vessel on coral reefs if I undertook to do so.

Confidentially, it would have been no easy matter finding anchorage every night. The hard work, too, of getting the sloop under way every morning was finished, I had hoped, when she cleared the Strait of Magellan. Besides that, the best of admiralty charts made it possible to keep on sailing night and day. Indeed, with a fair wind and in the clear weather of that season, the way through the Barrier Reef Channel (in all sincerity) was clearer than a highway in a busy city and — by all odds — less dangerous. But to anyone contemplating the voyage, I would say, beware of reefs day or night, or — remaining in the land — be wary still.

"The *Spray* came flying into port like a bird," said the longshore daily papers of Cooktown the morning after she arrived. "And it seemed strange," they added, "that only one man could be seen on board working the craft." The *Spray* was doing her best, to be sure, for it was near night, and she was in haste to find a perch before dark.

The *Spray* leaving Sydney, Australia, in the new suit of sails given by Commodore Foy of Australia.

Tacking inside of all the craft in port, I moored her at sunset nearly abreast the Captain Cook monument and next morning went ashore to feast my eyes on the very stones the great navigator had seen, for I was now on a seaman's consecrated ground. But there seemed a question in Cooktown's mind as to the exact spot where his ship, the *Endeavor*, hove down for repairs on her memorable voyage around the world. Some said it was not at all at the place where the monument now stood. A discussion of the subject was going on one morning where I happened to be, and a young lady present — turning to me as one of some authority in nautical matters — very flatteringly asked my opinion.

Well, I could see no reason why Captain Cook — if he made up his mind to repair his ship inland — couldn't have dredged out a channel to the place where the monument now stood — if he had a dredging-machine with him — and afterward fill it up again; for Captain Cook could do 'most anything, and nobody ever said that he hadn't a dredger along.

The young lady seemed to lean to my way of thinking and — following up the story of the historical voyage — asked if I had visited the point farther down the harbor where the great circumnavigator was murdered. This took my breath, but a bright school-boy coming along relieved my embarrassment, for — like all boys — seeing that information was wanted, he volunteered to supply it.

Said he: "Captain Cook wasn't murdered 'ere at all, ma'am. 'e was killed in Hafrica: a lion et 'im."

Here I was reminded of distressful days gone by. I think it was 1866 that the old steamship *Soushay*, from Batavia for Sydney, put in at Cooktown for scurvy-grass (as I always thought) and "incidentally" to land mails. On her sick-list was my fevered self, and so I didn't see the place till I came back on the *Spray* thirty-one years later. And now I saw coming into port the physical wrecks of miners from New Guinea, destitute and dying. Many had died on the way and had been buried at sea. He would have been a hardened wretch who could look on and not try to do something for them.

The sympathy of all went out to these sufferers, but the little town was already straightened from a long run on its benevolence. I thought of the matter, of the lady's gift to me at Tasmania — which I had promised myself I would keep only as a loan — but found now to my embarrassment that I had invested the money; however, the good Cooktown people wished to hear a story of the sea and how the crew of the *Spray* fared when illness got aboard of her. Accordingly the little Presbyterian church on the hill was opened for a conversation; everybody talked, and they made a roaring success of it. Judge Chester, the magistrate, was at the head of the gam, and so it was bound to succeed. He it was who annexed the island of New Guinea to Great Britain.

"While I was about it," said he, "I annexed the blooming lot of it." There was a ring in the statement pleasant to the ear of an old voyager; however, the Germans made such a row over the judge's mainsail haul that they got a share in the venture.

Well, I was now indebted to the miners of Cooktown for the great privilege of adding a mite to a worthy cause, and to Judge Chester all the town was indebted for a general good time. The matter standing so, I sailed on June 6, 1897, heading away for the north as before.

Arrived at a very inviting anchorage about sundown, the 7th, I came to for the night abreast the Claremont light-ship. This was the only time throughout the passage of the Barrier Reef Channel that the *Spray* anchored, except at Port Denison and at Endeavor River. On the very night following this, however (the 8th), I regretted keenly for an instant that I had not anchored before dark, as I might have done easily under the lee of a coral reef. It happened in this way. The *Spray* had just passed M Reef light-ship and left the light dipping astern, when — going at full speed with sheets off — she hit the M Reef itself on the north end, where I expected to see a beacon.

She swung off quickly on her heel, however, and with one more bound on a swell cut across the shoal point so quickly that I hardly knew how it was done. The beacon wasn't there; at least, I didn't see it. I hadn't time to look for it after she struck, and certainly it didn't much matter then whether I saw it or not.

But this gave her a fine departure for Cape Greenville, the next point ahead. I saw the ugly boulders under the sloop's keel as she flashed over them, and I made a mental note of it that the letter M — for which the reef was named — was the thirteenth one in our alphabet, and that thirteen — as noted years before — was still my lucky

135

number. The natives of Cape Greenville are notoriously bad, and I was advised to give them the go-by. Accordingly, from M Reef I steered outside of the adjacent islands to be on the safe side. Skipping along now, the *Spray* passed Home Island off the pitch of the cape soon after midnight and squared away on a westerly course. A short time later, she fell in with a steamer bound south, groping her way in the dark and making the night dismal with her own black smoke.

From Home Island, I made for Sunday Island and — bringing that abeam — shortened sail, not wishing to make Bird Island farther along before daylight, the wind being still fresh and the islands being low with dangers about them. Wednesday, June 9, 1897, at daylight, Bird Island was dead ahead two and a half miles, which I considered near enough. A strong current was pressing the sloop forward. I did not shorten sail too soon in the night! The first and only Australian canoe seen on the voyage was encountered here standing from the mainland, with a rag of sail set, bound for this island.

A long, slim fish that leaped on board in the night was found on deck this morning. I had it for breakfast. The spry chap was no larger around than a herring, which it resembled in every respect, except that it was three times as long. But that was so much better, for I am rather fond of fresh herring anyway. A great number of fisher-birds were about this day, which was one of the pleasantest on God's earth. The *Spray*, dancing over the waves, entered Albany Pass as the sun drew low in the west over the hills of Australia.

At 7:30P.M. the *Spray*, now through the pass, came to anchor in a cove in the mainland, near a pearl-fisherman called the *Tarawa*, which was at anchor, her captain from the deck of his vessel directing me to a berth. This done, he at once came on board to clasp hands. The *Tarawa* was a Californian, and Captain Jones, her master, was an American.

On the following morning, Captain Jones brought on board two pairs of exquisite pearl shells, the most perfect ones I ever saw. They were probably the best he had, for

Jones was the heart-yarn of a sailor. He assured me that if I would remain a few hours longer some friends from Somerset nearby would pay us all a visit, and one of the crew, sorting shells on deck, "guessed" they would. The mate "guessed" so, too. The friends came, as even the second mate and cook had "guessed" they would. They were Mr. Jardine, stockman, famous throughout the land, and his family. Mrs. Jardine was the niece of King Malietoa and cousin to the beautiful Faamu-Sami ("To make the sea burn"), who visited the *Spray* at Apia. Mr. Jardine was himself a fine specimen of a Scotsman. With his little family about him, he was content to live in this remote place, accumulating the comforts of life.

The fact of the *Tarawa* having been built in America accounted for the crew, boy Jim and all, being such good guessers. Strangely enough, though, Captain Jones himself, the only American aboard, was never heard to guess at all.

After a pleasant chat and good-bye to the people of the *Tarawa* — and to Mr. and Mrs. Jardine — I again weighed anchor and stood across for Thursday Island, now in plain view mid-channel in Torres Strait, where I arrived shortly after noon. Here the *Spray* remained over until June 24. Being the only American representative in port, this tarry was imperative, for on the 22d was the Queen's diamond jubilee. The two days over were (as sailors say) for "coming up."

Meanwhile, I spent pleasant days about the island. Mr. Douglas, resident magistrate, invited me on a cruise in his steamer one day among the islands in Torres Strait. This being a scientific expedition in charge of Professor Mason Bailey, botanist, we rambled over Friday and Saturday Islands, where I got a glimpse of botany. Miss Bailey, the professor's daughter, accompanied the expedition and told me of many indigenous plants with long names.

The 22d was the great day on Thursday Island, for then we had not only the jubilee, but a jubilee with a grand corroboree in it, Mr. Douglas having brought some four hundred native warriors and their wives and children

137

across from the mainland to give the celebration the true native touch, for when they do a thing on Thursday Island they do it with a roar.

The corroboree was, at any rate, a howling success. It took place at night, and the performers — painted in fantastic colors — danced or leaped about before a blazing fire. Some were rigged and painted like birds and beasts, in which the emu and kangaroo were well represented. One fellow leaped like a frog. Some had the human skeleton painted on their bodies, while they jumped about threateningly — spear in hand — ready to strike down some imaginary enemy. The kangaroo hopped and danced with natural ease and grace, making a fine figure. All kept time to music — vocal and instrumental — the instruments (save the mark!) being bits of wood (which they beat one against the other) and saucer-like bones held in the palm of the hands (which they knocked together, making a dull sound). It was a show at once amusing, spectacular, and hideous.

The warrior aborigines that I saw in Queensland were for the most part lithe and fairly well built, but they were stamped always with repulsive features, and their women were — if possible — still more ill favored.

I observed that on the day of the jubilee no foreign flag was waving in the public grounds except the Stars and Stripes, which — along with the Union Jack — guarded the gateway and floated in many places from the tiniest to the standard size. Speaking to Mr. Douglas, I ventured a remark on this compliment to my country.

"Oh," said he, "this is a family affair, and we do not consider the Stars and Stripes a foreign flag." The *Spray*, of course, flew her best bunting and hoisted the Jack, as well as her own noble flag, as high as she could.

On June 24, the *Spray* — well fitted in every way — sailed for the long voyage ahead down the Indian Ocean. Mr. Douglas gave her a flag as she was leaving his island. The *Spray* had now passed nearly all the dangers of the Coral Sea and Torres Strait, which indeed were not a few. And all ahead from this point was plain sailing and a straight course. The trade-wind was still blowing fresh and

could be safely counted on now down to the coast of
Madagascar — if not beyond that — for it was still early
in the season.

I had no wish to arrive off the Cape of Good Hope
before midsummer, and it was now early winter. I had
been off that cape once in July, which was, of course,

On board at St. Kilda, retracing on the chart
the course of the *Spray* from Boston.

midwinter there. The stout ship I then commanded
encountered only fierce hurricanes, and she bore them ill.
I wished for no winter gales now. It was not that I feared
them more, being in the *Spray* instead of a large ship, but
that I preferred fine weather in any case. It is true that
one may encounter heavy gales off the Cape of Good
Hope at any season of the year, but in the summer they
are less frequent and do not continue so long. And so,
with time enough before me to admit of a run ashore on
the islands en route, I shaped the course now for Keeling
Cocos, atoll islands, distant twenty-seven hundred miles.
Taking a departure from Booby Island, which the sloop
passed early in the day, I decided to sight Timor on the
way, an island of high mountains.

Booby Island I had seen before, but only once, and
that was when in the steamship *Soushay*, on which I was

139

"hove-down" in a fever. When she steamed along this way I was well enough to crawl on deck to look at Booby Island. Had I died for it, I would have seen that island.

In those days, passing ships landed stores in a cave on the island for shipwrecked and distressed wayfarers. Captain Airy of the *Soushay*, a good man, sent a boat to the cave with his contribution to the general store. The stores were landed in safety, and the boat brought back from the improvised post-office there a dozen or more letters — most of them left by whalemen with the request that the first homeward-bound ship would carry them along and see to their mailing — which had been the custom of this strange postal service for many years. Some letters brought back by our boat were directed to New Bedford, or some to Fairhaven, Massachusetts.

There is a light today on Booby Island and regular packet communication with the rest of the world, and the beautiful uncertainty of the fate of letters left there is a thing of the past. I made no call at the little island, but — standing close in — exchanged signals with the keeper of the light. Sailing on, the sloop was at once in the Arafura Sea, where for days she sailed in water milky white and green and purple. It was my good fortune to enter the sea on the last quarter of the moon, the advantage being that in the dark nights I witnessed the phosphorescent light effect at night in its greatest splendor. The sea, where the sloop disturbed it, seemed all ablaze so that by its light I could see the smallest articles on deck, and her wake was a path of fire.

On the 25th of June, the sloop was already clear of all shoals and dangers and was sailing on a smooth sea as steadily as before, but with speed somewhat slackened. I got out the flying-jib made at Juan Fernández and set it as a spinnaker from the stoutest bamboo that Mrs. Stevenson had given me at Samoa. The spinnaker pulled like a sodger, and — the bamboo holding its own — the *Spray* mended her pace.

Several pigeons flying across today from Australia toward the islands bent their course over the *Spray*. Smaller birds were seen flying in the opposite direction.

In the part of the Arafura that I came to first — where it was shallow — sea-snakes writhed about on the surface and tumbled over in the waves. As the sloop sailed farther on, where the sea became deep, they disappeared. In the ocean, where the water is blue, not one was ever seen.

In the days of serene weather, there was not much to do but read and take rest on the *Spray*, to make up as much as possible for the rough time off Cape Horn — which was not yet forgotten — and to forestall the Cape of Good Hope by a store of ease. My sea journal was now much the same from day to day — something like this of June 26 and 27, for example:

June 26, in the morning, it is a bit squally; later in the day blowing a steady breeze.

On the log at noon is . . . . 130 miles
Subtract correction for slip . . . <u>10 miles</u>
                          120 miles
Add for current . . . . <u>10 miles</u>
                          130 miles
Latitude by observation at noon, 10° 23′ S.
Longitude as per mark on the chart.

There wasn't much brain-work in that log, I'm sure. June 27 makes a better showing, when all is told:

First of all, today, was a flying-fish on deck; fried it in butter.

133 miles on the log.

For slip, off, and for current, on, as per guess, about equal — let it go at that.

Latitude by observation at noon, 10° 25′ S.

For several days now the *Spray* sailed west on the parallel of 10° 25′ S., as true as a hair. If she deviated at all from that through the day or night — and this may have happened — she was back, strangely enough, at noon at the same latitude. But the greatest science was in reckoning the longitude. My tin clock and only timepiece had lost its minute hand, but after I boiled her she told the hours and that was near enough on a long stretch.

On the 2d of July, the great island of Timor was in view away to the nor'ard. The following day, I saw Dana Island not far off, and a breeze came up from the land at night, fragrant of the spices or whatnot of the coast.

On the 11th, with the sail set and with the spinnaker still abroad, Christmas Island about noon came into view one point on the starboard bow. Before night, it was abeam and distant two and a half miles. The surface of the island appeared evenly rounded from the sea to a considerable height in the center. In outline it was as smooth as a fish, and a long ocean swell rolling up broke against the sides, where it lay like a monster asleep, motionless on the sea. It seemed to have the proportions of a whale, and as the sloop sailed along its side to the part where the head would be, there was a nostril even, which was a blow-hole through a ledge of rock where every wave that dashed threw up a shaft of water, lifelike and real.

It had been a long time since I last saw this island, but I remember my temporary admiration for the captain of the ship I was then in, the *Tanjore*, when he sang out one morning from the quarter-deck, well aft, "Go aloft there, one of ye, with a pair of eyes, and see Christmas Island." Sure enough, there the island was in sight from the royal-yard. Captain M— had thus made a great hit, and he never got over it. The chief mate, terror of us ordinaries in the ship, walking never to windward of the captain, now took himself very humbly to leeward altogether.

When we arrived at Hong Kong, there was a letter in the ship's mail for me. I was in the boat with the captain some hours while he had it. But do you suppose he could hand a letter to a seaman? No, indeed; not even to an ordinary seaman. When we got to the ship he gave it to the first mate; the first mate gave it to the second mate, and he laid it, michingly, on the capstan-head, where I could get it!

CHAPTER 16

A call for careful navigation – Three hours' steering in twenty-three days – Arrival at the Keeling Cocos Islands – A welcome from the children – Cleaning and painting the *Spray* on the beach – A blessing for a pot of jam – A risky adventure in a small boat – The governor calms the fears of the people – A convent in the hills.

TO the Keeling Cocos Islands was now only five hundred and fifty miles, but even in this short run it was necessary to be extremely careful in keeping a true course else I would miss the atoll.

On the 12th, some hundred miles southwest of Christmas Island, I saw anti-trade clouds flying up from the southwest very high over the regular winds — which weakened now for a few days — while a swell heavier than usual set in also from the southwest. A winter gale was going on in the directions of the Cape of Good Hope. Accordingly, I steered higher to windward, allowing twenty miles a day while this went on for change of current. And it was not too much, for on that course I made the Keeling Islands right ahead.

The first unmistakable sign of the land was a visit one morning from a white tern that fluttered very knowingly about the vessel and then took itself off westward with a businesslike air in its wing. The tern is called by the islanders the "pilot of Keeling Cocos." Farther on I came among a great number of birds fishing and fighting over whatever they caught. My reckoning was up and — springing aloft — I saw from half-way up the mast cocoanut-trees standing out of the water ahead. I expected to see this; still, it thrilled me as an electric shock might have done. I slid down the mast, trembling under the strangest sensations. And not able to resist the impulse, I sat on deck and gave way to my emotions. To folks in a parlor on shore this may seem weak indeed, but I am telling the story of a voyage alone.

143

I didn't touch the helm, for with the current and heave of the sea the sloop found herself at the end of the run absolutely in the fairway of the channel. You couldn't have beaten it in the navy! Then I trimmed her sails by the wind, took the helm, and flogged her up the couple of miles or so abreast of the harbor landing, where I cast anchor at 3:30P.M., July 17, 1897, twenty-three days from Thursday Island. The distance run was twenty-seven hundred miles as the crow flies. This would have been a fair Atlantic voyage. It was a delightful sail! During those twenty-three days I had not spent altogether more than three hours at the helm, including the time occupied in beating into Keeling harbor. I just lashed the helm and let her go. Whether the wind was abeam or dead aft, it was all the same: she always sailed on her course. No part of the voyage up to this point, taking it by and large, had been so finished as this.[1]

The Keeling Cocos Islands, according to Admiral Fitzroy, R.N., lie between the latitudes of 11° 50′ and 12° 12′ S., and the longitudes of 96° 51′ and 96° 58° E. They

[1]Mr. Andrew J. Leach, reporting, July 21, 1897, through Governor Kynnersley of Singapore, to Joseph Chamberlain, Colonial Secretary, said concerning the *Iphegenia's* visit to the atoll: "As we left the ocean depths of deepest blue and entered the coral circle, the contrast was most remarkable. The brilliant colors of the waters, transparent to a depth of over thirty-feet, now purple, now of the sky-blue, and now green, with the white crests of the waves flashing under a brilliant sun, the encircling . . . palm-clad islands, the gaps between which were to the south undiscernible, the white sand shores and the whiter gaps where breakers appeared, and, lastly, the lagoon itself, seven or eight miles across from north to south, and five to sex miles from east to west, presented a sight never to be forgotten. After some little delay, Mr. Sidney Ross, the eldest son of Mr. George Ross, came off to meet us, and soon after, accompanied by the doctor and another officer, we went ashore.

"On reaching the landing-stage, we found, hauled up for cleaning, etc., the *Spray* of Boston, a yawl of 12.70 tons gross, the property of Captain Joshua Slocum. He arrived at the island on the 17th of July, twenty-three days out from Thursday Island. This solitary traveler left Boston some two years ago single-handed, crossed to Gibraltar, sailed down to Cape Horn, passed through the Strait of Magellan to the Society Islands, thence to Australia, and through the Torres Strait to Thursday Island."

were discovered in 1608-9 by Captain William Keeling, then in the service of the East India Company. The southern group consists of seven or eight islands and islets and the atoll, which is the skeleton of what some day — according to the history of coral reefs — will be a continuous island. North Keeling has no harbor, is seldom visited, and is of no importance. The South Keelings are a strange little world with a romantic history all their own. They have been visited occasionally by the floating spar of some hurricane-swept ship, or by a tree that has drifted all the way from Australia, or by an ill-starred ship cast away, and finally by man. Even a rock once drifted to Keeling, held fast among the roots of a tree.

After the discovery of the islands by Captain Keeling, their first notable visitor was Captain John Cluni-Ross, who in 1814 touched in the ship *Borneo* on a voyage to India. Captain Ross returned two years later with his wife and family and his mother-in-law, Mrs. Dymoke, and eight sailor-artisans to take possession of the islands, but found there already one Alexander Hare, who meanwhile had marked the little atoll as a sort of Eden for a seraglio of Malay women which he moved over from the coast of Africa. It was Ross' own brother, oddly enough, who freighted Hare and his crowd of women to the islands, not knowing of Captain John's plans to occupy the little world. And so Hare was there with his outfit, as if he had come to stay.

On his previous visit, however, Ross had nailed the English Jack to a mast on Horsburg Island, one of the group. After two years, shreds of it still fluttered in the wind, and his sailors — nothing loath — began at once the invasion of the new kingdom to take possession of it, women and all. The force of forty women, with only one man to command them, was not equal to driving eight sturdy sailors back into the sea.[1]

From this time on Hare had a hard time of it. He and

[1]In the accounts given in Findlay's *Sailing Directory* of some of the events there is a chronological discrepancy. I follow the accounts gathered from the old captain's grandsons and from records on the spot.

Ross did not get on well as neighbors. The islands were too small and too near for characters so widely different. Hare had "oceans of money," and might have lived well in London, but he had been governor of a wild colony in Borneo and could not confine himself to the tame life that prosy civilization affords. And so he hung on to the atoll with his forty women — retreating little by little before Ross and his sturdy crew — till at last he found himself and his harem on the little island known to this day as Prison Island, where — like Bluebeard — he confined his wives in a castle.

The channel between the islands was narrow, the water was not deep, and the eight Scotch sailors wore long boots. Hare was now dismayed. He tried to compromise with rum and other luxuries, but these things only made matters worse. On the day following the first St. Andrew's celebration on the island, Hare — consumed with rage and no longer on speaking terms with the captain — dashed off a note to him, saying:

Dear Ross:
    I thought when I sent rum and roast pig to your sailors that they would stay away from my flower-garden.

In reply to which the captain — burning with indignation — shouted from the center of the island where he stood, "Ahoy, there, on Prison Island! You Hare, don't you know that rum and roast pig are not a sailor's heaven?" Hare said afterward that one might have heard the captain's roar across to Java.

The lawless establishment was soon broken up by the women deserting Prison Island and putting themselves under Ross' protection. Hare then went to Batavia, where he met his death.

My first impression upon landing was that the crime of infanticide had not reached the islands of Keeling Cocos. "The children have all come to welcome you," explained Mr. Ross, as they mustered at the jetty by hundreds of all ages and sizes. The people of this country were all rather shy, but — young or old — they never passed one or saw one passing their door without a salutation. In their musical voices they would say, "Are you walking?" ("Jalan, jalan?") "Will you come along?" one would answer.

The *Spray* ashore for "boot-topping" at the Keeling Islands.

For a long time after I arrived, the children regarded the "one-man ship" with suspicion and fear. A native man had been blown away to sea many years before, and they hinted to one another that he might have changed from black to white and returned in the sloop. For some time, every movement I made was closely watched. They were particularly interested in what I ate. One day, after I had been "boot-topping" the sloop with a composition of coal-tar and other stuff, and while I was taking my dinner

147

with the luxury of blackberry jam, I heard a commotion and then a yell and a stampede, as the children ran away yelling: "The captain is eating coal-tar! The captain is eating coal-tar!" But they soon found out that this same "coal-tar" was very good to eat and that I had brought a quantity of it. One day when I was spreading a sea-biscuit thick with it for a wide-awake youngster, I heard them whisper, "Chut-chut!" meaning that a shark had bitten my hand, which they observed was lame. Thenceforth, they regarded me as a hero, and I had not fingers enough for the little bright-eyed tots that wanted to cling to them and follow me about. Before this, when I held out my hand and said, "Come!" they would shy off for the nearest house and say, "Dingin" ("It's cold"), or "Ujan" ("It's going to rain"). But it was now accepted that I was not the returned spirit of the lost black, and I had plenty of friends about the island, rain or shine.

One day after this, when I tried to haul the sloop and found her fast in the sand, the children all clapped their hands and cried that a *kpeting* (crab) was holding her by the keel; and little Ophelia, ten or twelve years of age, wrote in the *Spray's* log-book:

> A hundred men with might and man
> > On the windlass hove, yeo ho!
> The cable only came in twain;
> > The ship she would not go;
> For, child, to tell the strangest thing,
> > The keel was held by a great kpeting.

This being so or not, it was decided that the Mohammedan priest, Sama the Emim, for a pot of jam should ask Mohammed to bless the voyage and make the crab let go the sloop's keel, which it did — if it had hold — and she floated on the very next tide.

On the 22d of July arrived H.M.S. *Iphegenia* with Mr. Justice Andrew J. Leach and court officers on board on a circuit of inspection among the Straits Settlements — of which Keeling Cocos was a dependency — to hear complaints and try cases by law, if any there were to try.

They found the *Spray* hauled ashore and tied to a cocoanut-tree. But at the Keeling Islands there had not been a grievance to complain of since the day that Hare migrated, for the Rosses have always treated the islanders as their own family.

If there is a paradise on this earth, it is Keeling. There was not a case for a lawyer, but something had to be done, for here were two ships in port: a great man-of-war and the *Spray*. Instead of a lawsuit, a dance was got up, and all the officers who could leave their ship came ashore. Everybody on the island came, old and young, and the governor's great hall was filled with people. All that could get on their feet danced, while the babies lay in heaps in the corners of the room, content to look on. My little friend Ophelia danced with the judge. For music, two fiddles screeched over and over again the old tune, "We Won't Go Home Till Morning." And we did not.

The women at the Keelings do not do all the drudgery, as in many places visited on the voyage. It would cheer the heart of a Fuegian woman to see the Keeling lord of creation up a cocoanut-tree. Besides cleverly climbing the trees, the men of Keeling build exquisitely modeled canoes. By far, the best workmanship in boat-building I saw on the voyage was here. Many finished mechanics dwelt under the palms at Keeling, and the hum of the band-saw and the ring of the anvil were heard from morning till night. The first Scotch settlers left there the strength of Northern blood and the inheritance of steady habits. No benevolent society has ever done so much for any islanders as the noble Captain Ross and his sons, who have followed his example of industry and thrift.

Admiral Fitzroy of the *Beagle* — who visited here, where many things are reversed — spoke of "these singular though small islands, where crabs eat cocoa-nuts, fish eat coral, dogs catch fish, men ride on turtles, and shells are dangerous man-traps," adding that the greater part of the sea-fowl roost on branches, and many rats make their nests in the tops of palm-trees.

My vessel being refitted, I decided to lead her with

the famous mammoth tridacna shell of Keeling, found in the bayou nearby. And right here, within sight of the village, I came near losing "the crew of the *Spray*" — not from putting my foot in a man-trap shell, however, but from carelessly neglecting to look after the details of a trip across the harbor in a boat.

Captain Slocum drifting out to sea.

I had sailed over oceans; I have since completed a course over them all and sailed round the whole world without so nearly meeting a fatality as on that trip across a lagoon, where I trusted all to someone else. And he — weak mortal that he was — perhaps trusted all to me. However that may be, I found myself with a thoughtless native in a rickety bateau that was fitted with a rotten sail, and this blew away in mid-channel in a squall that sent us drifting helplessly to sea, where we should have been incontinently lost.

With the whole ocean before us to leeward, I was dismayed to see while we drifted that there was not a paddle or an oar in the boat! There was an anchor, to be sure, but not enough rope to tie a cat, and we were already in deep water. By great good fortune, however, there was a pole. Plying this as a paddle with the utmost energy — and by the merest accidental flaw in the wind to favor us — the trap of a boat was worked into shoal water, where we could touch bottom and push her ashore. With Africa the nearest coast to leeward — three thousand miles away — with not so much as a drop of water in the boat and a lean and hungry native — well, cast the lot as one might, the crew of the *Spray* in a little while would have been hard to find. It is needless to say that I took no more such chances. The tridacna were afterward procured in a safe boat — thirty of them taking the place of three tons of cement ballast, which I threw overboard to make room and give buoyancy.

On August 22, the kpeting — or whatever else it was that held the sloop in the islands — let go its hold, and she swung out to sea under all sail, heading again for home. Mounting one or two heavy rollers on the fringe of the atoll, she cleared the flashing reefs. Long before dark, Keeling Cocos, with its thousand souls as sinless in their lives as perhaps it is possible for frail mortals to be, was left out of sight astern. Out of sight, I say, except in my strongest affection.

The sea was rugged, and the *Spray* washed heavily when hauled on the wind, which of course I took for the island of Rodriguez and which brought the sea abeam. The true course for the island was west by south, one quarter south, and the distance was nineteen hundred miles, but I steered considerably to the windward of that to allow for the heave of the sea and other leeward effects. My sloop on this course ran under reefed sails for days together. I naturally tired of the never-ending motion of the sea and, above all, of the wetting I got whenever I showed myself on deck. Under these heavy weather conditions, the *Spray* seemed to lag behind on her course; at least, I attributed to these conditions a discrepancy in the log, which by the fifteenth day out from Keeling amounted to one hundred and fifty miles between the rotator and the mental calculations I had kept of what she should have gone, and so I kept an eye lifting for land.

I could see about sundown this day a bunch of clouds that stood in one spot right ahead, while the other clouds floated on; this was a sign of something. By midnight, as the sloop sailed on, a black object appeared where I had seen the resting clouds. It was still a long way off, but there could be no mistaking this: it was the high island of Rodriguez. I hauled in the patent log, which I was now towing more from habit than from necessity, for I had learned the *Spray* and her ways long before this. If one thing was clearer than another in her voyage, it was that she could be trusted to come out right and in safety, though at the same time I always stood ready to give her the benefit of even the least doubt. The officers who are over-sure and "know it all like a book" are the ones who wreck the most ships and lose the most lives.

The cause of the discrepancy in the log was one often, namely, met with coming in contact with some large fish; two out of the four blades of the rotator were crushed or bent, the work probably of a shark. Being sure of the sloop's position, I lay down to rest and to think, and I felt better for it. By daylight the island was abeam about three miles away. It wore a hard, weather-beaten appearance all alone far out in the Indian Ocean, like land adrift. The windward side was uninviting, but there was a good port to leeward, and I hauled in now close on the wind for that. A pilot came out to take me into the inner harbor through a narrow channel among coral reefs.

It was a curious thing that at all of the islands some reality was insisted on as unreal, while improbabilities were clothed as hard facts. And so it happened here that the good abbé, a few days before, had been telling his people about the coming of Antichrist, and when they saw the *Spray* sail into the harbor — all feather-white before a gale of wind, and run all standing upon the beach, and with only one man aboard — they cried, "May the Lord help us, it is he, and he has come in a boat!" (which, I say, would have been the most improbably way of his coming.)

Nevertheless, the news went flying through the place. The governor of the island, Mr. Roberts, came down immediately to see what it was all about, for the little town was in a great commotion. One elderly woman, when she heard of my advent, made for her house and locked herself in. When she heard that I was actually coming up the street, she barricaded her doors and did not come out while I was on the island, a period of eight days. Governor Roberts and his family did not share the fears of their people, but came on board at the jetty where the sloop was berthed, and their example induced others also. The governor's young boys took charge of the *Spray's* dinghy at once, and my visit cost his Excellency — besides great hospitality to me — the building of a boat for them like the one belonging to the *Spray*.

My first day at this Land of Promise was to me like a fairy-tale. For many days I had studied the charts and counted the time of my arrival at this spot as one might his entrance to the Islands of the Blessed, looking upon it as the terminus of the last long run made irksome by the want of many things with which — from this time on — I could keep well supplied. And behold, here was the sloop, arrived and made securely fast to a pier in Rodriguez.

On the first evening ashore in the land of napkins and cut glass, I saw before me still the ghosts of hempen towels and of mugs with handles knocked off. Instead of tossing on the sea, however, as I might have been, here was I in a bright hall, surrounded by sparkling wit and dining with the governor of the island! "Aladdin," I cried, "where is your lamp? My fisherman's lantern — which I got at Gloucester — has shown me better things than your smoky old burner ever revealed."

The second day in port was spent receiving visitors. Mrs. Roberts and her children came first "to shake hands," they said, "with the *Spray*." No one was now afraid to come on board, except the poor old woman (who still maintained that the *Spray* had Antichrist in the hold — if, indeed, he had not already gone ashore.)

The governor entertained that evening and kindly invited the "destroyer of the world" to speak for himself. This he did, elaborating most effusively on the dangers of the sea (which, after the manner of many of our frailest mortals, he would have had smooth had he made it.) Also by contrivances of light and darkness, he exhibited on the wall pictures of the places and countries visited on the voyage (nothing like the countries, however, that he would have made) and of the people seen — savage and other — frequently groaning, "Wicked world! Wicked world!" When this was finished, his Excellency, speaking words of thankfulness, distributed pieces of gold.

On the next day, I accompanied his Excellency and family on a visit to San Gabriel, which was up the country among the hills. The good abbé of San Gabriel entertained us all royally at the convent, and we remained his guests until the following day. As I was leaving his place, the abbé said, "Captain, I embrace you, and of whatever religion you may be, my wish is that you succeed in making your voyage and that our Saviour the Christ be always with you!" To this good man's words I could only say, "My dear abbé, had all religionists been so liberal there would have been less bloodshed in the world."

At Rodriguez one may now find every convenience for filling pure and wholesome water in any quantity, Governor Roberts having built a reservoir in the hills and laid pipes to the jetty, where — at the time of my visit — there were five and a half feet at high tide. In former years well-water was used, and — more or less — sickness occurred from it. Beef may be had in any quantity on the island and at a moderate price. Sweet potatoes were plentiful and cheap; the large sack of them that I bought for about four shillings kept unusually well. I stored them in the sloop's dry hold. Of fruits, pomegranates were most plentiful. For two shillings I obtained a large sack of them, as many as a donkey could pack from the orchard, which — by the way — was planted by nature herself.

154

CHAPTER 17

A clean bill of health – Sailing the voyage over again in the opera-house – A newly discovered plant named in honor of the *Spray's* skipper – A party of young ladies – A warm reception at Durban – A friendly cross-examination by Henry M. Stanley – Three wise Boers seek proof of the flatness of the earth – Leaving South Africa.

ON the 16th of September, after eight restful days at Rodriguez — the mid-ocean land of plenty — I set sail, and on the 19th arrived at Mauritius, anchoring at quarantine about noon. The sloop was towed in later on the same day by the doctor's launch, after he was satisfied that I had mustered all the crew for inspection. Of this he seemed in doubt until he examined the papers, which called for a crew of one all told from port to port throughout the voyage. Then finding that I had been well enough to come thus far alone, he gave me pratique without further ado.

There was still another official visit for the *Spray* to pass farther in the harbor. The governor of Rodriguez, who had most kindly given me — besides some regular mail — private letters of introduction to friends, told me I should meet first of all Mr. Jenkins of the postal service, a good man.

"How do you do, Mr. Jenkins?" cried I, as his boat swung alongside.

"You don't know me," he said.

"Why not?" I replied.

"From where is the sloop?"

"From around the world," I again replied very solemnly.

"And alone?"

"Yes; why not?"

"And you know me?"

"Three thousand miles ago," cried I, "When you and I had a warmer job than we have now." (Even this was hot.)

"You were then Jenkinson, but if you have changed your name, I don't blame you for that."

Mr. Jenkins — forbearing soul — entered into the spirit of the jest, which served the *Spray* a good turn, for on the strength of this tale it got out that if any one

The *Spray* at Mauritius.

should go on board after dark the devil would get him at once. And so, I could leave the *Spray* without the fear of her being robbed at night. The cabin — to be sure — was broken into, but it was done in daylight, and the thieves got no more than a box of smoked herrings before "Tom" Ledson, one of the port officials, caught them red-handed — as it were — and sent them to jail. This was discouraging to pilferers, for they feared Ledson more than they feared Satan himself. Even Mamode Hajee Ayoob, who was the day-watchman on board — till an empty box fell over in the cabin and frightened him out of his wits — could not be hired to watch nights, or even till the sun went down.

156

"Sahib," he cried, "there is no need of it."

And what he said was perfectly true.

At Mauritius, where I drew a long breath, the *Spray* rested her wings, it being the season of fine weather. The hardships of the voyage — if there had been any — were not computed by officers of experience as nine tenths finished, and yet somehow I could not forget that the United States was still a long way off.

The kind people of Mauritius, to make me richer and happier, rigged up the opera-house, which they had named the "Ship *Pantai*."[1] All decks and no bottom was this ship, but she was as stiff as a church. They gave me free use of it while I talked over the *Spray's* adventures. His Honor, the mayor, introduced me to his Excellency, the governor, from the poop-deck of the *Pantai*. In this way I was also introduced again to our good consul, General John P. Campbell, who had already introduced me to his Excellency. I was becoming well acquainted and was in for it now to sail the voyage over again.

How I got through the story I hardly know. It was a hot night, and I could have choked the tailor who made the coat I wore for this occasion. The kind governor saw that I had done my part trying to rig like a man ashore, and he invited me to Government House at Reduit, where I found myself among friends.

It was winter still off stormy Cape of Good Hope, but the storms might whistle there. I determined to see it out in milder Mauritius, visiting Rose Hill, Curipepe, and other places on the island. I spent a day with the elder Mr. Roberts — father of Governor Roberts of Rodriguez — and with two of his friends: the Very Reverend Fathers O'Laughlin and McCarthy.

Returning to the *Spray* by way of the great flower conservatory near Moka, the proprietor — having only that morning discovered a new and hardy plant — to my great honor name it "Slocum," which he said Latinized it at once, saving him some trouble on the twist of a word. And the good botanist seemed pleased that I had come. How different things are in different countries! In Boston,

[1]Guinea-hen.

Massachusetts, at that time, a gentleman (so I was told) paid thirty thousand dollars to have a flower named after his wife, and it was not a big flower either, while "Slocum" — which came without the asking — was bigger than a mangel-wurzel!

I was royally entertained at Moka, as well as at Reduit and other places — once by seven young ladies, to whom I spoke of my inability to return their hospitality except in my own poor way of taking them on a sail in the sloop.

"The very thing! They very thing!" they call cried.

"Then please name the time," I said, as meek as Moses.

"To-morrow!" they all cried. "And, aunty, we may go, mayn't we, and we'll be real food for a whole week afterward, aunty! Say yes, aunty dear!"

All this after saying "To-morrow," for girls in Mauritius are, after all, the same as our girls in America.

And their dear aunt said, "Me, too" about the same as any really good aunt might say in my own country.

I was then in a quandary, it having recurred to me that on the very "to-morrow" I was to dine with the harbor-master, Captain Wilson; however, I said to myself, "The *Spray* will run out quickly into rough seas; these young ladies will have *mal de mer* and a good time, and I'll get in nearly enough to be at the dinner, after all."

But not a bit of it. We sailed almost out of sight of Mauritius, and they just stood up and laughed at seas tumbling aboard, while I was at the helm making the worst weather of it I could and spinning yarns to the aunt about sea-serpents and whales. But she, dear lady, when I had finished with stories of monsters, only hinted at a basket of provisions they had brought along — enough to last a week, for I had told them about my wretched steward.

The more the *Spray* tried to make these young ladies seasick, the more they all clapped their hands and said, "How lovely it is!" and "How beautifully she skims over the sea!" and "How beautiful our island appears from the distance!"

And they still cried, "Go on!"

We were fifteen miles or more at sea before they ceased the eager cry, "Go on!" Then the sloop swung round, I still hoping to be back to Port Louis in time to keep my appointment. The *Spray* reached the island quickly and flew along the coast fast enough, but I made a mistake in steering along the coast on the way home, for as we came abreast of Tombo Bay it enchanted my crew.

"Oh, let's anchor here!" they cried.

To this no sailor in the world would have said nay.

The sloop came to anchor ten minutes later as they wished, and a young man on the cliff abreast, waving his hat, cried, *"Vive la Spray!"*

My passengers said, "Aunty, mayn't we have a swim in the surf along the shore?"

Just then the harbor-master's launch hove in sight, coming out to meet us, but it was too late to get the sloop into Port Louis that night. The launch was in time, however, to land my fair crew for a swim, but they were determined not to desert the ship. Meanwhile, I prepared a roof for the night on deck with the sails, and a Bengali man-servant arranged the evening meal. That night the *Spray* rode in Tombo Bay with her precious freight. Next morning, bright and early, even before the stars were gone, I awoke to hear praying on deck.

The port officers' launch reappeared later in the morning — this time with Captain Wilson himself on board — to try his luck in getting the *Spray* into port, for he had heard of our predicament. It was worth something to hear a friend tell afterward how earnestly the good harbor-master of Mauritius said, "I'll find the *Spray*, and I'll get her into port."

A merry crew he discovered on her. They could hoist sails like old tars and could trim them, too. They could tell all about the ship's "hoods," and one should have seen them clap a bonnet on the jib. Like the deepest of deep-water sailors, they could heave the lead, and — as I hope to see Mauritius again! — any of them could have put the sloop in stays. No ship ever had a fairer crew.

The voyage was the event of Port Louis; such a thing as young ladies sailing about the harbor, even, was almost unheard of before.

While at Mauritius the *Spray* was tendered the use of the military dock free of charge and was thoroughly refitted by the port authorities. My sincere gratitude is also due other friends for many things needful for the voyage put on board, including bags of sugar from some of the famous old plantations.

The favorable season now set in, and thus well equipped on the 26th of October, the *Spray* put to sea. As I sailed before a light wind the island receded slowly, and on the following day I could still see the Puce Mountain near Moka. The *Spray* arrived next day off Galets, Réunion, and a pilot came out and spoke her. I handed him a Mauritius paper and continued on my voyage, for rollers were running heavily at the time, and it was not practicable to make a landing. From Réunion, I shaped a course direct for Cape St. Mary, Madagascar.

The sloop was now drawing near the limits of the trade-wind, and the strong breeze that had carried her with free sheets the many thousands of miles from Sandy Cape, Australia, fell lighter each day until October 30, when it was altogether calm and a motionless sea held her in a hushed world. I furled the sails at evening, sat down on deck, and enjoyed the vast stillness of the night.

October 31 a light east-northeast breeze sprang up, and the sloop passed Cape St. Mary about noon. On the 6th, 7th, 8th, and 9th of November in the Mozambique Channel, she experienced a hard gale of wind from the southwest. Here the *Spray* suffered as much as she did anywhere, except off Cape Horn. The thunder and lightning preceding this gale were very heavy. From this point until the sloop arrived off the coast of Africa, she encountered a succession of gales of wind, which drove her about in many directions, but on the 17th of November she arrived at Port Natal.

This delightful place is the commercial center of the "Garden Colony," Durban itself (the city) being the continuation of a garden. The signalman from the bluff station reported the *Spray* fifteen miles off. The wind was freshening, and when she was within eight miles, he said:

"The *Spray* is shortening sail; the mainsail was reefed and set in ten minutes. One man is doing all the work."

This item of news was printed three minutes later in a Durban morning journal, which was handed me when I arrived in port. I could not verify the time it had taken to reef the sail, for — as I have already said — the minute-hand of my time-piece was gone. I only knew that I reefed as quickly as I could.

The same paper, commenting on the voyage, said: "Judging from the stormy weather which has prevailed off this coast during the past few weeks, the *Spray* must have had a very stormy voyage from Mauritius to Natal." Doubtless, the weather would have been called stormy by sailors in any ship, but it caused the *Spray* no more inconvenience than the delay natural to head winds generally.

The question of how I sailed the sloop alone, often asked, is best answered, perhaps, by a Durban newspaper. I would shrink from repeating the editor's words but for the reason that undue estimates have been made of the amount of skill and energy required to sail a sloop of even the *Spray's* small tonnage. I heard a man who called himself a sailor say that "it would require three men to do what it was claimed" that I did alone and what I found perfectly easy to do over and over again. And I have heard that others made similar nonsensical remarks, adding that I would work myself to death. But here is what the Durban paper said:

As briefly noted yesterday, the *Spray*, with a crew of one man, arrived at this port yesterday afternoon on her cruise round the world. The *Spray* made quite an auspicious entrance to Natal. Her commander sailed his craft right up the channel past the main wharf and dropped his anchor near the old *Forerunner* in the creek, before any one had a chance to get on board. The *Spray* was naturally an object of great curiosity to the Point people, and her arrival was witnessed by a large crowd. The skillful manner in which Captain Slocum steered his craft about the vessels which were occupying the waterway was a treat to witness.

The *Spray* was not sailing in among greenhorns when she came to Natal. When she arrived off the port the pilot-ship — a fine, able steam-tug — came out to meet her and led the way in across the bar, for it was blowing a smart gale and was too rough for the sloop to be towed with safety. The trick of going in I learned by watching the steamer; it was simply to keep on the windward side of the channel and take the combers end on.

I found that Durban supported two yacht-clubs, both of them full of enterprise. I met all the members of both clubs and sailed in the crack yacht *Florence* of the Royal Natal, with Captain Spradbrow and the Right Honorable Harry Escombe, premier of the colony. The yacht's center-board plowed furrows through the mud-banks, which — according to Mr. Escombe — Spradbrow afterward planted with potatoes. The *Florence*, however, won races while she tilled the skipper's land.

After our sail on the *Florence*, Mr. Escombe offered to sail the *Spray* round the Cape of Good Hope for me and hinted at his famous cribbage-board to while away the hours. Spradbrow, in retort, warned me of it. Said he, "You would be played out of the sloop before you could round the cape." By others it was not thought probable that the premier of Natal would play cribbage off the Cape of Good Hope to win even the *Spray*.

It was a matter of no small pride to me in South Africa to find that American humor was never at a discount, and one of the best stories I ever heard was told by the premier. At Hotel Royal one day, dining with Colonel Saunderson, M.P., his son, and Lieutenant Tipping, I met Mr. Stanley. The great explorer was just from Pretoria and had already as good as flayed President Krüger with his trenchant pen. But that did not signify, for everybody has a whack at Oom Paul, and no one in the world seems to stand the joke better than he, not even the Sultan of Turkey himself.

The colonel introduced me to the explorer, and I hauled close to the wind to go slow, for Mr. Stanley was a nautical man once himself — on the Nyanza, I think — and of course my desire was to appear in the best light before a man of his experience. He looked me over carefully and said, "What an example of patience!"

"Patience is all that is required," I ventured to reply.

He then asked if my vessel had water-tight compartments. I explained that she was all water-tight and all compartment.

"What if she should strike a rock?" he asked.

"Compartments would not save her if she should hit the rocks lying along her course," said I, adding, "she must be kept away from the rocks."

After a considerable pause, Mr. Stanley asked, "What if a swordfish should pierce her hull with its sword?"

Of course, I had thought of that as one of the dangers of the sea and also of the chance of being struck by lightning. In the case of the swordfish, I ventured to say that "the first thing would be to secure the sword."

The colonel invited me to dine with the party on the following day that we might go further into this matter, and so I had the pleasure of meeting Mr. Stanley a second time, but got no more hints in navigation from the famous explorer.

It sounds odd to hear scholars and statesmen say the world is flat, but it is a fact that three Boers favored by the opinion of President Krüger prepared a work to support that contention. While I was at Durban, they came from Pretoria to obtain data from me, and they seemed annoyed when I told them that they could not prove it by my experience. With the advice to call up some ghost of the dark ages for research, I went ashore and left these three wise men poring over the *Spray's* track on a chart of the world, which, however, proved nothing to them, for it was on Mercator's projection and, behold, it was "flat."

The next morning I met one of the party in a clergyman's garb, carrying a large Bible, not different from the one I had read. He tackled me, saying, "If you respect the Word of God, you must admit that the world is flat."

"If the Word of God stands on a flat world —" I began.

"What!" cried he, losing himself in a passion and making as if he would run me through with an assagai. "What?" he shouted in astonishment and rage, while I jumped aside to dodge the imaginary weapon. Had this good — but misguided — fanatic been armed with a real weapon, the crew of the *Spray* would have died a martyr, there and then.

The next day, seeing him across the street, I bowed and made curves with my hands. He responded with a level, swimming movement of his hands, meaning "the world is flat." A pamphlet by these Transvaal geographers — made up of arguments from sources high and low to prove their theory — was mailed to me before I sailed from Africa on my last stretch around the globe.

While I feebly portray the ignorance of these learned men, I have great admiration for their physical manhood. Much that I saw first and last of the Transvaal and the Boers was admirable. It is well known that they are the hardest of fighters and as generous to the fallen as they are brave before the foe. Real stubborn bigotry with them is only found among old fogies and will die a natural death. And that, too, perhaps long before we ourselves are entirely free from bigotry. Education in the Transvaal is by no means neglected (English as well as Dutch being taught to all that can afford both), but the tariff duty on English school-books is heavy and from necessity the poorer people stick to the Transvaal Dutch and their flat world, just as in Samoa and other islands a mistaken policy has kept the natives down to Kanaka.

I visited many public schools at Durban and had the pleasure of meeting many bright children.

But all fine things must end, and December 14, 1897, the "crew" of the *Spray* — after having a fine time in Natal — swung the sloop's dinghy in on deck and sailed with a morning land-wind — which carried her clear of the bar — and again she was "off on her alone," as they say in Australia.

CHAPTER 18

Rounding the "Cape of Storms" in olden time – A rough Christmas –
The *Spray* ties up for rest at Cape Town – A railway trip to the
Transvaal – President Krüger's odd definition of the *Spray's* voyage
– Cocoa-nut fiber as a padlock – Courtesies from the admiral of
the Queen's navy – Land in sight.

THE Cape of Good Hope was now the most promi-
nent point to pass. From Table Bay I could count on
the air of brisk trades, and then the *Spray* would soon be
at home. On the first day out from Durban it fell calm,
and I sat thinking about these things and the end of the
voyage. The distance to Table Bay, where I intended to
call, was about eight hundred miles over what might
prove a rough sea.

The early Portuguese navigators — endowed with
patience — were more than sixty-nine years struggling to
round this cape before they got as far as Algoa Bay, and
there the crew mutinied. They landed on a small island —
now called Santa Cruz — where they devoutly set up the
cross and swore they would cut the captain's throat if he
attempted to sail farther. Beyond this they thought was
the edge of the world, which they too believed was flat.
And fearing that their ship would sail over the brink of it,
they compelled Captain Diaz, their commander, to
retrace his course, all being only too glad to get home. A
year later, Vasco da Gama sailed successfully round the
"Cape of Storms" — as the Cape of Good Hope was
called — and discovered Natal on Christmas or Natal
Day; hence, the name. From this point, the way to India
was easy.

Gales of wind sweeping round the cape even now
were frequent enough — one occurring, on an average,
every thirty-six hours — but one gale was much the same
as another, with no more serious result than to blow the
Spray along on her course when it was fair, or to blow her

back somewhat when it was ahead.

On Christmas, 1897, I came to the pitch of the cape. On this day the *Spray* was trying to stand on her head, and she gave me every reason to believe that she would accomplish the feat before night. She began very early in the morning to pitch and toss about in a most unusual manner, and I have to record that — while I was at the end of the bowsprit reefing the jib — she ducked me underwater three times for a Christmas box. I got wet and did not like it a bit. Never in any other sea was I put under more than once in the same short space of time, say three minutes. A large English steamer passing ran up the signal, "Wishing you a Merry Christmas." I think the captain was a humorist; his own ship was throwing her propeller out of water.

Two days later, the *Spray* — having recovered the distance lost in the gale — passed Cape Agulhas in company with the steamship *Scotsman*, now with a fair wind. The keeper of the light on Agulhas exchanged signals with the *Spray* as she passed and afterward wrote me at New York congratulations on the completion of the voyage. He seemed to think the incident of two ships of so widely different types passing his cape together worthy of a place on canvas, and he went about having the picture made. So I gathered from his letter. At lonely stations like this, hearts grow responsive and sympathetic, and even poetic. This feeling was shown toward the *Spray* along many a rugged coast, and reading many a kind signal thrown out to her gave one a grateful feeling for all the world.

One more gale of wind came down upon the *Spray* from the west after she passed Cape Agulhas, but that one she dodged by getting into Simons Bay. When it moderated, she beat around the Cape of Good Hope, where they say the *Flying Dutchman* is still sailing. The voyage then seemed as good as finished. From this time on, I knew that all — or nearly all — would be plain sailing.

Here I crossed the dividing-line of weather. To the north it was clear and settled, while south it was humid and squally, with often enough (as I have said) a treacherous gale. From the recent hard weather the *Spray* ran into a calm under Table Mountain, where she lay quietly till the generous sun rose over the land and drew a breeze in from the sea.

The steam-tug *Alert* — then out looking for ships — came to the *Spray* off the Lion's Rump and in lieu of a larger ship towed her into port. The sea being smooth, she came to anchor in the bay off the city of Cape Town, where she remained a day simply to rest clear of the bustle of commerce. The good harbor-master sent his steam-launch to bring the sloop to a berth in dock at once, but I preferred to remain for one day alone in the quiet of a smooth sea, enjoying the retrospect of the passage of the two great capes. On the following morning, the *Spray* sailed into the Alfred Dry-docks, where she remained for about three months in the care of the port authorities, while I traveled in the country over from Simons Town to Pretoria, being accorded by the colonial government a free railroad pass over all the land.

The trip to Kimberley, Johannesburg, and Pretoria was a pleasant one. At the last-named place, I met Mr. Krüger, the Transvaal president. His Excellency received me cordially enough, but my friend Judge Beyers — the gentlemen who presented me — by mentioning that I was on a voyage around the world unwittingly gave great offense to the venerable statesman, which we both regretted deeply.

Mr. Krüger corrected the judge rather sharply, reminding him that the world is flat. "You don't mean *round* the world," said the president. "It is impossible! You mean *in* the world. Impossible!" he said. "Impossible!" And not another word did he utter either to the judge or to me.

The judge looked at me, and I looked at the judge, who should have known his ground, so to speak, and Mr. Krüger glowered at us both. My friend the judge seemed embarrassed, but I was delighted; the incident pleased me more than anything else that could have happened. It was a nugget of information quarried out of Oom Paul, some of whose sayings are famous. Of the English he said, "They took first my coat and then my trousers." He also said, "Dynamite is the corner-stone of the South African Republic." Only unthinking people call the President dull.

Soon after my arrival at the cape, Mr. Krüger's friend Colonel Saunderson[1], who had arrived from Durban some time before, invited me to Newlands Vineyard, where I

Captain Slocum, Sir Alfred Milner (with the tall hat), and Colonel Saunderson, M.P., on the bow of the *Spray*.

met many agreeable people. His Excellency Sir Alfred Milner, the governor, found time to come aboard with a party. The governor, after making a survey of the deck, found a seat on a box in my cabin; Lady Muriel sat on a keg, and Lady Saunderson sat by the skipper at the wheel,

[1]Colonel Saunderson was Mr. Krüger's very best friend, inasmuch as he advised the president to avast mounting guns.

while the colonel — with his Kodak away in the dinghy — took snap shots of the sloop and her distinguished visitors. Dr. David Gill, astronomer royal, who was of the party, invited me the next day to the famous Cape Observatory.

An hour with Dr. Gill was an hour among the stars. His discoveries in stellar photography are well known. He showed me the great astronomical clock of the observatory, and I showed him the tin clock on the *Spray*, and we went over the subject of standard time at sea and how it was found from the deck of the little sloop without the aid of a clock of any kind.

Later, it was advertised that Dr. Gill would preside at a talk about the voyage of the *Spray:* that alone secured for me a full house. The hall was packed, and many were not able to get in. This success brought me sufficient money for all my needs in port and for the homeward voyage.

After visiting Kimberley and Pretoria and finding the *Spray* all right in the docks, I returned to Worcester and Wellington — towns famous for colleges and seminaries — passed coming in, still traveling as the guest of the colony. The ladies of all these institutions of learning wished to know how one might sail round the world alone, which I thought augured of sailing-mistresses in the future instead of sailing-masters. It will come to that yet if we men-folk keep on saying we "can't."

On the plains of Africa, I passed through hundreds of miles of rich but still barren land, save for scrub-bushes on which herds of sheep were browsing. The bushes grew about the length of a sheep apart, and they (I thought) were rather long of body, but there was still room for all. My longing for a foothold on land seized upon me here, where so much of it lay waste. But instead of remaining to plant forests and reclaim vegetation, I returned again to the *Spray* at the Alfred Docks, where I found her waiting for me with everything in order, exactly as I had left her.

I have often been asked how it was that my vessel and all appurtenances were not stolen in the various ports when I left her for days together without a watchmen in charge. This is just how it was: The *Spray* seldom fell among thieves. At the Keeling Islands, at Rodriguez, and at many such places, a wisp of cocoa-nut fiber in the door latch — to indicate that the owner was away — secured the goods against even a longing glance. But when I came to a great island nearer home, stout locks were needed. The first night in port, the things which I had always left uncovered disappeared, as if the deck on which they were stowed had been swept by a sea.

A pleasant visit from Admiral Sir Harry Rawson of the Royal Navy and his family brought to an end the *Spray's* social relations with the Cape of Good Hope. The admiral — then commanding the South African Squadron and now in command of the great Channel fleet — evinced the greatest interest in the diminutive *Spray* and her behavior off Cape Horn, where she was not an entire stranger. I have to admit that I was delighted with the trend of Admiral Rawson's questions and that I profited by some of his suggestions, notwithstanding the wide difference in our respective commands.

On March 26, 1898, the *Spray* sailed from South Africa, the land of distances and pure air, where she had spent a pleasant and profitable time. The steam-tug *Tigre* towed her to sea from her wonted berth at the Alfred Docks, giving her a good offing. The light morning breeze, which scantily filled her sails when the tug let go the tow-line, soon died away altogether and left her riding over a heavy swell in full view of Table Mountain and the high peaks of the Cape of Good Hope. For a while, the grand scenery served to relieve the monotony. One of the old circumnavigators — Sir Frances Drake, I think — when he first saw this magnificent pile sang, "'T is the fairest thing and the grandest cape I've seen in the whole circumference of the earth."

The view was certainly fine, but one has no wish to linger long to look in a calm at anything, and I was glad to note, finally, the short heaving sea, precursor of the wind which followed on the second day. Seals playing about the *Spray* all day — before the breeze came — looked with large eyes when at evening she sat no longer like a lazy bird with folded wings. They parted company now, and the *Spray* soon sailed the highest peaks of the mountains

Reading day and night.

out of sight, and the world changed from a mere panoramic view to the light of a homeward-bound voyage.

Porpoises and dolphins, and such other fishes as did not mind making a hundred and fifty miles a day, were her companions now for several days. The wind was from the southeast; this suited the *Spray* well, and she ran along steadily at her best speed, while I dipped into the new books given me at the cape, reading day and night. March 30 was for me a fast-day in honor of them. I read on — oblivious of hunger or wind or sea — thinking that

171

all was going well, when suddenly a comber rolled over the stern and slopped saucily into the cabin, wetting the very book I was reading. Evidently, it was time to put in a reef, that she might not wallow on her course.

March 31 the fresh southeast wind had come to stay. The *Spray* was running under a single-reefed mainsail, a whole jib, and a flying-jib besides set on the Vailima bamboo, while I was reading Stevenson's delightful *Inland Voyage*. The sloop was again doing her work smoothly, hardly rolling at all, but just leaping along among the white horses, a thousand gamboling porpoises keeping her company on all sides. She was again among her old friends the flying-fish, interesting denizens of the sea. Shooting out of the waves like arrows — and with outstretched wings — they sailed on the wind in graceful curves; then falling again, they touched the crest of the waves to wet their delicate wings and renew the flight. They made merry the livelong day. One of the joyful sights on the ocean of a bright day is the continual flight of these interesting fish.

One could not be lonely in a sea like this. Moreover, the reading of delightful adventures enhanced the scene. I was now in the *Spray* and on the Oise in the *Arethusa* at one and the same time. And so the *Spray* reeled off the miles, showing a good run every day till April 11, which came almost before I knew it. Very early that morning, I was awakened by that rare bird, the booby, with its harsh quack, which I recognized at once as a call to go on deck. It was as much as to say, "Skipper, there's land in sight." I tumbled out quickly and — sure enough — away ahead in the dim twilight about twenty miles off was St. Helena.

My first impulse was to call out, "Oh, what a speck in the sea!" It is in reality nine miles in length and two thousand eight hundred and twenty-three feet in height. I reached for a bottle of port-wine out of the locker and took a long pull from it to the health of my invisible helmsman — the pilot of the *Pinta*.

CHAPTER 19

In the isle of Napoleon's exile – Two lectures – A guest in the ghost-room at Plantation House – An excursion to historic Longwood – Coffee in the husk, and a goat to shell it – The *Spray's* ill luck with animals – A prejudice against small dogs – A rat, the Boston spider, and the cannibal cricket – Ascension Island.

I T was about noon when the *Spray* came to anchor off Jamestown, and "all hands" at once went ashore to pay respects to his Excellency the governor of the island, Sir R.A. Sterndale. His Excellency, when I landed, remarked that it was not often nowadays that a circumnavigator came to his way, and he cordially welcomed me and arranged that I should tell about the voyage: first at Garden Hall to the people and then at Plantation House — the governor's residence, which is in the hills a mile or two back — to his Excellency and the officers of the garrison and their friends. Mr. Poole, our worthy consul, introduced me at the castle and in the course of his remarks asserted that the sea-serpent was a Yankee.

Most royally was the crew of the *Spray* entertained by the governor. I remained at Plantation House a couple of days, and one of the rooms in the mansion — called the "west room" — being haunted, the butler, by command of his Excellency, put me up in that — like a prince. Indeed, to make sure that no mistake had been made, his Excellency came later to see that I was in the right room and to tell me all about the ghosts he had seen or heard of. He had discovered all but one, and — wishing me pleasant dreams — he hoped that I might have the honor of a visit from the unknown one of the west room. For the rest of the chilly night, I kept the candle burning and often looked from under the blankets, thinking that maybe I should meet the great Napoleon face to face. But I saw only furniture and the horseshoe that was nailed over the door opposite my bed.

St. Helena has been an island of tragedies — tragedies that have been lost sight of in wailing over the Corsican. On the second day of my visit, the governor took me by carriage-road through the turns over the island. At one point of our journey, the road — in winding around spurs and ravines — formed a perfect W within the distance of a few rods. The roads, though tortuous and steep, were fairly good, and I was struck with the amount of labor it must have cost to build them. The air on the heights was cool and bracing. It is said that — since hanging for trivial offenses went out of fashion — no one has died there, except from falling over the cliffs in old age, or being crushed by stones rolling on them from the steep mountains!

Witches at one time were persistent at St. Helena, as with us in America in the days of Cotton Mather. At the present day, crime is rare in the island. While I was there, Governor Sterndale, in token of the fact that not one criminal case had come to court within the year, was presented with a pair of white gloves by the officers of justice.

Returning from the governor's house to Jamestown, I drove with Mr. Clark, a countryman of mine, to "Longwood," the home of Napoleon. M. Morilleau, French consular agent in charge, keeps the place respectable and the buildings in good repair. His family at Longwood, consisting of wife and grown daughters, are natives of courtly and refined manners and spend here days, months, and years of contentment, though they have never seen the world beyond the horizon of St. Helena.

On the 20th of April, the *Spray* was again ready for sea. Before going on board, I took luncheon with the governor and his family at the castle. Lady Sterndale had sent a large fruit-cake early in the morning from Plantation House to be taken along on the voyage. It was a great high-decker, and I ate sparingly of it (as I thought), but it did not keep as I had hoped it would. I ate the last of it along with my first cup of coffee at Antigua, West Indies, which after all was quite a record. The one my own sister made me at the little island in the

Bay of Fundy at the first of the voyage kept about the same length of time; namely, forty-two days.

After luncheon, a royal mail was made up for Ascension, the island next on my way. Then Mr. Poole and his daughter paid the *Spray* a farewell visit, bringing me a basket of fruit. It was late in the evening before the anchor was up, and I bore off for the west, loath to leave my new friends. But fresh winds filled the sloop's sails once more, and I watched the beacon-light at Plantation House — the governor's parting signal for the *Spray* — till the island faded in the darkness astern and became one with the night, and by midnight the light itself had disappeared below the horizon.

When morning came, there was no land in sight, but the day went on the same as days before, save for one small incident. Governor Sterndale had given me a bag of coffee in the husk, and Clark (the American) — in an evil moment — had put a goat on board "to butt the sack and hustle the coffee-beans out of the pods." He urged that the animal — besides being useful — would be as companionable as a dog. I soon found that my sailing-companion — this sort of dog with horns — had to be tied up entirely. The mistake I made was that I did not chain him to the mast instead of tying him with grass ropes less securely, and this I learned to my cost.

Except for the first day, before the beast got his sea-legs on, I had no peace of mind. After that — actuated by a spirit born, maybe, of his pasturage — this incarnation of evil threatened to devour everything from flying-jib to stern-davits. He was the worst pirate I met on the whole voyage. He began depredations by eating my chart of the West Indies in the cabin one day while I was about my work for'ard, thinking that the critter was securely tied on deck by the pumps. Alas! there was not a rope in the sloop proof against that goat's awful teeth!

In was clear from the very first that I was having no luck with animals on board. There was the tree-crab from the Keeling Islands. No sooner had it got a claw through its prison-box than my sea-jacket, hanging within reach, was torn to ribbons. Encouraged by this success, it

175

smashed the box open and escaped into my cabin, tearing up things generally and finally threatening my life in the dark. I had hoped to bring the creature home alive, but this did not prove feasible. Next, the goat devoured my straw hat, and so when I arrived in port I had nothing to wear ashore on my head. This last unkind stroke decided his fate.

On the 27th of April, the *Spray* arrived at Ascension, which is garrisoned by a man-of-war crew, and the boatswain of the island came on board. As he stepped out of his boat, the mutinous goat climbed into it and defied boatswain and crew. I hired them to land the wretch at once, which they were only too willing to do, and there he fell into the hands of a most excellent Scotchman, with the chances that he would never get away. I was destined to sail once more into the depths of solitude, but these experiences had no bad effect upon me; on the contrary, a spirit of charity and even benevolence grew stronger in my nature through the meditations of these supreme hours on the sea.

In the loneliness of the dreary country about Cape Horn I found myself in no mood to make one life less in the world — except in self-defense — and as I sailed this trait of the hermit character grew till the mention of killing food-animals was revolting to me. However well I may have enjoyed a chicken stew afterward at Samoa, a new self rebelled at the thought suggested there of carrying chickens to be slain for my table on the voyage, and Mrs. Stevenson, hearing my protest, agreed with me that to kill the companions of my voyage and eat them would be indeed next to murder and cannibalism.

As to pet animals, there was no room for a noble large dog on the *Spray* on so long a voyage, and a small cur was for many years associated in my mind with hydrophobia. I witnessed once the death of a sterling young German from that dreadful disease and about the same time heard of the death — also by hydrophobia — of the young gentleman who had just written a line of insurance in his company's books for me. I have seen the whole crew of a ship scamper up the rigging to avoid a dog racing about the decks in a fit. It would never do, I thought, for the crew of the *Spray* to take a canine risk. And with these just prejudices indelibly stamped on my mind, I have (I'm afraid) answered impatiently too often the query, "Didn't you have a dog?" with, "I and the dog wouldn't have been very long in the same boat, in any sense."

A cat would have been a harmless animal, I dare say, but there was nothing for puss to do on board, and she is an unsociable animal at best. True, a rat got into my vessel at the Keeling Cocos Islands and another at Rodriguez, along with a centiped stowed away in the hold. But one of them I drove out of the ship, and the other I caught. This is how it was: for the first one with infinite pains I made a trap, looking to its capture and destruction, but the wily rodent — not to be deluded — took the hint and got ashore the day the thing was completed.

It is — according to tradition — a most reassuring sign to find rats coming to a ship, and I had a mind to abide the knowing one of Rodriguez, but a breach of discipline decided the matter against him. While I slept one night — my ship sailing on — he undertook to walk over me, beginning at the crown of my head, concerning which I am always sensitive. I sleep lightly. Before his impertinence had got him even to my nose, I cried, "Rat!" had him by the tail, and threw him out of the companion-way into the sea.

As for the centiped, I was not aware of its presence till the wretched insect — all feet and venom — beginning (like the rat) at my head, wakened me by a sharp bite on the scalp. This also was more than I could tolerate. After a few applications of kerosene, the poisonous bite (painful at first) gave me no further inconvenience.

From this on for a time, no living thing disturbed my solitude; no insect even was present in my vessel, except the spider and his wife from Boston with a family of young spiders. Nothing, I say, till sailing down the last stretch of the Indian Ocean, where mosquitoes came by hundreds from rain-water poured out of the heavens. Simply a barrel of rain-water stood on deck five days, I think, in the sun, then music began. I knew the sound at once; it was the same as heard from Alaska to New Orleans.

Again at Cape Town, while dining out one day, I was taken with the song of a cricket, and Mr. Branscombe, my host, volunteered to capture a pair of them for me. They were sent on board next day in a box labeled, "Pluto and Scamp." Stowing them away in the binnacle in their own snug box, I left them there without food till I got to sea — a few days. I had never heard of a cricket eating anything. It seems that Pluto was a cannibal, for only the wings of poor Scamp were visible when I opened the lid, and they lay broken on the floor of the prison-box. Even with Pluto it had gone hard, for he lay on his back stark and stiff, never to chirrup again.

Ascension Island, where the goat was marooned, is called the Stone Frigate, R.N., and is rated "tender" to the South African Squadron. It lies in 7° 55′ south latitude and 14° 25′ west longitude, being at the very heart of the southeast tradewinds and about eight hundred and forty miles from the coast of Liberia. It is a mass of volcanic matter, thrown up from the bed of the ocean to the height of two thousand eight hundred and eighteen feet at the highest point above sea-level. It is a strategic point and belonged to Great Britain before it got cold.

In the limited, but rich soil at the top of the island among the clouds, vegetation has taken root, and a little scientific farming is carried on under the supervision of a gentleman from Canada. Also a few cattle and sheep are pastured there for the garrison mess. Water storage is made on a large scale. In a word, this heap of cinders and lava rock is stored and fortified and would stand a siege.

Very soon after the *Spray* arrived, I received a note from Captain Blaxland, the commander of the island, conveying his thanks for the royal mail brought from St. Helena and inviting me to luncheon with him and his wife and sister at headquarters, not far away. It is hardly necessary to say that I availed myself of the captain's hospitality at once. A carriage was waiting at the jetty when I landed, and a sailor with a broad grin led the horse carefully up the hill to the captain's house, as if I were the lord of the admiralty and a governor besides. And he led it as carefully down again when I returned.

On the following day, I visited the summit among the clouds, the same team being provided and the same old sailor leading the horse. There was probably not a man on the island at that moment better able to walk than I. The sailor knew that. I finally suggested that we change places.

"Let me take the bridle," I said, "and keep the horse from bolting."

"Great Stone Frigate!" he exclaimed, as he burst into a laugh, "this 'ere 'oss wouldn't bolt no faster nor a turtle. If I didn't tow 'im 'ard, we'd never get into port."

I walked most of the way over the steep grades, whereupon my guide — every inch a sailor — became my friend. Arriving at the summit of the island, I met Mr. Schank, the farmer from Canada, and his sister, living very cozily in a house among the rocks, as snug as conies and as safe. He showed me over the farm, taking me through a tunnel which led from one field to the other, divided by an inaccessible spur of mountain. Mr. Schank said that he had lost many cows and bullocks, as well as sheep, from breakneck over the steep cliffs and precipices. One cow, he said, would sometimes hook another right over a precipice to destruction and go on feeding unconcerned. It seemed that the animals on the island farm — like mankind in the wide world — found it all too small.

On the 26th of April, while I was ashore, rollers came in which rendered launching a boat impossible; however, the sloop being securely moored to a buoy in deep water outside of all breakers, she was safe, while I — in the best of quarters — listened to well-told stories among the officers of the Stone Frigate. On the evening of the 29th, the sea having gone down, I went on board and made preparations to start again on my voyage early next day, the boatswain of the island and his crew giving me a hearty handshake as I embarked at the jetty.

For reasons of scientific interest, I invited in mid-ocean the most thorough investigation concerning the crew-list of the *Spray*. Very few had challenged it — and perhaps few ever will do so henceforth — but for the benefit of the few that may, I wished to clench beyond doubt the fact that it was not at all necessary in the expedition of a sloop around the world to have more than one man for the crew, all told, and that the *Spray* sailed with only one person on board.

And so, by appointment, Lieutenant Eagles, the executive officer — in the morning just as I was ready to sail — fumigated the sloop, rendering it impossible for a person to live concealed below and proving that only one person was on board when she arrived. A certificate to this effect — besides the official documents from the many consulates, health offices, and custom-houses — will seem to many superfluous, but this story of the voyage may find its way into hands unfamiliar with the business of these offices and of their ways of seeing that a vessel's papers and — above all — her bills of health are in order.

The lieutenant's certificate being made out, the *Spray*, nothing loath, now filled away clear of the sea-beaten rocks, and the trade-winds — comfortably cool and bracing — sent her flying along on her course. On May 8, 1898, she crossed the track homeward bound that she made October 2, 1895, on the voyage out. She passed Fernando de Noronha at night, going some miles south of it, and so I did not see the island. I felt a contentment in knowing that the *Spray* had encircled the globe — and even as an adventure alone I was in no way discouraged as to its utility — and said to myself, "Let what will happen, the voyage is now on record." A period was made.

CHAPTER 20

In the favoring current off Cape St. Roque, Brazil – All at sea regarding the Spanish-American War – An exchange of signals with the battle-ship *Oregon* – Off Dreyfus' prison on Devil's Island – Reappearance to the *Spray* of the north star – The light on Trinidad – A charming introduction to Grenada – Talks to friendly auditors.

ON May 10 there was a great change in the condition of the sea; there could be no doubt of my longitude now, if any before had existed in my mind. Strange and long-forgotten current ripples pattered against the sloop's sides in grateful music; the tune arrested the car, and I sat quietly listening to it while the *Spray* kept on her course. By these current ripples I was assured that she was now off St. Roque and had struck the current which sweeps around that cape. The trade-winds — we old sailors say — produce this current, which, in its course from this point forward, is governed by the coastline of Brazil, Guiana, Venezuela, and — as some would say — by the Monroe Doctrine.

The trades had been blowing fresh for some time, and the current now at its height amounted to forty miles a day. This — added to the sloop's run by the log — made the handsome day's work of one hundred and eighty miles on several consecutive days. I saw nothing of the coast of Brazil, though I was not many leagues off and was always in the Brazil current.

I did not know that war with Spain had been declared and that I might be liable, right there, to meet the enemy and be capture. Many had told me at Cape Town that — in their opinion — war was inevitable, and they said: "The Spaniard will get you! The Spaniard will get you!" To all this I could only say that, even so, he would not get much. Even in the fever-heat over the disaster to the *Maine* I did not think there would be war, but I am no politician.

181

Indeed, I had hardly given the matter a serious thought when, on the 14th of May, just north of the equator and near the longitude of the river Amazon, I saw first a mast with the Stars and Stripes floating from it, rising astern as if poked up out of the sea, and then rapidly appearing on the horizon, like a citadel, the *Oregon!* As she came near, I saw that the great ship was flying the signals "C B T," which read, "Are there any men-of-war about?" Right under these flags, and larger than the *Spray's* mainsail, so it appeared, was the yellowest Spanish flag I ever saw. It gave me nightmare some time after when I reflected on it in my dreams.

I did not make out the *Oregon's* signals till she passed ahead, where I could read them better, for she was two miles away, and I had no binoculars. When I had read her flags, I hoisted the signal "No," for I had not seen any Spanish men-of-war; I had not been looking for any. My final signal — "Let us keep together for mutual protection" — Captain Clark did not seem to regard as necessary. Perhaps my small flags were not made out; anyhow, the *Oregon* steamed on with a rush, looking for Spanish men-of-war, as I learned afterward. The *Oregon's* great flag was dipped beautifully three times to the *Spray's* lowered flag as she passed on. Both had crossed the line only a few hours before. I pondered long that night over the probability of a war risk now coming upon the *Spray* after she had cleared all — or nearly all — the dangers of the sea, but a strong hope mastered my fears.

On the 17th of May, the *Spray* — coming out of a storm at daylight — made Devil's Island, two points on the lee bow, not far off. The wind was still blowing a stiff breeze on shore. I could clearly see the dark-gray buildings on the island as the sloop brought it abeam. No flag or sign of life was seen on the dreary place.

Later in the day, a French bark on the port tack, making for Cayenne, hove in sight, close-hauled on the wind. She was falling to leeward fast. The *Spray* was also close-hauled and was lugging on sail to secure an offing on the starboard tack, a heavy swell in the night having thrown her too near the shore, and now I considered the matter of supplicating a change of wind. I had already enjoyed my share of favoring breezes over the great oceans, and I asked myself if it would be right to have the wind turned now all into my sails while he was bound the other way. A head current — which he stemmed — together with a scant wind was bad enough for him. And so I could only say in my heart, "Lord, let matters stand as they are, but do not help the Frenchman any more just now, for what would suit him well would ruin me!"

I remembered that when a lad I heard a captain often say in meeting that in answer to a prayer of his own the wind changed from southeast to northwest, entirely to his satisfaction. He was a good man, but did this glorify the Architect — the Ruler of the winds and the waves? Moreover, it was not a trade-wind, as I remember it, that changed for him, but one of the variables which will change when you ask it, if you ask long enough. Again, this man's brother maybe was not bound the opposite way, well content with a fair wind himself, which made all the difference in the world.[1]

On May 18, 1898, is written large in the *Spray's* log-book: "To-night, in latitude 7° 13′ N., for the first time in nearly three years I see the north star." The *Spray* on the day following logged one hundred and forty-seven miles. To this I add thirty-five miles for current sweeping her onward. On the 20th of May, about sunset, the island of Tobago, off the Orinoco, came into view, bearing west by north, distant twenty-two miles. The *Spray* was drawing rapidly toward her home destination.

Later at night, while running free along the coast of Tobago — the wind still blowing fresh — I was startled by the sudden flash of breakers on the port bow and not far off. I luffed instantly offshore and then tacked, heading in for the island. Finding myself, shortly after, close in with the land, I tacked again offshore, but without much altering the bearings of the danger. Sailing whichever way

[1]The Bishop of Melbourne (commend me to his teachings) refused to set aside a day of prayer for rain, recommending his people to husband water when the rainy season was on. In like manner, a navigator husbands the wind, keeping a weather-gauge where practicable.

I would, it seemed clear that if the sloop weathered the rocks at all it would be a close shave, and I watched with anxiety while beating against the current, losing ground.

So the matter stood hour after hour, while I watched the flashes of light thrown up as regularly as the beats of the long ocean swells, and always they seemed just a little nearer. It was evidently a coral reef — of this I had not the slightest doubt — and a bad reef at that. Worse still, there might be other reefs ahead forming a bight into which the current would sweep me and where I should be hemmed in and finally wrecked.

I had not sailed these waters since a lad and lamented the day I had allowed on board the goat that ate my chart. I taxed my memory of sea lore, of wrecks on sunken reefs, and of pirates harbored among coral reefs where other ships might not come, but nothing I could think of applied to the island of Tobago, save the one wreck of Robinson Crusoe's ship in the fiction, and that gave me little information about reefs. I remembered only that in Crusoe's case he kept his powder dry.

"But there she booms again," I cried, "and how close the flash is now! Almost aboard was that last breaker! But you'll go by, *Spray*, old girl! 'Tis abeam now! One surge more! and oh, one more like that will clear your ribs and keel!"

And I slapped her on the transom — proud of her last noble effort to leap clear of the danger — when a wave greater than the rest threw her higher than before, and, behold, from the crest of it was revealed at once all there was of the reef. I fell back in a coil of rope — speechless and amazed — not distressed, but rejoiced. Aladdin's lamp! My fisherman's own lantern! It was the great revolving light on the island of Trinidad, thirty miles away, throwing flashes over the waves, which had deceived me! The orb of the light was now dipping on the horizon, and how glorious was the sight of it!

But, dear Father Neptune, as I live, after a long life at sea and much among corals, I would have made a solemn declaration to that reef! Through all the rest of the night I saw imaginary reefs and — not knowing what moment the sloop might fetch up on a real one — I tacked off and on till daylight, as nearly as possible in the same track, all for the want of a chart. I could have nailed the St. Helena goat's pelt to the deck.

My course was now for Grenada, to which I carried letters from Mauritius. About midnight of the 22d of May, I arrived at the island and cast anchor in the roads off the town of St. George, entering the inner harbor at daylight on the morning of the 23d, which made forty-two days' sailing from the Cape of Good Hope. It was a good run, and I doffed my cap again to the pilot of the *Pinta*.

Lady Bruce, in a note to the *Spray* at Port Louis, said Grenada was a lovely island, and she wished the sloop might call there on the voyage home. When the *Spray* arrived, I found that she had been fully expected.

"How so?" I asked.

"Oh, we heard that you were at Mauritius," they said, "and from Mauritius, after meeting Sir Charles Bruce, our old governor, we knew you would come to Grenada." This was a charming introduction, and it brought me in contact with people worth knowing.

The *Spray* sailed from Grenada on the 28th of May and coasted along under the lee of the Antilles, arriving at the island of Dominica on the 30th, where — for the want of knowing better — I cast anchor at the quarantine ground, for I was still without a chart of the islands, not having been able to get one even at Grenada.

Here I not only met with further disappointment in the matter, but was threatened with a fine for the mistake I made in the anchorage. There were no ships either at the quarantine or at the commercial roads, and I could not see that it made much difference where I anchored. But an island chap, a sort of deputy harbor-master, coming along, thought it did, and he ordered me to shift to the other anchorage, which, in truth, I had already investigated and did not like, because of the heavier roll there from the sea. And so instead of springing to the sails at once to shift, I said I would leave outright as soon as I could procure a chart, which I begged he would send and get for me.

"But I say you mus' move befo' you gets anyt'ing't all," he insisted, and raising his voice so that all the people alongshore could hear, he added, "An' jes now!"

Then he flew into a towering passion when they on shore snickered to see the crew of the *Spray* sitting calmly by the bulwark instead of hoisting sail.

"I tell you dis am quarantine," he shouted, very much louder than before.

"That's all right, general," I replied. "I want to be quarantined anyhow."

"That's right, boss," some one on the beach cried, "that's right. You get quarantined," while others shouted to "make de white trash move 'long out o' dat."

They were about equally divided on the island for and against me. The man who had made so much fuss over the matter gave it up when he found that I wished to be quarantined and sent for an all-important fellow, who soon came alongside, starched from clue to earing. He stood in the boat as straight up and down as a fathom of pump-water — a marvel of importance.

"Charts!" cried I, as soon as his shirt-collar appeared over the sloop's rail. "Have you any charts?"

"No, sah," he replied with much-stiffened dignity. "No-sah. Ch'ts do's n't grow on dis island."

Not doubting the information, I tripped anchor immediately, as I had intended to do from the first, and made sail for St. John, Antigua, where I arrived the 1st of June, having sailed cautiously in midchannel all the way.

The *Spray* — always in good company — now fell in with the port officers' steam-launch at the harbor entrance, having on board Sir Francis Fleming, governor of the Leeward Islands, who — to the delight of "all hands" — gave the officer in charge instructions to tow my ship into port. On the following day, his Excellency and Lady Fleming, along with Captain Burr, R.N., paid me a visit. The court-house was tendered free to me at Antigua, as was done also at Grenada, and at each place a highly intelligent audience filled the hall to listen to a talk about the seas the *Spray* had crossed and the countries she had visited.

186

CHAPTER 21

Clearing for home – In the calm belt – A sea covered with sargasso –
The jibstay parts in a gale – Welcomed by a tornado off Fire Island
– A change of plan – Arrival at Newport – End of a cruise of over
forty-six thousand miles – The *Spray* again at Fairhaven.

ON the 4th of June, 1898, the *Spray* cleared from the
United States consulate, and her license to sail
single-handed, even round the world, was returned to her
for the last time. The United States consul, Mr. Hunt,
before handing the paper to me, wrote on it — as General
Roberts had done at Cape Town — a short commentary
on the voyage. The document, by regular course, is now
lodged in the Treasury Department at Washington, D.C.

On June 5, 1898, the *Spray* sailed for a home port,
heading first direct for Cape Hatteras. On the 8th of
June, she passed under the sun from south to north; the
sun's declination on that day was 22° 54´, and the latitude
of the *Spray* was the same just before noon. Many think it
is excessively hot right under the sun. It is not necessarily
so. As a matter of fact, the thermometer stands at a
bearable point whenever there is a breeze and a ripple on
the sea, even exactly under the sun. It is often hotter in
cities and on sandy shores in higher latitudes.

The *Spray* was booming joyously along for home now,
making her usual good time, when all of a sudden she
struck the horse latitudes, and her sail flapped limp in a
calm. I had almost forgotten this calm belt, or had come
to regard it as a myth. I now found it real, however, and
difficult to cross. This was as it should have been, for,
after all of the dangers of the sea — the dust-storm on the
coast of Africa, the "rain of blood" in Australia, and the
war risk when nearing home — a natural experience
would have been missing had the calm of the horse
latitudes been left out. Anyhow, a philosophical turn of

thought now was not amiss, else one's patience would have given out almost at the harbor entrance. The term of her probation was eight days. Evening after evening during this time I read by the light of a candle on deck. There was no wind at all, and the sea became smooth and monotonous. For three days I saw a full-rigged ship on the horizon, also becalmed.

Sargasso — scattered over the sea in bunches, or trailed curiously along down the wind in narrow lanes — now gathered together in great fields, strange sea animals, little and big, swimming in and out, the most curious among them being a tiny seahorse which I captured and brought home preserved in a bottle. But on the 18th of June a gale began to blow from the southwest, and the sargasso was dispersed again in the windrows and lanes.

On this day there was soon wind enough and to spare. The same might have been said of the sea. The *Spray* was in the midst of the turbulent Gulf Stream itself. She was jumping like a porpoise over the uneasy waves. As if to make up for lost time, she seemed to touch only the high places. Under a sudden shock and strain, her rigging began to give out. First the main-sheet strap was carried away, and then the peak halyard-block broke from the gaff. It was time to reef and refit, and so when "all hands" came on deck I went about doing that.

The 19th of June was fine, but on the morning of the 20th another gale was blowing, accompanied by cross-seas that tumbled about and shook things up with great confusion. Just as I was thinking about taking in sail, the jibstay broke at the masthead and fell — jib and all — into the sea. It gave me the strangest sensation to see the bellying sail fall, and where it had been suddenly to see only space; however, I was at the bows with presence of mind to gather it in on the first wave that rolled up before it was torn or trailed under the sloop's bottom.

I found by the amount of work done in three minutes' or less time that I had by no means grown stiff-jointed on the voyage; anyhow, scurvy had not set in, and being now within a few degrees of home, I might complete the voyage, I thought, without the aid of a doctor. Yes, my health was still good, and I could skip about the decks in a lively manner, but could I climb?

The great King Neptune tested me severely at this time, for — the stay being gone — the mast itself switched about like a reed and was not easy to climb. But a gun-tackle purchase was got up, and the stay set taut from the masthead — for I had spare blocks and rope on board with which to rig it — and the jib with a reef in it was soon pulling again like a "sodger" for home. Had the *Spray's* mast not been well stepped, however, it would have been "John Walker" when the stay broke. Good work in the building of my vessel stood me always in good stead.

On the 23d of June I was at last tired, tired, tired of baffling squalls and fretful cobble-seas. I had not seen a vessel for days and days, where I had expected the company of at least a schooner now and then. As to the whistling of the wind through the rigging and the slopping of the sea against the sloop's sides, that was well enough in its way, and we could not have got on without it, the *Spray* and I. But there was so much of it now, and it lasted so long!

At noon of that day, a winterish storm was upon us from the nor'west. In the Gulf Stream thus late in June, hailstones were pelting the *Spray*, and lightning was pouring down from the clouds — not in flashes alone, but in almost continuous streams. By slants, however, day and night I worked the sloop in toward the coast, where on the 25th of June off Fire Island, she fell into the tornado which an hour earlier had swept over New York City with lightning that wrecked buildings and sent trees flying about in splinters; even ships at docks had parted their moorings and smashed into other ships, doing great damage.

It was the climax storm of the voyage, but I saw the unmistakable character of it in time to have all snug aboard and receive it under bare poles. Even so, the sloop shivered when it struck her, and she heeled over unwillingly on her beam ends, but rounding to with a sea-anchor ahead, she righted and faced out the storm. In

189

the midst of the gale I could do no more than look on, for what is a man in a storm like this?

I had seen one electric storm on the voyage off the coast of Madagascar, but it was unlike this one. Here the lightning kept on longer, and thunderbolts fell in the sea all about. Up to this time, I was bound for New York, but when all was over, I rose, made sail, and hove the sloop round from starboard to port tack to make for a quiet harbor to think the matter over. And so, under short sail she reached in for the coast of Long Island, while I sat thinking and watching the lights of coasting-vessels which now began to appear in sight.

Reflections of the voyage so nearly finished stole in upon me now; many tunes I had hummed again and again came back once more. I found myself repeating fragments of a hymn often sung by a dear Christian woman of Fairhaven when I was rebuilding the *Spray*. I was to hear once more and only once, in profound solemnity, the metaphorical hymn:

By waves and wind I'm tossed and driven.

And again:

But still my little ship outbraves
The blust'ring winds and stormy waves.

After this storm, I saw the pilot of the *Pinta* no more.

The experiences of the voyage of the *Spray* — reaching over three years — had been to me like reading a book, and one that was more and more interesting as I turned the pages, till I had come now to the last page of all, and the one more interesting than any of the rest.

When daylight came, I saw that the sea had changed color from dark green to light. I threw the lead and got soundings in thirteen fathoms. I made the land soon after — some miles east of Fire Island — and sailing thence before a pleasant breeze along the coast, made for Newport. The weather after the furious gale was remarkably fine. The *Spray* rounded Montauk Point early in the afternoon; Point Judith was abeam at dark; she fetched in at Beavertail next.

Sailing on, she had one more danger to pass — Newport Harbor was mined. The *Spray* hugged the rocks along where neither friend, nor foe could come if drawing much water and where she would not disturb the guard-ship in the channel. It was close work, but it was safe enough so long as she hugged the rocks close and not the mines.

Flitting by a low point abreast of the guard-ship, the dear old *Dexter*, which I knew well, some one on board of her sang out, "There goes a craft!" I threw up a light at once and heard the hail, "*Spray* ahoy!" It was the voice of a friend, and I knew that a friend would not fire on the *Spray*.

I eased off the main-sheet now, and now the *Spray* swung off for the beacon-lights of the inner harbor. At last she reached the port in safety, and there at 1A.M. on June 27, 1898, cast anchor, after the cruise of more than forty-six thousand miles round the world, during an absence of three years and two months, with two days over for coming up.

Was the crew well? Was I not? I had profited in many ways by the voyage. I had even gained flesh and actually weighed a pound more than when I sailed from Boston. As for aging, why, the dial of my life was turned back till my friends all said, "Slocum is young again." And so I was, at least ten years younger than the day I felled the first tree for the construction of the *Spray*.

My ship was also in better condition than when she sailed from Boston on her long voyage. She was still as sound as a nut and as tight as the best ship afloat. She did not leak a drop — not one drop! The pump, which had been little used before reaching Australia, had not been rigged since that at all.

The first name on the *Spray's* visitor book in the home port was written by the one who always said, "The *Spray* will come back." The *Spray* was not quite satisfied till I sailed her to her birthplace, Fairhaven, Massachusetts, farther along. I had myself a desire to return to the place

of the very beginning when I had, as I have said, renewed my age. So on July 3, with a fair wind, she waltzed beautifully round the coast and up the Acushnet River to Fairhaven, where I secured her to the cedar spile driven in the bank to hold her when she was launched. I could bring her no nearer home.

If the *Spray* discovered no continents on her voyage, it may be that there were no more continents to be discovered; she did not seek new worlds, or sail to powwow about the dangers of the seas. The sea has been much maligned. To find one's way to lands already discovered is a good thing, and the *Spray* made the discovery that even the worst sea is not so terrible to a well-appointed ship. No king, no country, no treasury at all was taxed for the voyage of the *Spray*, and she accomplished all that she undertook to do.

To succeed, however, in anything at all, one should go understandingly about his work and be prepared for every emergency. I see — as I look back over my own small achievement — a kit of not too elaborate carpenter's tools, a tin-clock, and some carpet-tacks — not a great many — to facilitate the enterprise as already mentioned in the story. But above all to be taken into account were some years of schooling, where I studied with diligence Neptune's laws, and these laws I tried to obey when I sailed overseas; it was worth the while.

And now, without having wearied my friends, I hope, with detailed scientific accounts, theories, or deductions, I will only say that I have endeavored to tell just the story of the adventure itself. This — in my own poor way — having been done, I now moor ship, weather-bitt cables, and leave the sloop *Spray*, for the present, safe in port.

Sail-plan of the *Spray*.
The solid lines represent the sail-plan of the Spray on starting for the long voyage. With it, she crossed the Atlantic to Gibraltar, and then crossed again southwest to Brazil. In South American waters the bowsprit and boom were shortened and the jigger-sail added to form the yawl-rig with which the rest of the trip was made, the sail-plan of which is indicated by the dotted lines. The extreme sail forward is a flying-jib occasionally used, set to a bamboo stick fastened to the bowsprit. The manner of setting and bracing the jigger-mast is not included in this drawing.

APPENDIX
LINES AND SAIL-PLAN OF THE *SPRAY*
Her pedigree as known – The Lines of the *Spray* – Her self-steering qualities – Sail-plan and steering-gear – An unprecedented feat – A final word of cheer to would-be navigators.

FROM a feeling of diffidence toward sailors of great experience, I refrained in the preceding chapters (as prepared for serial publication in the *Century Magazine*) from entering fully into the details of the *Spray's* build and of the primitive methods employed to sail her. Having had no yachting experience at all, I had no means of knowing that the trim vessels seen in our harbors and near the land could not all do as much — or even more — than the *Spray*, sailing, for example, on a course with the helm lashed.

I was unaware that no other vessel had sailed in this manner around the globe, but would have been loath to say that another could not do it, or that many men had sailed vessels of a certain rig in that manner as far as they wished to go. I was greatly amused, therefore, by the flat assertions of an expert that it could not be done.

The *Spray*, as I sailed her, was entirely a new boat, built over from a sloop which bore the same name and which — tradition said — had first served as an oysterman about a hundred years ago on the coast of Delaware. There was no record in the custom-house of where she was built. She was once owned at Noank, Connecticut; afterward in New Bedford; and when Captain Eben Pierce presented her to me at the end of her natural life, she stood — as I have already described — propped up in a field at Fairhaven.

Her lines were supposed to be those of a North Sea fisherman. In rebuilding timber by timber and plank by plank, I added to her freeboard twelve inches amidships,

Deck plan of the *Spray*.

eighteen inches forward, and fourteen inches aft, thereby increasing her sheer and making her (as I thought) a better deep-water ship. I will not repeat the history of the rebuilding of the *Spray* — which I have detailed in my first chapter — except to say that, when finished, her dimensions were thirty-six feet nine inches over all, fourteen feet two inches wide, and four feet two inches deep in the hold, her tonnage being nine tons net, and twelve and seventy one-hundredths tons gross.

I gladly produce the lines of the *Spray* with such hints as my really limited fore-and-aft sailing will allow, my seafaring life having been spent mostly in barks and ships. No pains have been spared to give them accurately. The *Spray* was taken from New York across to Bridgeport, Connecticut, and under the supervision of the Park City Yacht Club was hauled out of the water and very carefully measured in every way to secure a satisfactory result. Captain Robins produced the model. Our young yachtsmen — pleasuring in the "lilies of the sea" — very naturally will not think favorably of my craft. They have a right to their opinion, while I stick to mine. They will take exceptions to her short ends, the advantage of these being most apparent in a heavy sea.

Some things about the *Spray's* deck might be fashioned differently without materially affecting the vessel. I know of no good reason why for a party-boat a cabin trunk might not be built amidships instead of far aft like the one on her, which leaves a very narrow space between the wheel and the line of the companionway. Some even say that I might have improved the shape of her stern. I do not know about that. The water leaves her run sharp after bearing her to the last inch, and no suction is formed by undue cutaway.

Smooth-water sailors say, "Where is her overhang?" They never crossed the Gulf Stream in a nor'easter, and they do not know what is best in all weathers. For your life, build no fantail overhang on a craft going offshore. As a sailor judges his prospective ship by a "blow of the eye" when he takes interest enough to look her over at all, so I judged the *Spray*, and I was not deceived.

In a sloop-rig the *Spray* made that part of her voyage reaching from Boston through the Strait of Magellan, during which she experienced the greatest variety of weather conditions. The yawl-rig then adopted was an improvement only in that it reduced the size of a rather heavy mainsail and slightly improved her steering qualities on the wind. When the wind was aft, the jigger was not in use; invariably, it was then furled. With her boom broad off and with the wind two points on the quarter, the *Spray* sailed her truest course. It never took long to find the amount of helm or angle of rudder required to hold her on course, and — when that was found — I lashed the wheel with it at that angle. The mainsail then drove her, and the main-jib — with its sheet boused flat amidships or a little to one side or the other — added greatly to the steadying power. Then if the wind was even strong or squally, I would sometimes set a flying-jib also — on a pole rigged out on the bowsprit — with the sheets hauled flat amidships, which was a safe thing to do even in a gale. A stout downhaul on the gaff was a necessity, because without it the mainsail might not have come down when I wished to lower it in a breeze. The amount of helm required varied according to the amount of wind and its direction. These points are quickly gathered from practice.

Briefly, I have to say that when close-hauled in a light wind under all sail she required little or no weather helm. As the wind increased, I would go on deck (if below) and turn the wheel up a spoke more or less, relash it or (as sailors say) put it in a becket, and then leave it as before.

To answer the questions that might be asked to meet every contingency would be a pleasure, but it would overburden my book. I can only say here that much comes to one in practice, and that — with such as love sailing — mother-wit is the best teacher, after experience. Labor-saving appliances? There were none. The sails were hoisted by hand; the halyards were rove through ordinary ships' blocks with common patent rollers. Of course, the sheets were all belayed aft.

The windlass used was in the shape of a winch, or

crab, I think it is called. I had three anchors: weighing forty pounds, one hundred pounds, and one hundred and eighty pounds respectively. The windlass and the forty-pound anchor, and the "fiddlehead" — or carving on the end of the cutwater — belonged to the original *Spray*. The ballast (concrete cement) was stanchioned down securely. There was no iron or lead or other weight on the keel.

If I took measurements by the rule, I did not set them down, and after sailing even the longest voyage in her I could not tell offhand the length of her mast, boom, or

Steering-gear of the *Spray*.
The dotted lines are the ropes used to lash the wheel.
In practice, the loose ends were belayed, one over the other,
around the top spokes of the wheel.

gaff. I did not know the center of her effort in her sails, except as it hit me in practice at sea, nor did I care a rope yarn about it. Mathematical calculations, however, are all right in a good boat, and the *Spray* could have stood them. She was easily balanced and easily kept in trim.

Some of the oldest and ablest shipmasters have asked how it was possible for her to hold a true course before the wind, which was just what the *Spray* did for weeks together. One of these gentlemen — a highly esteemed shipmaster and friend — testified as government expert in a famous murder trial in Boston — not long since — that a ship would not hold her course long enough for the steersman to leave the helm to cut the captain's throat. Ordinarily it would be so. One might say that with a square-rigged ship it would always be so. But the *Spray* — at the moment of the tragedy in question — was sailing around the globe with no one at the helm, except at intervals more or less rare; however, I may say here that this would have had no bearing on the murder case in Boston. In all probability, Justice laid her hand on the true rogue. In other words, in the case of a model and rig similar to that of the tragedy ship, I should myself testify as did the nautical experts at the trial.

But see the run the *Spray* made from Thursday Island to the Keeling Cocos Islands: twenty-seven hundred miles distant in twenty-three days with no one at the helm in that time — save for about one hour — from land to land. No other ship in the history of the world ever performed under similar circumstances the feat on so long and continuous a voyage. It was, however, a delightful midsummer sail.

No one can know the pleasure of sailing free over the great oceans save those who have had the experience. It is not necessary — in order to realize the utmost enjoyment of going around the globe — to sail alone, yet for once and the first time there was a great deal of fun in it. My friend — the government expert and saltiest of salt sea-captains — standing only yesterday on the deck of the *Spray* was convinced of her famous qualities, and he spoke enthusiastically of selling his farm on Cape Cod and putting to sea again.

To young men contemplating a voyage, I would say go. The tales of rough usage are for the most part exaggerations, as also are the stories of sea danger. I had a fair schooling in the so-called "hard ships" on the hard Western Ocean, and in the years there I do not remember having once been "called out of my name." Such recollections have endeared the sea to me. I owe it further to the officers of all the ships I ever sailed in as boy and man to say that not one ever lifted so much as a finger to me. I did not live among angels, but among men who could be roused. My wish was, though, to please the officers of my ship wherever I was, and so I got on. Dangers there are, to be sure, on the sea as well as on the land, but the intelligence and skill God gives to man reduce these to a minimum. And here comes in again the skillfully modeled ship worthy to sail the seas.

Body-plan of the *Spray*.

To face the elements is, to be sure, no light matter when the sea is in its grandest mood. You must know the sea and know that you know it and not forget that it was made to be sailed over.

I have given in the plans of the *Spray* the dimensions of such a ship as I should call seaworthy in all conditions of weather and on all seas. It is only right to say, though, that to insure a reasonable measure of success, experience should sail with the ship. But in order to be a successful navigator or sailor, it is not necessary to hang a tar-bucket about one's neck. On the other hand, much thought concerning the brass buttons one should wear adds nothing to the safety of the ship.

I may some day see reason to modify the model of the dear old *Spray*, but out of my limited experience I strongly recommend her wholesome lines over those of pleasure-fliers for safety. Practice in a craft such as the *Spray* will teach young sailors and fit them for the more

Lines of the *Spray*.

important vessels. I myself learned more seamanship, I think, on the *Spray* than on any other ship I ever sailed. And as for the patience, the greatest of all the virtues, even while sailing through the reaches of the Strait of Magellan, between the bluff mainland and dismal Fuego — where through intricate sailing I was obliged to steer — I learned to sit by the wheel, content to make ten miles a

Plan of the after cabin of the *Spray*.

day beating against the tide. And when a month at that was all lost, I could find some old tune to hum while I worked the route all over again, beating as before. Nor did thirty hours at the wheel in storm overtax my human endurance, and to clap a hand to an oar and pull into or out of port in a calm was no strange experience for the crew of the *Spray*. The days passed happily with me wherever my ship sailed.

FURTHER READING

Andrade, Cipriano, Jr. "A Critical Analysis of the Yawl *Spray*," *The Rudder*. June, 1909.

Blondin, Robert. *The Solitary Slocum*. Halifax, Nova Scotia: Nimbus Publishing, 1992.

Culler, R.D. *Skiffs & Schooners*. Camden, Maine: International Marine, 1974.

Day, Thomas Fleming. "On Capt. Joshua Slocum." *The Rudder*. Reprinted in *The Rudder Treasury*, Tom Davin (ed.), Dobbs Ferry, New York: Sheridan House, 1953.

Degnon, Dom. "The Age of Small Sail." *SAIL*. December, 1994.

de Graff, J. *Great Voyages in Small Boats: Solo Circumnavigations*. Clinton Corners, New York: 1976.

Fortman, Janis L. *First to Sail the World Alone: Joshua Slocum*. New York, NY: Contemporary Perspectives, Inc., 1978.

Garland, Jos. E. *Down to the Sea*. Boston, Massachusetts: David R. Godine, 1973.

Johnson, Clifton. "Captain Joshua Slocum: The Man Who Sailed Around the World in a Thirty-Seven-Foot Boat." *Outing*. October, 1902.

————. "The Cook Who Sailed Alone." *Good Housekeeping*. February, 1903.

Kovacs, Deborah. *Midnight on the River*. New York, New York: Viking Press, 1993.

Lopes, Myra. *Captain Joshua Slocum: A Centennial Tribute*. New Bedford, Massachusetts: RPI, 1994.

Ransome, Arthur. Introduction to *Sailing Alone Around the World*. (Mariners Library No. 1) Rupert Hart-Davis: London, England, 1948.

Roberts-Goodson, R. Bruce. "*Spray* and Her Sisters." *SAIL*. December, 1994.

————. *Spray: The Ultimate Cruising Boat*. Saverna Park, Maryland: Bruce Roberts, Ltd., 1995.

Slack, Kenneth E. *In the Wake of the Spray*. New Brunswick, NJ: Rutgers University Press, 1966.

Slocum, Joshua. *Around the World in the Sloop Spray*. New York, New York: Charles Scribner's Sons, 1914.

————. *Sailing Alone Around the World*. New York, New York: Century Company, 1900.

————. *Spray Souvenir Book*. Boston, Massachusetts: Published by Slocum in conjunction with his appearance at the Pan American Exposition, 1901.

————. *Voyage of the Destroyer from New York to Brazil*. Boston, Massachusetts: Robinson Printing Company, 1894.

Slocum, Victor. *Capt. Joshua Slocum: The Life and Voyages of America's Best Known Sailor*. Dobbs Ferry, New York: Sheridan House, 1950.

Teller, Walter Magnes. "Any Word on Captain Slocum?" *Vineyard Gazette*, 19 June 1953.

Teller, Walter Magnes. *Joshua Slocum*. New Brunswick, New Jersey: Rutgers University Press, 1971.

————. "Postscripts to *The Search for Captain Slocum*." *American Neptune*. July 1958.

————. *The Search for Captain Slocum: A Biography*. New Brunswick, New Jersey: Rutgers University Press, 1956.

————. *The Voyages of Joshua Slocum*. New Brunwsick, New Jersey: Rutgers University Press, 1958.

FURTHER READING

Papers of Joshua Slocum

Letters from Capt. Joshua Slocum to Roberts Brothers, publishers of Boston
PHILLIPS LIBRARY
Peabody Essex Museum
East India
Salem, Massachusetts

Letters from Capt. Joshua Slocum to Century Company, publishers of New York
THE CENTURY COLLECTION
Manuscript Room
New York Public Library
New York, New York

Letters of Joshua Slocum to the Smithsonian Institution
SMITHSONIAN INSTITUTION
Department of Engineering and Industries
Washington, D.C.

Letters of Capt. Joshua Slocum
NATIONAL ARCHIVES
Records of the Department of State
Record Group 59
Washington, D.C.

Papers of Walter Magnes Teller

Photographs, letters, and notes of interviews used in research of books and articles about Joshua Slocum.
OLD DARTMOUTH HISTORICAL SOCIETY WHALING MUSEUM
18 Johnny Cake Hill
New Bedford, Massachusetts

DUKES COUNTY HISTORICAL SOCIETY
School Street
Edgartown, Massachusetts

.

INDEX

— A —

Acushnet River *ix*,193
Africa 38,39,145,151,160,plains 169,187
after-cabin plan 202
aground 45-50
Airy, Captain 139
Akbar 126-8
Alan Erric Island 88
Alaska *xiii*,178
Albany Pass 136
Alert 42,167
Alfred Dry-docks 167,169,170
Algoa Bay 165
Amazon River *x*,*xxii*,182
Amen Rocks 11
American Museum of Natural History *xxi*
Amethyst xiv,*xvi*
Annapolis Valley 1
anonymous gift 121,134
Antarctic 118
Antichrist, mistaken for 152-3
Antigua 174,186
Antilles 185
Aoele 104
Apia, Samoa 103,104,108,111, 112,137
Aquidneck xvi,*xvii*,1,50
Aquidneck Island *xvi*
Arafura Sea 124,140
Arethusa 172
Argentina *xvi*
Ascension Island 175,176,178
astronomy (cf. *Cape Observatory* and *nautical astronomy*)
Atlantic 16,20
Atlantic Ocean *ix*,*xv*,15,31,35,43, meets Pacific 81

Australia *vii*,2,110,112-21,140,fn 144,164,191
Azores 20,21,52,92,102
Azopardo 87

— B —

B. Aymar xiii
Bahamas *xxi*
Bahia Blanca 56
Bailey, Prof. Mason 137
Balfour 32
Baltimore *xvi*
Bass Strait 115,118
Batavia 146
Bay of Fundy *x*,1,12,175
Beaconsfield 121
Beagle xix,70,149
Beauty Point 121
Beavertail 191
Bird Island 136
Black Pedro 62,78-9,80,87
Bluebird 10
body-plan 201
Boers 163-4 (cf. *flat earth*)
Bonet Island 82
booby 172
Booby Island 139
Boomerang 131
Boreas 60,72
Borgia Bay 63,82,83
Borneo 146
Borneo 145
Boston 2,7,23,43,131,157,177, 191,198,200
Bowen 131
Brazil current 181
Bridgeport 196
Brier Island *x*,*xi*,12-14
British Columbia *xii*

Bruce, Admiral 31,32
Buenos Aires *xvi-xvii*,51,52-55
Buffalo 43
Buffalo, NY *xxi*
Buzzards Bay *ix,xx*,6

— C —

Caini, Samoa 106-7
California coast 81
Campbell, Gen. John P. 157
Canada 178,179
Canary Islands 38
Cannibal Islands 112
Cape Agulhas 166
Cape Ann *xvii*,12
Cape Bundooro 116,124
Cape Cod *ix,xi*,51,200
Cape Froward 60,66,70,76
Cape Greenville 135-6
Cape Hatteras 187
Cape Hawk 126,127
Cape Horn *xii*,43,55-7,67-9,75-
    80,83,87,89,112,140, fn 144,
    160,170,176
Cape Howe 124
Cape Leeuwin 115,118-9
Cape Observatory 169
Cape of Good Hope *xii,xv*,23,42,
    139,140, 143,157,162,165-6,
    170,185
"Cape of Storms" 165
Cape Pillar 64,67,68,86,89,90
Cape Quod 83
Cape Sable 14-5,18,20,21,31
Cape St. Mary 160
Cape Town 77,167,178,181,187
Cape Verde Islands 40,126
Cape Virgins 56-57
Captain Joshua Slocum xxii
Caribbean *xi,xxi*
carpet-tacks 59,70,193
Carrington, Sir F. 32,33
Carroza, Manuel 92,94,96,102
Cashes Ledge 11
Castillo Chicos 49
Catherton 114
Century Illustrated Magazine xx,95,
    195
Cervantes, Miguel de *xix*
Chamberlain, Joseph 144
Charles Island 61,77,80
charts 23,65,110
Chebucto Head 15

Chilmark *xviii*
China 2
Christmas Island 141,142,143
chronometer (cf. *tin clock*)
Churchill, General & Mrs. 103
Cinque Ports 95
circumnavigators 126,170,180
Claremont Lightship 135
Cleveland, President Grover *xx*
Cliff Island 116
Cluni-Ross, Capt. John 145-7,149
Cockburn Channel 70,75
Cody, Buffalo Bill *xxi*
Coffee Island 61,77
Colimbia 81
Collingwood 32
Colombia 80-1,83,102
Columbus, Christopher 27,29,30,
    38
Condor 87
Constitution xiii
Cook, Capt. 133-4
Cook, John 4
Cooke Inlet *xiii*
Cooktown 128,132-5
coral reef 183-4
Coral Sea 124,127,138
Cormorant 32
corroboree 137-138
course (cf. *true course*)
Crescent Head 128
Crow Island *ix*
Crusoe, Robinson (cf. *Selkirk*) 91,
    97,183
Curipepe 157

— D —

da Gama, Vasco 165
Dana Island 141
Danger Point 129,130
Dartmouth *ix*
Darwin, Charles *xix*,70
deck plan 197
Deer Island x,8
Delaware *ix*,195
Destroyer xviii,43
Devil's Island 182
Devonport 122-4
Dexter 191
Digby Neck *xi*
doldrums 40-41
dolphins 41-42,171
Dominica 185

210

INDEX

Drake, Sir Francis 170
Dublin *xii*
Duke 95
Durban 160-164,168
Dusen, Professor 87

— E —

East Boston *x,xvii*,7
Eastern Point 11
East India Company 145
Echo Mountain 77
Elizabeth Islands *ix*
Endeavor 133-4
Endeavor River 128,132,135
English Bank 55
equator, crossing 43
Escombe, Harry 162
Evangelista Islands 89

— F —

Faamu-Sami 112,137
Fairhaven *ix,x,xviii*,3,4,6,139,190,
  191-3,195
Falkland Islands 68
Famine Reach 73
Fayal 20-21,26
Fernando de Noronha Island 180
Fiji 113
Findlay's *Sailing Directory* fn 145
Fire Island 189-190
fish 11,30,41-42,50
flat earth 163-4,165,167
Fleming, Sir Francis 186
Florence 162
Flores Island 20
Flying Dutchman 166
flying-fish 37,39,40,103,141,142
Forerunner 161
Fortescue Bay 60,80,82
Fort Teresa 49
Friday Island 137
Frisco *xii*
fruit-cake 174-5
Fuegian encounters 52,59,61,62,
  71,76,86
Fuerteventura Island 38
Fury Island 69

— G —

Gannet Island (Rock) 12
Gantes, Juan 19
George's Island 15

Georgetown 122
ghost 173
Gibraltar 22-3,32-5,43,129,fn 144
Gill, Dr. David 168-9
Gloucester, MA *x*,8-11,153
Gloucester Island 131
Gray Gables *xx*
Great Barrier Reef 119,126,129-
  130,132,135
Great Britain 178
Great Sandy Cape 129
Greenland 4
Grenada 185,186
Guiana 181
Gulf of St. George 56
Gulf of St. Matias 56
Gulf Stream 16,storm 188-9,196

— H —

Hadden, J. Cuthbert fn 95
Hairby, Sir Edward 53
Halifax, NS 15
Hall, Basil 112
Hampden, Lord 121-2
Hannibal, Chief Mate 80
Hare, Alexander 145-7,149
Hebe 32
Henderson, Capt. 80
Hesperus 8
Hobson's Bay 118
Home Island 136
homeward bound 180,187
Hong Kong *xiv*,142
Honolulu *xiii,xiv*
Horn Islands 113
Horsburg Island 145
horse latitudes 187-8
Horta 22-25,26,31
Howard, Capt. 51-52,55
Howard, Farmer 3
Howard, Tom 118
Huemel 64
hydrophobia 176-7

— I —

India 145
Indian Ocean 104,138,152,177
Inland Voyage 172
Iphegenia 144,148
Ironbound Island 15
Irving, Washington *xix*
Island of Birds 12

211

Island of Frogs 12
Island of Tragedies (Sable) 16

— J —

Jamestown 173-4
Java 146
Java 19-20
Johannesburg 167
Juan Fernández Island 90-97,98,
 101,102,140

— K —

Keeling Cocos Islands 4,139,143-
 151,169,175,177,200
Keeling, William 145
Kimberley 167,169
King Malietoa 111-112,137
Kodak 168
Krakatau volcano *xv*
Krüger, President 162,163-4,167

— L —

Lady Elliott Light 129
Langara Cove 83
Langley, Samuel P. *xi,xxi*
La Vaguisa 19
Leach, Andrew J. 144,148
Leeward Islands 186
Liberdade *xvii*,2
Liberia 178
lines of the *Spray* 202
Line Wall House 33
Lion's Rump 167
Lisbon 22
Liverpool, NS 15
Liverpool, UK *xii,xv*
log entry 140,183
London Missionary Society 112
Long Island 190
Longwood 174

— M —

M Reef 135-6
MacKinley, President William *xx*
Madagascar 139,160,190
Maine 181
Maldonado 50
Malietoa (cf. *King Malietoa*)
Manila *xv*,80
man in the moon 16-17
Manly 114

Manning, General 26
Marblehead 8
Marion *ix*
Marquesas Islands 97-100
Martha's Vineyard *ix,xi,xxi*
Mary 116
Massachusetts Bay 8
Mather, Cotton 174
Mattapoisett *ix*
Mauritius 115,155-160,161,185
Mediterranean Sea 35,104
Melbourne 117-8
Menemsha *xxii*
Mercator's projection 163
Mersey River 122
Miami *xi,xxi*
Milky Way 69-70
Milner, Sir Alfred 168
mirage 57
Missionary Review 112
Mohammed 36
Moka 157-8,159
Monhegan Light 12
Monroe Doctrine 181
Montauk Point 190
Montevideo 49,51
Morocco 33
Mozambique 160
Mulannah 122
Murrumbidgee River 127
mutiny quelled *xv*

— N —

Nahant 8
Nansen, Dr. Fridtjof 13
Nantasket 41
Nantucket *ix,xi*
Napoleon 173,174
nautical astronomy 99-100
Neptune 16,20,184,189,193
New Bedford *ix,x*,3,4,22,92,102,
 139,195
New Caledonia 113
Newcastle 113,114,127
New England *xi*
New Guinea 127,128,134,135
Newlands Vineyard 168
New Orleans 178
Newport *xvi,xx*,94,190,191
New South Wales 113,129
New York *xv*,2,43,80,166,189,196
Nictheroy 43
Noank *x*,195

INDEX

Norfolk, VA 43
Norman's Woe 8
Northern Light xiv-xvi,2,80
North Mountain 1
North Sea 195
north star 183
North Star 43
Notch Cove 64
Nova Scotia x,xv,1,12-14
Nukahiva Island 99,101
Nully Nully 131
Nyanza River 162

— O —

ocean meteorology 98
Olinda Point, Brazil 43
Olympia 20
Oom Paul 162,167
Ophelia's poem 148
Oregon 182
Orinoco River xxii,183
Orlando 114,132
Osbourne, Lloyd 104,112
Oyster Bay xx
Oxford Village x

— P —

Pacific Ocean xii,xv,60,entering
   67,69,73,75,meets Atlantic 81,
   86,98,102,103,129-130
Palmer Island ix
Panama 81
Pan American Exposition xxi
Papauta College 108
Paranaguá Bay xvii
Pardo 123
Paris 94
Paris Exposition 122
Park City Yacht Club (NY) 196
Parramatta 125
Patagonia 56
Pato xiv,xvi
Patrician 113
Pemaquid 12
Pernambuco, Brazil xvi,42,43,117
pets 176-8
Phillipine Islands xiii
phosphorescent light 140
Pico Island 21,25
Pierce, Capt. Eben xviii,3,6,195
Pinta, pilot of 26-29,51,125,172,
   185,190

pirates 35-37,43,50,184
Plantation House 173-4
poems 148
Point Judith 191
Popes Island ix
porpoises 18,20,171-2,188
Port Angosto 85-88
Port Denison 131-2,135
Port Elizabeth, South Africa xv
Port Heads 119
Port Indio 55
Port Jackson 125
Portland, OR xiv
Port Louis 159,185
Port Macquarie 126,127
Port Natal 160,161,165
Port Stanley 68
Port Stevens 126
Port Tamar 64,66,67
Poverty Point ix
Pretoria 162,167,169
Prince of Monaco 26
Prison Island 146
Puce Mountain 160
Puget Sound xii
Punta Arenas (cf. *Sandy Point*)

— Q —

Queen Margaret of Manua 111
Queensland 131,138

— R —

Racer 117,118
"rain of blood" 119,187
Rawson, Sir Harry 170
reading 30,39,97,126,171-2,188,
   voyage like 190
Red Sea 35,43
Reduit 157
Réunion 160
Reynolds, Commander 32
Rìo de Janeiro 43,45,92
Rìo de la Plata (River Plate) xvi,39,
   51,55
Rìo Negro xxii
Robinson Crusoe Bay 95
Rock of Lamentations (Sambro) 15
Rodriguez Island 151-5,157,169,
   177
Roosevelt, President Theodore xx
Rose Hill 157
Ross (cf. *Cluni-Ross*)

213

Round Pond Harbor 12
Royal Mail Steamship Company 51

— S —

Sable Island 16
Sagamore Hill *xx*
Sagamore Village *xx*
Sailing Alone Around the World *xx*
St. Antonio 40
St. Felix 97
St. George 185
St. Helena 172-9
St. John 186
St. Kilda 117,119-120
St. Mary's Bay *xii*,14
St. Michael's 25
St. Nicholas Bay 60,72
St. Roque 181
Samblich, Capt. Pedro 59,70,79
Sambro (Rock of Lamentations) 15
Samoa 10,101-12,118,140,164
Sandy Cape 160
Sandy Point (Punta Arenas) 58,60,
  71,73,75,78,79,87
San Francisco *xii*,*xiii*,80
San Gabriel 154
Santa Cruz Island 165
Santa Maria 38
Saturday Island 137
Saunderson, Col. 168
Scotsman 166
seahorse 188
Seal Rocks 114,126
Seattle *xii*
Secret 116
Selkirk, Alexander 94,95
Shakespeare, William *xix*
sharks 41-42,90,101,118,119-120,
  148,152
Shelcote 114
Sherman 128
Simons Bay 166
sister 175
Slocum plant 157-8
Slocum, Benjamin Aymar *xiii*
Slocum, Henrietta (Elliott) *xvii*,*xx*,
  xxi,*xxii*
Slocum, James Garfield *xiii*,*xvii*
Slocum, Jesse *xiii*
Slocum, John *xi*,*xv*,*xvi*
Slocum, Joshua *ix-xiii*
Slocum, Sarah Jane (Southern) *xi*
Slocum, Victor *xiii*,*xvii*,*xxii*

Slocum, Virginia Albert (Walker)
  xii,*xiii*,*xvi*
Smithsonian Institution *xxi*
Snug Bay 76-7
Society Islands fn 144
Soushay 134,139
South Africa 162-170
South China Sea *xiii*
Southern Cross 97
Southern Cross 80
South Pacific *ix*,87
South Solitary Island 129
South Wales 45
Southwest Point, Nova Scotia *xi*
Spain 31
Spanish-American War 181,187
Spice Islands 2
spider-fight 77
Sprague, Hon. Horatio J. 34
Standard 53
Stanley, Henry M. 162-3
steering-gear design 199
Stevenson, Robert Louis *xix*,172
Stevenson, Fanny (Mrs. R.L.) 104-
  5,112-3, 140,176
Stone Frigate, R.N. (cf. *Ascension
  Island*) 178
Strait of Gibraltar 31
Strait of Magellan 23,55-6,57-67,
  chart 65,69-75,87,88,90,93, 118,
  132,fn 144,198,202
Suez Canal 35
Sunday Island 136
swordfish 43,163
Sydney, Australia *xii*,*xvi*,114-5,
  116,125,133

— T —

Table Bay 165
Table Mountain 167,170
Taloa 105,106,107
Tamar River 119,122
Tanjore *xii*,142
Tarawa 136
Tarifa 31
Tasmania 116,119-124,134
Teller, Walter Magnes *xviii*,*xxii*
Tennyson, Alfred Lord *xix*
Thatcher's Island 11
Thieves' Bay 70
Three Island Cove 62-3
Thursday Island 127,137,144, &
  fn, 200

INDEX

Tierra del Fuego 51,59,62,67,69, 71,88
Tigre 170
tin clock 10,20,14,141,169,193
Timor Island 140,141
Tisbury *xxii,xxiii*
Tobago Island 183-4
Topaze 95
tornado 189
Torres Strait 119,137,138,fn 144
trade-winds 39,40,42,43,97,98, 113, 129,132,138,160,180-1,183
Trafalgar 31
Transvaal 164
tridacna 150-1
Trinidad 184
true course 52,141,143,152,153
Turkey, Sultan of 162
turtles 30,149
Tusitala 104
Twain, Mark *xix*
Tweed River 129
Twofold Bay 116

— U —

Uruguay *xvi*,49,50

— V —

Vailima 104,112-113,172
Valparaiso 91,92
Venetian 7
Venezuela 181
Victoria Museum of Launceston 119
Vineyard Haven *x,xxii*
Vineyard Sound *ix,xxii*
Voyage of Joshua Slocum xviii
Voyage of the Liberdade xviii

— W —

Wagnall, Adam *xix*
Wagnall, Mabel *xix*
Washington xii,xiii
Washington, DC *xvii*
Waterloo Bay 116
Watson's Bay 125,126
wave (dangerous) 56,166, 171
Wellington 169
West Indies 175
Westport, MA *ix*
Westport, NS *xi*,12,13
West Tisbury *xxi*

Weymouth 95
whales 11,12,42,101,102,116-7,127,141
Whitsunday Pass
williwaw 60,64,71-3
Wilmot, Nova Scotia *x*
Wilson, John 24
Wilson's Promontory 116
Wing, Joe (John) 22
Worcester 169

— Y —

yammerschooner 61,78,80,81
Yarmouth, NS 14-15
Yarrow River 117
Young, A. 111
Young, Margaret (cf. *Queen Margaret*)

ACKNOWLEDGMENTS

A S with the preparation and production of any book, there are countless people who lend their time and support to those whose names appear in larger print. Certainly, this edition of Joshua Slocum's *Sailing Alone Around the World* remains no exception, and there can never be enough thanks in the world to fulfill our debts of gratitude.

We have deeply appreciated the cooperation in New Bedford by both Judith Lund and Ann Brengle at the Old Dartmouth Historical Society Whaling Museum, as well as by Benjamin Baker at Baker Books; in Fairhaven, by Don Tucker and Roy Greenson of the Joshua Slocum Centennial Committee; in Edgartown, by Larry Michie at *The Vineyard Gazette*, as well as by Bruce Andrews at the Dukes County Historical Society; in Vineyard Haven, by Randi Vega at the Martha's Vineyard Chamber of Commerce; in Westport, Massachusetts, by Jan Hall at Partners Village Store and in Westport, Nova Scotia, by Carol Welch; in Mattapoisett, by master boatbuilder Peter Duff; in Boston, by Rob Eckhart at *SAIL Magazine*; in Salem, by John Coza at the Peabody-Essex Museum, as well as by David Dunn of the educational sailing program, *Chasing Joshua*; in Baltimore, by Elizabeth Downs; in Washington, D.C., by Jeff Meeks, by Terri Short at the National Archives, as well as Jerome Callahan at the Smithsonian Museum of American History; in San Francisco, by Cate Schley and Ben Manilla; and in Chatham, by Andy Scherding.

216